Disarming Military Industries

Turning an Outbreak of Peace into an Enduring Legacy

Peter Southwood

M
MACMILLAN

First published 1991

Published by
MACMILLAN PRESS LTD
Houndmills, Basingstoke, Hampshire RG21 2XS
and London
Companies and representatives
throughout the world

Printed in Great Britain by
  WBC Print Ltd., Bridgend

Typeset by Footnote Graphics
Warminster, Wiltshire

British Library Cataloguing in Publication Data
Southwood, Peter
Disarming military industries: turning an
outbreak of peace into an enduring legacy.
1. Western world. Military equipment industries
I. Title
338.47623091821
ISBN 0–333–52393–8

DISARMING MILITARY INDUSTRIES

yet much remains
To conquer still; peace hath her victories
No less renowned than war

John Milton

Contents

List of Figures

List of Tables

List of Abbreviations

ABM	– Anti-ballistic missile
ACDA	– Arms Control and Disarmament Agency
BWB	– Federal Office of Military Technology and Procurement
CBO	– Congressional Budget Office
DoD	– Department of Defense (US)
EAC	– Economic Adjustment Committee
EC	– European Community
EIU	– Economist Intelligence Unit
FRG	– Federal Republic of Germany
GDP	– Gross Domestic Product
GNP	– Gross National Product
HMSO	– Her Majesty's Stationery Office
ICBM	– Intercontinental ballistic missile
IECC	– International Economic Conversion Conference
MIRV	– Multiple independently targetable re-entry vehicle
MoD	– Ministry of Defence (UK)
NATO	– North Atlantic Treaty Organisation
OEA	– Office of Economic Adjustment
R&D	– Research and development
RDT&E	– Research, development, testing and evaluation
SALT	– Strategic Arms Limitation Talks
SIPRI	– Stockholm International Peace Research Institute
SLBM	– Submarine-launched ballistic missile
UK	– United Kingdom
UN	– United Nations
UNESCO	– United Nations Educational, Scientific and Cultural Organisation
USA	– United States of America
USSR	– Union of Soviet Socialist Republics
WTO	– Warsaw Treaty Organisation

Conventions

$	– United States dollars
billion	– thousand million

Preface

Some time ago I was having lunch in the company of a retired official from the British Ministry of Defence. Conversation turned to the prospects for disarmament. He said that this could never be possible as 'millions' of people in the United Kingdom depended on the manufacture of armaments for their jobs. In reply I pointed out that, far from employing millions, just 400 000 were directly or indirectly engaged in the production of weapons for the British armed forces, which was a significant but not overwhelming number. This news clearly surprised him but the view that disarmament would be a threat to vast numbers of jobs remains an enduring illusion shared, I suspect, by a great many people despite so much evidence to the contrary.

During a period in which a window of opportunity has opened up for significant cuts in the nuclear and conventional forces of the major global powers, it has become more important than ever to demonstrate that the conversion of military industries to peaceful purposes is indeed feasible. Further pressures to pursue this path arise from a variety of sources. There is the seemingly unstoppable escalation in the costs associated with each new generation of defence equipment at a time when defence ministries can barely maintain, or are even forced to cut, their budgets in real terms. Reinforcing these constraints is the dramatic reduction in public support, since the early 1980s, for higher military spending in countries like the USA and UK, particularly in the face of President Gorbachev's 'peace offensive' and the Soviet Union's numerous unilateral initiatives to cut their armed forces and weaponry. Finally, there is likely to be a growing recognition that, if the strategic threat from the East has diminished, then there are sound economic and social reasons for switching resources from the military to the civilian economy.

This book sets out to present the evidence that the West can cope successfully with disarmament and to identify the strategies and policies which need to be adopted in furtherance of that end. It is, therefore, addressed directly to policy-makers and practitioners as well as to scholars and to peace researchers, in particular. I also believe that this work is sufficiently free of jargon to be comprehensible to the interested lay reader.

Underlying this narrower question of defence conversion is the grander theme of peace itself. For those concerned with the bigger questions of peace theory and peace research the Introduction and the second part of Chapter 7, in particular, are intended to set conversion in a wider context. (Conversely those uninterested in such matters might prefer to ignore these sections.) I am conscious that in my efforts to face 'reality', but not to be so enslaved by it as to be unable to change it, I may have ended up satisfying no one: the practitioner will disdain the Utopian, the Utopian the practical. However, in my world there is room for both.

This perception of the world has been greatly influenced by the seven years I have spent at the School of Peace Studies, University of Bradford, first as an undergraduate and later as a postgraduate undertaking the doctoral research which formed the basis for this book. It would be impossible to exaggerate the value to me of that experience. I lighted on the School as one who, emerging from the darkness of the night, finds a temporary shelter which he never imagined could have existed there at all. The excitement at the intellectual freedom, and the challenge of a subject so much at the centre of thought and action, has turned every previous difficulty to advantage. For this I owe a lasting debt of gratitude to the School, its staff and students, and to the Quakers who did so much to make it possible.

I would like, in particular, to offer a special thanks to my former supervisor Dr Tom Woodhouse for his encouragement and constructive comments both on the original thesis and an earlier draft of the book. During the actual research many other individuals were also very helpful, including my colleagues Steve Schofield and Russell Fleming and all those involved in the Arms Conversion Group. They ensured that I was always able to work in a stimulating environment and was never isolated intellectually. Whatever merits this book has owes much to them – its faults are, of course, mine alone.

The entire research programme was funded by a generous grant from the Joseph Rowntree Social Service Trust to whom I extend my sincere thanks. The interest and encouragement of one of the Trustees, Chris Greenfield, was much appreciated.

I am very grateful to Louise Rhodes who, having played a major role in typing my long thesis, willingly agreed to take on the further task of typing the manuscript for this book. Addition-

Preface

ally, I offer my thanks to the Graphics Department of Bradford University for undertaking the artwork.

The interest and support of my parents and other relations and friends during the writing of this book was also appreciated.

Finally, thanks are due to the following sources who kindly agreed to allow me to use certain excerpts in this work: Figures 2.1 and 2.2 are reproduced with the permission of the Stockholm International Peace Research Institute (SIPRI); Figure 10.1 is reproduced with the permission of Macmillan Press; Figure 10.2 is reproduced with the permission of Professor Peter Wallensteen and Olof Frensborg; Table 1.1 is Crown copyright and reproduced with the permission of the Controller of Her Majesty's Stationery Office (HMSO); Tables 5.2–5.4 are based on SIPRI data reproduced with the permission of Oxford University Press; and Table 8.1 is reproduced with the permission of the Bulletin of Peace Proposals.

Grittenham, Wiltshire   PETER SOUTHWOOD

Introduction

In so far as there is a popular notion of the conversion of military industries it is generally associated with that of beating 'swords into plowshares', an idea derived from Old Testament prophecies. This turning of the instruments of war into the instruments of peace symbolises the link between conversion and the concept of peace itself. Although the meaning of conversion and how far it does, or does not, relate to achieving disarmament and the establishment of a peaceful society can only be made clearer later in the book, it will be apposite now to provide a preliminary overview of the relevance of conversion to research into peace issues.

The meaning of peace has been an object of much controversy. Wiberg, in a review of peace theories and findings derived from articles published in the *Journal of Peace Research* between 1964 and 1980, noted that the concept was usually defined in terms of either positive or negative peace. 'Negative peace' refers simply to the absence of violence or war, whether at the international or any other level. 'Positive peace' has changed its meaning over time, at first being seen in terms of the integration of human society and increased cooperation, while later the notion of structural violence emerged, (especially under the influence of Galtung), and positive peace was redefined as the absence of such violence.[1] This structural violence, though much criticised for lacking an empirical basis and for its normative content, was useful in highlighting the causes of human suffering (like poverty and starvation) arising not from physical violence but from the character of specific human institutions. A society could not really be described as peaceful while such suffering existed, even if no actual physical violence were present.

Another way of looking at the question of positive peace is to consider the oft-repeated statement that 'nuclear weapons have kept the peace in Europe for the last forty years'. Just as a room full of armed men from two opposing sides could scarcely be described as an example of a 'peaceful relationship', even if there was no actual fighting going on, so a world dominated by nuclear arsenals with immense destructive potential could not, in terms of positive peace, be construed as an acceptable basis for peaceful relations between nations.

Nevertheless it is probably true to say that most emphasis, within peace research, has been given to negative peace. As will become evident later in this book, the conversion of military industries is implicitly allied to this notion of peace and has been criticised by some peace researchers for being wedded to an armaments-based security concept and for its inattention to the underlying causes of arms races and wars.

The study of the post-Second World War arms race, as a process, has been the subject of much research, including the development of mathematical models based on the work of Richardson and others. These models concentrated on inter-action between the parties involved, though by the 1970s greater interest was shown in domestic forces in arming nations, especially the power of military–industrial complexes. This, too, had a bearing on the conversion debate which, in the 1960s, had tended to be technical and economistic without taking sufficient account of political constraints on turning military industries to peaceful purposes. Allied to this topic is a major and recurrent theme in peace research: the economic consequences of arma-ments and disarmament. A key question here is the role of high levels of military expenditure in national economies and whether it is essential for, or detrimental to, the overall performance of the economy.[2] The burgeoning arms trade, particularly between the industrialised countries and the Third World, forms a subsidiary but significant aspect of this issue.

Leading on from this study of arms races is the related concern of peace researchers with understanding the causes of war (though whether arms races themselves cause wars is doubtful, but worthy of more attention).[3] In terms of conversion the focus of attention ought, perhaps, to be on the functional alternatives to war and the building of peace structures to tilt the world in a more peaceful direction. It might be expected that non-violence, which has been on the agenda of peace research from the beginning, would feature prominently in building positive con-ditions for peace. In fact, though, only the most radical versions of conversion (known in this book as peace conversion) have even touched on these options; this provides further evidence that the conversion of military industries has been overwhelm-ingly allied to negative peace and, so far, has contributed little or nothing to an understanding of positive peace. There are reasons for this which will become evident later in the book but, for now, it will suffice to note that conversion has not, in general, been a particularly radical let alone a Utopian concept. Now and again, though, proponents of defence conversion have made genuine efforts to grapple with the deep-rooted issues of arms races and the war-making machinery, suggesting that conversion need not necessarily be tied solely to negative peace.

There is, though, a real difficulty in relating traditional and more radical approaches to conversion, analogous to Wiberg's observation that the relationship between positive and negative peace is not well understood, and that little has been learnt on how to create the former without sacrificing the latter.[4] His view might equally well be applied to the relationship between the conversion of military industries and peace conversion and whether the latter can be pursued without losing whatever prospects there might be for the former.

Thus the major contribution of conversion, so far, has been to demonstrate, not the condition for peace, but that the economic consequences of disarmament (whether partial or complete) are manageable and would most likely be beneficial to the civilian economy. More recently it has been argued that conversion does not even have to wait upon disarmament; conversion planning can begin immediately, and such planning will actually help create the political pre-conditions for disarmament by reassuring those whose livelihoods currently depend on the arms race.

So the central theme of this book is conversion as a process and, specifically, the scope for implementing conversion programmes and the effectiveness of current conversion policies. The emphasis throughout is on assessing the forces for and against conversion at both the macro- and the micro-level, rather than on a purely economic or organisational exercise.

There is a further significant dimension. Labour unions in the Western defence industries have taken an increasingly positive attitude to defence industry conversion since the mid-1970s (though apathy and even hostility are still very evident). This raises the question of industrial democracy and whether trade union initiatives on conversion, within individual factories, have any scope for successful implementation. While only a subordinate theme in this book it is one of relevance to short- and long-term perspectives for conversion programmes at the micro-level. Additionally it helps to explain the emphasis in the book on diversification and conversion within military industries and companies, rather than through closure of defence firms or bases and the dispersal of human and material resources to new civilian industries. While the two types of conversion are complementary (rather than exclusive) the obvious preference of the unions for the factory-based variety has been evident in the writings of peace researchers and labour organisers over the last decade.

When the 1980s began the prospects for disarmament had rarely looked bleaker but, at the time of writing, when the decade is drawing to its close the possibilities for deep cuts in the level of nuclear and conventional armaments have, arguably, never been better in post-war history. These recent developments have heightened awareness of the conversion issue. Yet this book is not primarily concerned with tracing the causes, progress or prospects of current disarmament and arms control negotiations. Rather its objective is to try to provide a deeper understanding of how far the opportunities for conversion of military industries can be utilised, and the barriers overcome, in widely varying circumstances. In that sense the perspective is a longer-term one, at once sensitive to the issues of the moment while also transcending them, in that a theoretical framework is offered that will take account of pervading economic and social structures as well as rapidly changing technologies and markets, and shifts in policies and opinions.

Before this can be done, though, there is a need to look back over the last forty years or so and ask, much as Wiberg did of peace: 'What have we learnt about conversion?'

1 The Study of Defence Conversion since 1945

The conversion of armaments has a long history stretching back into biblical times. The vision of a society without war, in which military industries and armed forces could be turned to peaceful purposes, has recurred in many traditions, secular and religious, as a powerful inspiration to those seeking an end to violence and injustice. The appeal of conversion is such that, at first sight, this idea has the ability to cross political, cultural and ideological barriers which little else could traverse. On how many other issues could Isaiah's prophetic utterance:

> ... and they shall beat their swords into plowshares, and their spears into pruninghooks: nation shall not lift up sword against nation, neither shall they learn war any more ... [1]

find a modern counterpart in Trotsky's record of events in Russia in 1917:

> ... As they approached the [attainment of] power the workers also approached more and more concretely the problems of industry. The artillery conference even established a special centre for the study of methods of transition from munition factories to peaceful production. [2]

Yet the very differences of style emphasise the fact that each statement was made under completely different historical conditions, that it was the product of quite separate cultures and traditions and the precise meaning of the conversion envisaged represented contrasting religious and secular ideals. So just as we use the word 'state' to describe both the far-flung Roman Empire of imperial times and also the modern nation-state, knowing that each institution was in precise details quite different, in the same way the term 'conversion' needs to be applied to a historically specific period if more than a very abstract notion of the concept is to be achieved.

Hence the first task will be to outline the scope of this book and present a modern definition of the term – conversion – which is central to the whole work. Even so it should be borne in mind that there is no generally agreed term for describing the process of turning military industries to peaceful purposes and different writers will use different terms. Where this is significant in any quotation within this work an appropriate comment or qualification will be made at the time.

The forty years since the end of the Second World War provide a sufficient historical context for the purposes of understanding the scope and nature of defence conversion. Indeed, the primary focus will be on the last thirty years or so, roughly corresponding to the period of growing world-wide concern about the nuclear and conventional arms race and the consequent emergence of modern peace movements in many of the Western democracies. Whilst the nature and extent of the conversion, or reconversion, process after the cessation of hostilities in 1945 will be given some attention, the circumstances of the time were too different from the current position to be able to draw any close parallel.

It seems appropriate, therefore, to concentrate on the period from the late 1950s, which also corresponds to a tremendous outpouring of ideas and writings on, amongst other subjects, the economics of disarmament which is so closely linked to the question of conversion. Peace researchers, economists, government experts and even a few trade union leaders all made their contributions to the debate on what would happen to the economy if the objective of general and complete disarmament were achieved. While there were some important writings from the United Kingdom (UK) and other Western European and Scandinavian countries, it was from the United States of America (USA) that the most influential investigations emerged. Consequently it is crucial to any analysis of conversion prospects in specific Western countries to examine, first, the international post-war developments in thinking on conversion which have had a major impact on progress in those countries.

The main purpose of this book is to evaluate the most important contributions to Western literature, written or translated into the English language,[3] on the main topic of defence conversion and the economics of disarmament. However, before this can be done it will be necessary to discuss, in this chapter, how the task can best be undertaken, given the various sources of knowledge on, and approaches taken to, this subject. Moreover, the economics of disarmament cannot be divorced from an understanding of the main features of the global arms race and its economic and social consequences (to be assessed in Chapters 2–4), since it is the growth of the armaments sector which provides the rationale for having a conversion policy in the first place. As the defence industries of the major Western states are the focal points for conversion policies it will also be appropriate to offer a comparative study of their industries (in Chapter 5). This will also serve to confirm that the structure of each major Western defence industry is sufficiently similar to allow the lessons drawn from conversion studies in one country to be generally applicable to the others. These matters will then form the background to the extensive review of conversion literature (in Chapters 6–12).

Thus the major part of this book will put the main Western countries, with indigenous defence industries, in their proper international context and enable (in the final Chapters 14–15) a theoretical framework to be established for assessing the prospects for conversion in any of these states. This framework will also form the basis for a more comprehensive concluding statement on the prospects for conversion in the West, during the years ahead, than would otherwise have been possible. In the same way it is hoped that conversion researchers in individual Western countries with major defence industries will find the framework a useful starting point for the comprehensive national studies which will be essential if the economic and social opportunities presented by disarmament are to be grasped.[4]

THE MEANING OF CONVERSION AND RELATED TERMS

The use of terms like economic conversion, arms conversion or conversion has not been very consistent in the post-war period. Some clarification of the meaning of these concepts is essential here to avoid confusion later in this book. It will then also be clearer what kind of conversion occurred after the ending of hostilities in 1945 and why this example is of only limited relevance to contemporary circumstances. Having, therefore, decided to concentrate on writings and experience from the late 1950s onwards a novel categorisation of the relevant literature will be proposed as the basis for eventually deriving an appropriate theoretical framework. This categorisation, although centred on various approaches to conversion, extends also to the various studies of the economic and social consequences of the arms race, to which the economics of disarmament and conversion ought to be linked.

The starting point for discussing the question of definition is the broader concept of *economic conversion*. Kenneth Boulding defined this in 1960 as:

> ... the problem of how to adjust the structure of production in the economy – that is, the commodity mix of total output – to shifts in the structure of total demand, public and private.[5]

However, particularly in the USA, the term economic conversion has tended, amongst advocates of defence conversion programmes, to take a more specific and limited meaning. Seymour Melman, gave one of the fullest definitions:

> Economic conversion from military to civilian economy is the formulation, planning and execution of organisational, technical, occupational and economic changes required to turn industry, laboratories, training institutions, bases, and other facilities from military to civilian use.[6]

In effect this is (more or less) what *arms conversion* means in the UK, where the term is more commonly used, and care needs to be taken to recognise the distinction between economic conversion, in the broader non-military sense of the term, and this special case of economic conversion involving military industries.

Melman is concerned with conversion as a process (not simply a problem) which forms an integral part of reversing the arms race. But the extent of the change involved is brought home even more forcefully by comparing conversion with *diversification*. Gilmore and Coddington provided such a distinction in 1966:

> Diversification has been defined by Stanley S. Miller as 'entry into a substantially different business field, either through internal research or through acquisition.'[7]

In the case of defence diversification a 'substantially different business field' was taken to be a non-defence, non-aerospace field. On the other hand:

Conversion by a firm or by an entire industry entails the abandonment (usually under extreme market pressure) of one set of products and markets in favour of an entirely different set.[8]

This point was also emphasised by the UK Labour Party Defence Study Group report in 1977:

> *Conversion* refers to the process by which part of our military industrial capacity would move into a different field of manufacture – a once and for all change. *Diversification* implies a widening of the base of activity – alternating military and non-military work for unconverted capacity.[9]

Yet these relatively straightforward definitions of conversion, and their distinction from the more limited changes involved in diversification, do not bring out the full subtleties and complexities of the word conversion even when applied within an economic context. As Ulrich Albrecht claimed:

> Conversion entails considerably more than the mere change of products in some plants. The economic problems of adaption [*sic*], which commonly provide for the issue area in conversion research, are also but one segment of a far broader affair.[10]

Albrecht proceeded to include a body of knowledge derived from theology and philosophy, especially dogmatics, in order to provide useful insights into the concept of conversion. In dogmatics conversion involves a principal change leading to a reorientation towards commonality as opposed to an ideological or formal change without any practical consequences. This means that as armaments industries developed from general social reproduction so their reversal towards common civilian goods should, according to Albrecht, more appropriately be called 'reversion' rather than 'conversion'. Indeed Melman partly covered this point by speaking of *reconversion* of firms after the Second World War:

> At that time, the issue was reconversion; the firms could and did go back to doing the work they had been involved in before the war. They could literally draw the old sets of blueprints and tools from the shelf and go to work on the old products.[11]

However, Melman argued that the term conversion is appropriate now:

> At the present time, the bulk of military production is concentrated in industries, firms, or plants that have been specialised for this work, and frequently have no prior history of civilian work. Therefore, the problem is one of conversion – redesigning the total operation of enterprises and parts of enterprises.[12]

According to Albrecht, a conversion process requires: positive change of the conversion object (which in the case of industries also means labour conversion) that does not require destruction of its former substance; the convertite increases his quality through losing those features which distinguish him from commonality. In principle the capacity to convert is to be found in any segment of society. Albrecht listed the main consequences of adopting the conversion concept to military activities as follows: priority is placed on implementation of conversion efforts; conversion is assumed to be manageable without annihilation of the essence of the conversion object (in particular, without making redundant the human resources tied up in the firms and industries concerned); the characteristic for successful conversion is a greater degree of commonality in features, both of the convertite and society (i.e. the firms and industries re-enter the civilian fold). What is more, a conversion process is part of a larger structure and may occur not just as a result of general and complete disarmament but of even partial arms reduction measures. Politically, conversion of military activities to civilian efforts is a reformist concept, as reflected in the great preponderance of 'liberal' writers on the subject.[13]

A more radical view of conversion was presented by Oberg. This will be discussed in greater detail in Chapter 8 but he made the point:

> Literally, the term 'conversion' means to turn around, to transform, to change faith or values. It is a deep change. This is what conversion studies should be about ...[14]

Following Kaldor's thinking he argued:

> In other words, we would hold it highly unlikely that conversion will lead to real disarmament unless it is part of a *larger*

strategy which encompasses (a) a converted attitude among decision-makers as to what *security* is about, (b) a fundamental democratic control of the *social driving forces behind armament* and (c) a concern for the human and social development brought about through *the structural transformation and dissolution of those conflict formations that lead to war.*[15] (Emphasis in the original.)

This *peace conversion* approach, as Woodhouse described it, is a criticism of studies which fail to take account of the politics of conversion and the need to develop a view of an alternative society, where economic and political power is more decentralised and amenable to democratic control.[16]

For the most up-to-date views on the range of meanings of conversion it is necessary to turn, finally, to the first International Economic Conversion Conference (IECC) that took place at Boston College, Massachusetts, from 22 to 24 June 1984. This conference brought together 750 trade unionists, peace activists and representatives from the churches and groups working for economic justice. Participants came from thirteen different countries, forty-one states of the USA and four Canadian provinces.

The IECC defined conversion, first of all, in traditional terms as '... the process of planning for the outbreak of peace'.[17] However, the diversity of meanings that could be attached to the concept soon became evident. Advance planning, including blueprinting the redesign for civilian work and occupational conversion, was stressed by Melman. Barry Bluestone emphasised the distinction between corporate conversion, which goes on constantly in any capitalist economy, and socially beneficial conversion, which involves workers and their communities and can take place in military or civilian production facilities. Democratic planning not just at a national but an international level, given the existence of collaborative arms projects, was seen as crucial to winning workers' support for disarmament proposals. Additionally, conversion was linked to the following: development issues and the struggles of workers in developing countries; strategies that could help society cope constructively with economic decline and structural unemployment; the fight for economic justice for the poor and minority people. Finally a Canadian bishop expressed the need for moral as well as economic conversion.

In a sense the IECC graphically illustrated the burden placed upon the word conversion when it is defined in the broadest possible terms. The more radical the concept the greater the weight of requirements placed upon it and the more difficult to find a definition that is rigorous. The more reformist the concept the easier it is to define but the less it has to contribute to disarmament, and the establishment of a peaceful society, because the structures that lead to the arms race, and support militarism, are left unchallenged.

No entirely satisfactory resolution of these difficulties is possible given that different writers and speakers use the same, or similar, words differently. However, this book will differentiate the various terms as follows using the authorities cited previously. These definitions seem to fit in as well as can be expected with the way the terms have developed in post-Second World War Western history:

- *Economic conversion*. The process of adjusting the structure of production in the economy – that is, the commodity mix of total output – to shifts in the structure of total demand, public and private.
- *Conversion/defence conversion*. A special case of economic conversion, in the broader sense defined above. It is the formulation, planning and execution of the organisational, technological, occupational, and economic changes required to completely turn part or all of given military industries, firms and other facilities from defence to civilian use.

  In the USA the term 'economic conversion' is also used to describe this special case, whilst in the UK the term 'arms conversion' is most frequently used by proponents of conversion.
- *Peace conversion*. Links defence conversion to a wider disarmament strategy, based on a largely non-military security concept, involving the structural transformation and dissolution of those conflict formations that lead to war and democratic participation in the conversion process by workers and their communities.
- *Reconversion*. The process by which certain industries, firms and other facilities return to civilian activities after a temporary involvement in military activities due to war or some other national or international crisis.

● *Diversification.* The entry of a firm into a substantially different business field, either through internal changes or through
acquisition, without abandoning its original business field. In
the case of military firms this implies a widening of the base of
activity – alternating military and non-military work for
unconverted capacity.

It is now necessary to consider the relevance to contemporary
society of the last major conversion – or, more accurately,
reconversion – programme in Western history.

THE POST-SECOND WORLD WAR RECONVERSION EXPERIENCES

Prior to the Second World War of 1939–45 defence expenditure
in both the United States and the UK had generally never been
of great significance during peacetime. In the UK during the last
two decades of the nineteenth century it had hovered around 2.5
per cent of net national income and even in 1913, the year before
the outbreak of the First World War, it was only 3.7 per cent.
After falling back to less than 3 per cent of net national income in
1923 and 1933, defence expenditure rose to 5.3 per cent in
1938.[18] Meanwhile in the USA defence spending was less than 2
per cent of Gross National Product (GNP) at the time of the
early build-up in production for European needs during the
Second World War. Prior to that no full-scale defence industry
existed in the private sector of the economy. Throughout the
nineteenth century government arsenals and private firms
shared the manufacture of guns and ships and only during actual
war was there a significant level of arms production. Immediately
after the ending of hostilities there would be sharp cut-backs in
defence spending and production. This pattern continued up to
the Second World War.[19]
  During the 1939–45 war UK government current expenditure, which had accounted for 14.9 per cent of net national
expenditure in 1938, rose to 54.3 per cent in 1944, mainly on
military account. Personal expenditure on consumers' goods and
services accounted for 80.4 per cent of net national expenditure
in 1938 but this declined to 56.7 per cent in 1944.[20] After the war
ended in August 1945 government current expenditure declined

Table 1.1   Changes in United Kingdom employment, 1939–47

| | Working population in Great Britain (thousands) | | | |
	Mid 1939	Mid 1945	End 1946	End 1947
Civil work	16 730	12 586	17 816	18 537
Production for forces	1 270	3 830	460	350
HM Forces	480	5 090	1 440	1 113
Unemployed	1 270	103	398	300
Demobilised but not yet employed	—	40	300	123
Total	19 750	21 649	20 414	20 423
Men	14 656	14 881	14 629	14 659
Women	5 094	6 768	5 785	5 764
	19 750	21 649	20 414	20 423

Source: Anon., 'Planning for Victory', *Labour Research*, 74, no. 5 (May 1985), p. 119, citing *Ministry of Labour Gazette*, March 1948.

rapidly to 46.5 per cent of net national expenditure and then, more sharply still, to 25.2 per cent in 1946. However, net national expenditure as a whole declined by only 4.5 per cent over the period 1944–46. Thereafter in 1947 and 1948 total output rose both in current and constant prices. Hence it may be stated that the disarmament programme after the war did not result in anything but a minor and short-lived reduction in the total level of economic activity.

As far as employment was concerned Table 1.1 illustrates the extent of the changes which occurred from the outbreak of war in 1939 until the major part of demobilisation was complete in 1947.

Over 3.5 million men and women were demobilised from the armed forces and the number of workers engaged in arms manufacture fell by over 3.25 million during the year and a half from VE day. Workers involved in arms production and members of the armed services who had accounted for 42 per cent of the working population at the beginning of the period only accounted for less than 10 per cent at the end of the period.[21] Even so unemployment remained below 4 per cent of the working population, including demobilised service personnel not immediately found work, but this was at a time when a far greater redeployment of the working population was being accomplished than would be required now.

The increase in the numbers employed on civilian work did not, however, match the run-down in defence employment since the size of the working population declined. This was due, first, to nearly one million women leaving the paid workforce altogether by December 1947 and, secondly, to a number of persons past the normal age of retirement who also left the labour force once war ended. During the three years from 1945 to 1948 expansion of employment was greatest in construction (709 000), services (656 000), manufacturing (491 000) and distribution (433 000).[22] Amongst the major industries only metals, engineering, vehicles and shipbuilding suffered a large decline in employment, i.e. the industries which had been most involved in the war effort.

As the Economist Intelligence Unit put it:

> From the viewpoint of both output and employment, therefore, the disarmament programme at the end of the 1939–1945 war was carried out with a minimum of friction and dislocation. Moreover this transition to a mainly peacetime economy was achieved without the government having to take massive steps to ease the changeover and to support the level of demand. Income taxes were reduced, refunds were made of excess profit taxes, substantial out-payments were made in the form of war damage compensation and a policy of cheap money was adopted, but, for the most part, the government used its very considerable powers during the period to channel demand into particular fields of activity, as there was little need to sustain it. There were, of course, many difficulties experienced during this period, but they were only indirectly attributable to the demobilisation programme.[23]

Why did this reconversion programme proceed fairly smoothly? Two factors in particular are generally agreed to have been significant. First, there was a backlog of demand accumulated during the wartime years as a result of destruction and the lack of many goods and services. Secondly, most of the population had money to turn these demands into actual purchases. This was itself the consequence of nearly full employment during the war years coupled with a comparative absence of ways in which to spend the money earned. So savings rose rapidly until 1945 and then fell sharply over the next few years as consumer expenditure dramatically increased. Real disposable incomes increased only moderately in 1946.[24]

Government policy, cited previously, was clearly a factor, too, in helping the process of reconversion and reconstruction. An article in *Labour Research* also stressed the importance of planning, based on prior wartime experience, as well as pressure from the labour movement and workers in the armed forces who were unwilling to countenance a return to the high levels of unemployment typical of the 1930s.[25] Whilst the extent of government intervention in the transition to a peacetime economy was no doubt less than in wartime planning, as many wartime controls were abandoned in the years after the end of hostilities, it is clearly right that these political and psychological factors be given due weight in addition to the favourable economic matters discussed earlier.

At the level of individual companies, the point has been made by Melman and others that firms could and did go back to doing the work they had been involved in before the war. This was probably more true for the USA than the UK where a private sector defence industry was more developed. Professor Brown issued a cautionary note concerning the extent to which demobilisation after the war was simply a reversion to the status quo:

> ... it would be easy to exaggerate the extent to which this was so in 1945–6, and to underrate the extent to which the equipment was run down, the men were without previous industrial experience, and the pattern of demand, and of industry, that emerged was different from that before the war.[26]

Another area that would merit consideration in any detailed analysis of post-Second World War reconversion experience is the whole question of technological development. Although there had been massive advances in weapons capabilities during the war arms technology was still less advanced and specialised than it is today and conversion, or reconversion, difficulties were less than they would be now.

American reconversion experiences were, in most respects, similar to those in the UK. Defence expenditures had leapt from less than 2 per cent to over 40 per cent of GNP at the high point of wartime production. However, between 1945 and 1946 expenditures on national security (in constant 1960 dollars) were reduced by 80 per cent. This was equivalent to about 30 per cent of 1945 GNP. During the period between June 1945 and June 1946 over nine million men were demobilised from the armed forces yet unemployment in the immediate post-war years remained below 4 per cent of the labour force. Private domestic investment, consumption and non-defence government expenditures all increased between 1945 and 1946 (in constant 1960 dollars) while net exports of goods and services moved from deficit into surplus. As a result the decline in real aggregate demand was less than half the decline in defence spending.[27] The reasons why the US economy adjusted so quickly to demobilisation are similar to those given for the UK experience and need not be repeated here.

Nevertheless, in one respect, the Second World War was a watershed in the history of the US defence industry. Whilst there was a short period at the end of the war during which it seemed that the traditional pattern of reductions in spending to low peacetime levels would be repeated, two major influences altered the historical cycle. The cold war between the United States and the Soviet Union (USSR), followed by the start of the Korean War in 1950, led to a great surge in defence spending that was only partly related to the war itself. A high and relatively steady level of spending on defence, with bulges caused by the Vietnam War and, more recently, an upward trend since 1976, has formed the basis for the establishment of a permanent defence industry.[28]

The second major influence on the US defence industry was the greatly enhanced rate of technological change in weapons systems during and after the Second World War. The new technologies – relating to nuclear weapons, advanced jet aircraft, missiles and so on – did not have a sound base in the existing US arsenal system and it was felt that the in-house laboratories lacked the flexibility in terms of salary levels and hiring practices to cope with rapid developments in advanced technologies. These influences, combined with inter-service rivalries over new weapon systems, led to the development of a large-scale peacetime defence industry in the USA largely supplanting the in-house laboratories and arsenals that had previously dominated weapons development and production.[29]

So whilst the post-Second World War reconversion experience was being completed a new institutional basis for defence procurement began to arise that would change, to a considerable extent, the whole nature of the conversion problem in the Western world's leading political and industrial state. Nor could the post-Korean War experience provide many lessons for today. As the US government itself put it:

> Despite the mildness of the 1954 recession it is now clear that fiscal and monetary policies might have been applied with more vigor. The reason they were not is that the decline in defense spending following the Korean War was not treated by the policymakers as a major demobilization requiring strong compensatory action. For this reason the 1953–1954 period does not provide a significant guide to the behavior of the American economy in a disarmament program during the 1960s.[30]

The reconversion experiences of both the United Kingdom and the United States demonstrate that where favourable political and economic circumstances and a positive climate of opinion prevail, a disarmament programme of far greater proportions than would now be entailed, even if general and complete disarmament were agreed, could be implemented without causing an economic depression. Unfortunately, though, none of the factors prevailing in 1945 are present today. There is no backlog of demand arising from the war years – quite the contrary in some cases, where markets are saturated. Savings are not running at high levels due to any lack of spending opportunities. The political commitment and planning apparatus to support a conversion programme is largely lacking. And, finally, the post-war optimism and radicalism amongst working people is largely absent in the advanced, Western countries both in terms of achieving major disarmament objectives or reviving the national or international economies.

This is not to say that conversion programmes cannot or will not be carried out but only to stress that the question must be examined in the context of more recent history and not that of post-Second World War or post-Korean War disarmament experiences.

CATEGORISATION OF THE CONVERSION LITERATURE

Over the last thirty years a very extensive literature has emerged on the subject of conversion. As long ago as 1978 Albrecht referred to some three thousand titles that he knew to have been published since the early 1960s, and many more have appeared since then. This poses the question of how best to categorise and evaluate such an extensive literature.

Various authors have attempted this task before. Saltman, in 1972, chose the simplest method, a chronological one, further subdividing the titles according to three perspectives: world considerations, regional considerations, and specific industrial and occupational considerations.[31] However appropriate this approach may have been at that time a more sophisticated methodology is needed to cope with a much greater diversity in the foci of conversion studies published since then. Albrecht himself proposed a more innovative approach which he applied to his own review of conversion literature in June 1978.[32] His idea was to structure this field of literature into methodological classes, in particular arms industries as the object of conversion, econometric analysis, and political and social problems. This served to highlight the emphasis, in the literature, placed on the economic consequences of reduced military expenditure but the relative neglect of key areas like the political problems of conversion. Finally, in 1985, Ball considered what had been learnt from conversion studies about the problems facing governments, specific industries and defence employees arising from any future decline in military expenditure. Her thorough review[33] is premised on a framework for conversion which largely follows that adopted by the United Nations, in its various reports on the arms race and disarmament.

What this book will seek to do is to provide a classification of the literature, based on a set of approaches to conversion (somewhat different to that of Albrecht), in order to arrive at a revised framework for analysing conversion prospects. The distinctiveness of this framework will lie in its utility in identifying both the factors which improve, and those which reduce, the likelihood of successful conversion programmes at national, regional, industrial or company level. This, in turn, will be very relevant to an evaluation of conversion policies. So whereas

Ball's review was based on one particular model of conversion, this review will, by critically assessing the main approaches adopted in the literature, work towards – as it turns out – a modified version of this framework for conversion, particularly suited to policy formation.

To achieve this process of reappraisal it is necessary to identify not only the main approaches taken to studying conversion, but also the sources of knowledge from which these approaches are derived. This will have the effect of focusing attention on the primary architects of modern conversion strategies. These sources of knowledge can be categorised as follows: peace researchers and other academics; the United Nations (UN) and various individual Western governments; the labour movements, whose written contributions have frequently been made via sympathetic academics; and defence managers, whose views have also been refracted through scholars, often attached to research institutes. Naturally these repositories of knowledge, on the defence industry and conversion, have exerted varying degrees of influence on each other and one of the subsidiary purposes of this review of the literature will be to identify these reciprocal effects, and their historical significance in the development of ideas on conversion.

Despite the breadth and extent of the literature, from these various sources there appear to be just three principal approaches to conversion and, additionally, a radical critique of the dominant one of these three categories. This pre-eminent category is described here as the 'economic approach to conversion', which normally involves certain political assumptions about the degree of reduction in armaments anticipated. The economics of disarmament has been the prime concern of this approach but, from the mid to late 1960s, the harmful economic and social consequences of the arms race were increasingly emphasised to strengthen the case for disarmament and conversion. The study of defence industries has also been integral to this approach to conversion. It is principally from peace researchers and other academics, and from the United Nations and individual Western governments, that the main advances in knowledge have come. Their political assumptions on the degree of disarmament or the extent of military spending reductions involved have varied according to time and place, as will be described in detail in Chapters 6 and 7.

This approach has been criticised by orthodox Marxists and theorists of the military–industrial complex. More significantly, for the purposes of this book, even some peace researchers have developed an insightful critique of the traditional approach to conversion, and this radical alternative is called 'peace conversion' (as defined earlier in this chapter). Its distinguishing feature is the explicit treatment of the political problems of conversion which are generally, but not always, presumed to be solvable by reformist, economic studies of defence conversion.

Since the early 1980s some peace researchers have turned their attention to the alternative defence policies which would be needed if nuclear weapons were completely dispensed with or the military were strictly confined to defence. Instead of assuming disarmament agreements or military spending reduction measures as occurs in the economic approach to conversion, a different defence policy is proposed and the economic consequences are evaluated later. This will be described as the 'defence policy approach to conversion'.

Both the economic and the defence policy approaches to conversion involve primarily macro-level studies. Although the more comprehensive treatments of the economics of disarmament and conversion do consider the problems faced by individual defence companies, the main emphasis is on the national or regional economies and on specific industrial sectors. There is, however, a body of knowledge to draw upon, derived from the direct work experiences of managers and trade unionists in the Western defence industries. This has led to what will be known as the 'industrial approach to conversion' because it is concerned with a deeper understanding of the practical problems of defence industry diversification and conversion at the level of individual factories. This approach will require a discussion of past and current managerial initiatives together with the advent of labour organisations' involvement in conversion issues, and the extent to which such involvement has influenced, and been influenced by, peace researchers.

Thus a complex but coherent matrix of categories has been presented to serve as the basis for an evaluation of conversion literature. For ease of reference this categorisation has been summarised in Figure 1.1. Some further subdivisions, by historical period and country, will be introduced, as appropriate, to highlight different economic and national conditions. Although

Sources of knowledge	Category

United Nations ⟶ Economic approach to conversion (Chapters 6–7)

National governments ⟶ Peace conversion (Chapter 8)

Peace researchers ⟶ Defence policy approach to conversion (Chapter 9)

Other academics ⟶ Industrial approach to conversion (Chapters 10–12)

Defence industry managers

Labour organisers

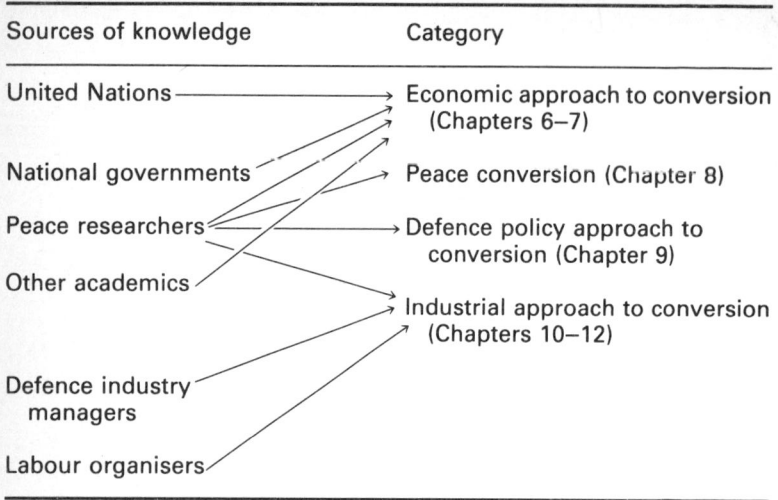

Figure 1.1   Categorisation of Western conversion literature

this classification has not been used before it is hoped that its value, to the analyst of conversion policies, will be more clearly established by the end of the book.

The starting point for this review is to provide some assessment of the arms race and its economic and social consequences, since this provides an indispensable link to an analysis of Western defence industries and the economic approach to conversion.

2 The Global Arms Race

A concise study of the arms race is important for three reasons: to identify general trends in post-war history; to understand the main causative factors behind the strength and dynamism of the armaments build-up; and to appreciate the implications of developments in the arms race for disarmament and, therefore, conversion. For this specific purpose a number of United Nations reports on the economic and social consequences of the arms race and on the relationship between disarmament and development provide an authoritative source of data and analysis. These reports will be used to examine the main quantitative and qualitative features of the arms race over the last forty years and some analysis, by no means comprehensive, of its causes. Then the relevance of this examination to the structure and content of this book will be summarised.

PRINCIPAL FEATURES

The latest UN report on the arms race, in 1982,[1] revealed that annual world military expenditure in 1981 stood at between US $550–600 billion (in 1982 prices). This represented roughly 6 per cent of total world output, being a smaller share than in the early 1960s. Figure 2.1 illustrates the changes which have occurred in world military expenditure in constant (1978) prices and exchange rates between 1949 and 1982. The six main military spenders – the USA, USSR, China, France, UK and the Federal Republic of Germany (FRG) – accounted for about 70 per cent of the total. Together the two major military alliances – the North Atlantic Treaty Organisation (NATO) and the Warsaw Treaty Organisation (WTO) – were responsible for over 70 per cent of global military expenditure. The developing countries accounted for about 16 per cent. Figure 2.2 shows how global military expenditure has been split between the main groups of countries described, in constant (1979) prices, during the period 1972–81.

World military expenditure on research and development (R&D) in 1980 was estimated to be $35 billion or more, being

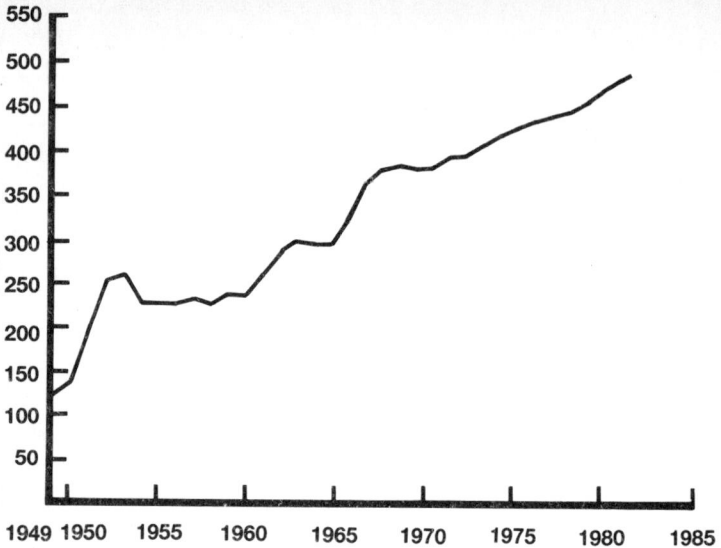

Figure 2.1   World military expenditure, 1949–82. US $ thousand million, in
constant (1978) prices and exchange rates

Sources: *Economic and Social Consequences of the Arms Race and of Military
Expenditures*, A/37/386 (New York, 1983), Chart 1 adapted from SIPRI,
World Armaments and Disarmament: SIPRI Yearbook 1981 (London, 1981), p. 3.

roughly one quarter of total world R&D expenditure for all
activities. The USA and USSR alone accounted for about 85 per
cent of global military R&D expenditure. Related to the R&D
intensity of military work was the estimate that approximately
20 per cent of the world's qualified scientists and engineers were
engaged in military work during the 1970s.[2] However, as with
military expenditure *in toto*, the share was less than during the
1960s.

An earlier UN report estimated that the total number of
people directly engaged by the military to provide specialised
goods and services world-wide was 43.5 million people, although
this estimate was subject to a very wide margin of error. This
estimate included some 25 million people employed in the
world's regular armed forces; about 10 million in paramilitary
forces having similar functions to those of regular armies;

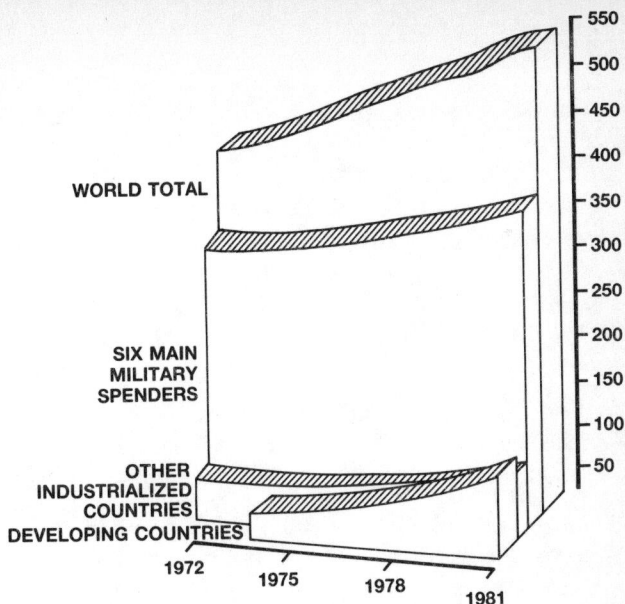

Figure 2.2   Military expenditures, 1972–81: world total and selected groups of countries. US $ thousand million (1979 prices)

Sources: *Economic and Social Consequences of the Arms Race and of Military Expenditures*, A/37/386 (New York, 1983), Chart 2 based on SIPRI, *World Armaments and Disarmament: SIPRI Yearbook 1982* (London, 1982), Appendix 5B.

approximately 4 million workers employed in defence departments world-wide; roughly 500 000 scientists and engineers engaged in military R&D world-wide; and about 4 million workers directly engaged in the production of weapons and other specialised military equipment.[3] This was the size of the labour force, concentrated in the six main military spenders cited previously, which was of prime concern in the context of disarmament and conversion. Additionally, further workers are engaged in supplying civilian goods and services to the military and also indirect employment arises from military purchases. Attempts to quantify these categories were even more difficult and the results will not be reported here. All the UN reports commented on the paucity and unreliability of information available, concerning resources devoted to military purposes, and this will be the subject of further discussion later in the book.

While the sheer size and distribution of global military expenditure and the resources it absorbs are highly significant in the event of progress being made towards the goal of general and complete disarmament, the point has been made that the qualitative features of the arms race are, if anything, even more important. It is to these that attention must now be turned.

The focus of the arms race is the competition in armaments between the largest military powers. As the 1971 UN report commented:

> In a period in which no major nations have been at all-out war with each other, it is a new departure for the world to devote so large a proportion of its resources to military uses.[4]

Compared to previous periods of history two principal changes have occurred: there are larger standing armies; and those armies have been equipped with weapons which are far more lethal, expensive and complex as a result of qualitative changes in weaponry. The trend to produce and accumulate yet more sophisticated, costly and deadly weapons, which began in the late 1940s, continued uninterruptedly into the 1960s impelling a growing number of states, including smaller and developing countries, along its path. This decade was distinguished by a greater spread, and a more extensive technological development, of military equipment than any which preceded it.

During the 1960s supersonic aircraft became unexceptional even in military forces of developing countries; the nuclear weapons in the armouries of a few major powers (the USA, USSR, UK) were diversified and multiplied with an attendant massive accumulation of destructive power; the development of ballistic missiles, coupled with the sophistication of their guidance and control systems, made possible precise attacks by nuclear warheads on any chosen target; and space technology brought a new dimension to the whole area of military communications and surveillance.[5] In addition France and China became nations with a nuclear capability.

In the 1970s, particularly after the 1973 oil price crisis, many countries experienced deep recession and high inflation. Most other countries were indirectly affected by its impact on international trade and the international system of payments. Many governments resorted to scaling down their programmes in the social and economic areas. Additionally the problems of resource conservation and preserving the environment became issues of public concern. Yet, while these factors made the wastage of the arms race even more evident, they did not serve to restrain it – indeed from the mid 1970s global military expenditure rose again in real terms.

While the Disarmament Decade – as the 1970s were called – did lead, at least in its first part, to the consolidation of *détente* between the USA and USSR, in particular, by the adoption of a number of partial arms limitation agreements, these neither turned nor even arrested the tide of the arms race.

In the nuclear weapons field there was widespread concern by the end of the 1960s that a new arms race spiral might occur as a result of the development of anti-ballistic missile (ABM) systems and from counter measures in the shape of greater numbers of launchers and warheads per launcher to saturate the ABM systems.[6] The latter counter measures were called multiple and independently targetable re-entry vehicles (MIRVs).

The first strategic arms limitation agreement (SALT I), signed in May 1972, set ceilings on the number of ABM sites and intercontinental and submarine-launched ballistic missile launchers. While this did succeed in halting deployment of ABM systems it did not prevent vigorous R&D programmes on improved ABMs being maintained. Also SALT I had no discernible impact on the extent of MIRV deployment, with the attendant result that the number of nuclear warheads delivered by intercontinental ballistic missiles (ICBMs) and submarine-launched ballistic missiles (SLBMs) rose by about one thousand every year, even though the number of ICBM and SLBM launchers remained relatively constant after 1972.[7]

Other nuclear weapons developments were equally ominous for disarmament prospects. As ballistic missile attacks became capable of increasing accuracy it was, and is, possible to consider using them to destroy the military installations of the enemy or even to conduct a supposedly 'limited' nuclear war. Long-range cruise missiles – small, very manoeuvrable, pilotless aircraft equipped with nuclear or conventional warheads – increase the verification problems of future arms limitation agreements, since it would be impossible to determine beforehand which kind of warhead they carried. Also, because cruise missiles cost much less than ICBMs, smaller countries might be able to afford them, so increasing risks of nuclear proliferation. The potential, and in some cases actual, development of small, low-yield nuclear weapons, enhanced radiation weapons and tactical concepts for their use in battlefield situations may together make the step from non-nuclear to nuclear war that much less difficult to take.[8] If used on the battlefield, escalation to full-scale nuclear war may prove unstoppable.

Many of these developments have been made possible, or strengthened, by developments in satellite technology. These have given the main military powers an immense superiority through their impact, first on target identification, navigation and damage assessment in relation to 'counterforce' nuclear strategies (concentrating on military not civilian targets) or conventional warfare, and secondly on global intelligence gathering and surveillance of the military programmes of other countries. Whilst this latter capability could help to verify arms control agreements it could also be used for assistance in aggression and other harmful purposes.[9]

In the conventional weapons arena developments had also been far-reaching in the 1970s. New precision guided munitions with very high accuracy, and remotely piloted vehicles for reconnaissance missions, had become accessible to many countries because of both the type of technology involved and the relatively low costs. New weapons based on blast, fragmentation and incendiary effects were developed and, as used in carpet-bombing raids in the Indo-China War, had destructive and ecological effects almost as serious as those caused by nuclear weapons. Also such technical and operational constraints on the deployment of chemical weapons as remained, could be eroded through the development of binary nerve gases and their munitions.[10]

Arms exports then provided the mechanism by which these technological changes spread rapidly from the major powers to the rest of the world:

In addition to the constant pressure on importing countries to modernize their stocks of weapons and equipment, the qualitative character of the arms race gives rise to various pressures in the main producing countries to raise exports, including the need to dispose of obsolete inventories, to achieve large-scale economies, and to lengthen production runs in order to lower unit costs and finance further research and development efforts.[11]

The latter half of the 1970s and the early 1980s witnessed a severe deterioration in the politico-strategic and socio-economic context. In 1979 the USA and USSR did agree a second strategic arms limitation treaty but the US Congress was unwilling to ratify it. The 1980s began with major setbacks to the process of *détente* epitomised by the Conference at Madrid, a follow-up to the Helsinki Accords in 1977 which had consolidated the process of *détente* in inter-European relations. Serious difficulties arose at the follow-up meetings of the Conference in sustaining the *détente* policy.[12] Increasing tension and aggressive stances between the leading arms race participants worsened the position in various crisis areas around the world. Unsurprisingly, in this climate, the 1980s inherited a situation of virtual stalemate in disarmament negotiations which was only broken after the less confrontational postures adopted in Geneva, during the Gorbachev–Reagan Summit, in November 1985.

Since that Summit there has been one major breakthrough in negotiations over armaments reductions: the signing of a treaty between the USA and USSR on the elimination of inter-mediate-range and shorter-range nuclear missiles on 8 December 1987.[13] For the first time in the long history of arms control negotiations an entire category of weapons was removed from the arsenals of both sides. Militarily this represented only a small proportion of all nuclear stockpiles but politically it has created the impetus for negotiations across a whole range of other categories including, very significantly, conventional forces and equipment.

While it must surely be hoped that further agreements on disarmament will be reached, the vulnerability of the whole process to any deterioration in international relations should be readily apparent. Consequently some attention now needs to be given to the underlying causes of the arms race, and the reasons why disarmament has proved so elusive a goal, since these factors have important implications for conversion.

CONSEQUENCES FOR DISARMAMENT AND CONVERSION

The qualitative nature of the arms race and its significance for arms limitation agreements has already been noted but requires fuller elaboration. In the 1977 UN report the factors underlying the arms race were identified as follows:

> The strong qualitative momentum of the current arms race has a number of important consequences for the way it develops, the insecurity it generates and in terms of the possibilities for disarmament. In an arms race where the emphasis is on quantity, where technological development is slow and of little consequence, countries may be expected to match their armament efforts to the stocks or the growth rates of the military forces of their opponents. There is room for saturation levels or for mutually agreed ceilings and reductions. Under conditions of rapid military innovation, on the other hand, the decisive factor in the military procurement plans of countries at the forefront of the technological arms race is not so much the actual military strength of their opponents but rather those technological advances which opponents might be able to achieve over the next decade or so (10 years being the typical gestastion period for a major technological advance). Inevitably, as the apprehensions of military planners shift from the force levels towards the R&D efforts of their opponents, it is increasingly on the R&D efforts of their own country, which are known, that they will have to base their plans.[14]

So by a subtle process the arms race, which appears as an action–reaction phenomenon, becomes to some extent a result of internal rather than external pressures. The 1977 report went on to appraise the situation as follows:

> Each country is actively seeking means of defeating its own most advanced weapons and of neutralizing its own most recent defences, thus conferring on the development of military technology a momentum and a rate of obsolescence much greater than in comparable civilian applications. A qualitative arms race with its long lead time and its emphasis on future possibilities rather than current realities tends to move in one

direction only: one country's advances in weaponry will be emulated by others, but its self-restraint need not be. Similarly an increase in international tension may accelerate the arms race, but an improvement of the international climate will not necessarily suffice to slow it down.[15]

The internal and external pressures which serve to maintain the momentum of the arms race are further aided by the nature of the defence market[16] and the problem of surplus industrial capacity. Weapons procurement is more concerned with achieving very high technical specifications and meeting early delivery schedules than with minimising cost, as the escalating unit costs for each new generation of weapon systems and the large cost overruns on many advanced military projects bear eloquent testimony. As a result of these characteristics of the defence market, an increasing volume of R&D is needed for each new generation of weapons which, in turn, means that staff must be expanded rather than simply extending the design cycle, if weapons are not to be obsolete by the time they enter service. This trend in the qualitative arms race causes problems of surplus capacity in both design and production areas unless military procurement expands for each new generation of weapons.[17] Employment can only be maintained with rapid design and development provided production cycles are kept short and weapon systems are frequently being replaced. While abandonment of major military equipment programmes after a great deal of money has been spent on development helps to lessen this problem it makes the arms race a particularly wasteful process.

Other domestic factors have also been proposed in identifying the powerful forces behind the arms race: internal social discontent resulting in an expansion of the armed forces; the inertia of established institutions and the coalitions of interest which can arise between political, military, industrial and professional groups; compromise arrangements between various institutional pressures and inter-service rivalries.[18]

The processes behind the arms race are, at present, inadequately comprehended. This lack of understanding is partly due to the fact that different forces sustain the arms race in different regions of the globe. Most studies are confined to the USA and Europe where sufficient information is available. The serious consequences of the sheer complexity and multitude of pressures which sustain the arms race, in terms of the implications for disarmament (and hence conversion), are again clearly spelled out in the UN's 1977 report:

> ... if effective progress towards disarmament is to be achieved *it will clearly be insufficient to regard the arms race merely as an action–reaction phenomenon, and disarmament as simply a question of political will at the highest decision-making levels.* The arms race is not only becoming more dangerous; it is also more complex and more firmly entrenched. *It is sustained by a variety of forces acting together, and it must be expected that to remove one of them is not sufficient to reverse its course. In fact, it may be assumed that it is not one or a few single factors but precisely their multiplicity which confers upon the arms race its great inertia and which has rendered it so intractable from the point of view of disarmament, any limited successes in one field tending to be offset very quickly by developments in other sectors of the arms race.*[19] (Emphasis added.)

This quotation emphasises three points which will be of crucial significance later in analysing the economic approach to conversion: disarmament is not simply a matter of political will; removing one of the forces behind the arms race will be insufficient to reverse its course; and success in one area of the disarmament field can very soon be counteracted by developments elsewhere in the arms race.

The foregoing description and analysis of the arms race, albeit highly abbreviated, provides the background for subsequent discussion of its economic and social consequences, the main Western arms industries and the economics of disarmament. The Eastern state socialist countries will not be dealt with since their detailed conversion problems will be different owing to the fact that they are mostly centrally planned economies (albeit moving towards a greater market orientation) and information on conversion questions is anyway very limited. The general principles are, though, applicable and the USSR appears to be giving serious attention to conversion of its own military industries for the first time since 1945.[20] Also the conversion problems of developing countries, as relatively few of them have their own substantial defence industries and those that do operate in a rather different economic and political climate to the Western industrialised countries, are not considered here. Some reference will, though, be made to the relationship between disarmament and development.

Consequently it is the major Western industrialised states – those with their own indigenous defence industries – which offer, within limits, some insights into conversion opportunities and problems in any of the main private enterprise economies. The smaller West European countries, with less substantial domestic defence industries,[21] are not discussed explicitly in this book but many of the lessons learnt concerning conversion will be applicable to them as well.

3 The Impact of High Military Expenditures (I)

The socio-economic consequences of the post-war armaments build-up became a topic of major concern to peace researchers and the United Nations from the late 1960s onwards. Previously the economics of disarmament had tended, with the notable exception of Melman in the USA, to be considered in isolation from this broader issue. Yet the economic burden of military expenditure came to be recognised as a major issue because the wastefulness of spending on armaments, if it harmed rather than aided the economy as a whole, provided a source of additional pressure for restraining and then turning the tide of the arms race. How powerful, or otherwise, this argument against high levels of defence expenditure is likely to be will be a matter for discussion at the end of the next chapter.

The literature on this subject is considerable and only a summary of the results of research and the areas of contention will be possible. Moreover, it is the national, rather than the international, consequences of the arms race which has received most attention within the major Western market economies, so it is this aspect which will be emphasised here. The United Nations' view will be examined first and afterwards the main findings of peace research will be assessed. The latter includes work derived from scholars interested in defence economics *per se* and·not directly focusing on disarmament or conversion. The writings of one individual in particular, within the peace research field, will be considered separately and in more detail: Seymour Melman's ideas on the 'permanent war economy' provide a distinct and influential approach to conversion (or economic conversion, in the American sense of the term defined in Chapter 1). The discussion of his work in the next chapter, and that of the United Nations here, will be essential background material for the subsequent assessment of their respective contributions to the economics of disarmament and conversion in Chapters 6 and 7.

One final point will need to be covered. Both the United Nations and most peace researchers are agreed that military spending is harmful to the economy and, in general, take what has been termed a 'liberal' perspective.[1] In opposition to this are the views of orthodox Marxists who in the 1960s (and, indeed, from the early twentieth century) argued that military spending is an essential prop to, and regulator of, the capitalist economies. The merits of this argument will be weighed carefully in Chapter 4 since the logical consequence is that capitalist economies cannot afford to disarm and conversion is, therefore, an irrelevance.

UNITED NATIONS REPORTS

The United Nations' view on the national economic and social consequences of the arms race has stressed the opportunity costs of high military expenditures in terms of resources that might otherwise have been used to meet major human needs. As the saying goes, 'the choice is between guns and butter'. It is not possible to have both, at least not with the same resources at the same time. The lack of resources in meeting areas of human need is obvious and many examples are cited: poverty, lack of adequate housing or health services, better educational provisions, protection of the environment.[2]

The later UN reports discussed these issues more fully in the context of the 'stagflation' of the mid to late 1970s and early 1980s. The contrast between that environment and the boom years which preceded it is important. For whereas during the boom years the harmful economic effects of defence spending on consumption and investment are directly measured by the volume of resources absorbed for military purposes since the factors of production are fully utilised, the processes at work are quite different in a period of deep recession and high inflation, in which some factors of production are idle.[3] The reason for this is that in a recession unemployed resources could be drawn upon when increasing military expenditure without directly withdrawing resources from civilian use (except in some bottleneck situations), and it might be argued that such spending benefits the economy as a whole.

The 1977 UN report rejected this view and claimed that increasing expenditure on arms was not an efficient way of combating recession because it might lead to economies in the areas of health, education and welfare, with resulting harmful social consequences, and it would also intensify the problems of inflation and the balance of payments. Instead the report argued for increasing expenditures on education, health, housing and social welfare.[4]

This question of the contribution of military expenditure in stimulating inflation was elaborated upon in the 1977 report because, although it could not be quantified, it seemed to be 'not inconsequential'.[5] It was argued that prolonged high levels of military expenditure were likely to aggravate upward pressure on price levels in several ways. First, military expenditure is inherently inflationary since it results in effective demand being created but the military equipment thus produced is neither consumable nor capable of being used to increase productive capacity, i.e. it has little or no economic value. (However, against this proposition, it could be argued that arms exports may generate foreign currency[6] and there may also be some civilian spin-offs from expenditure on military R&D – to be discussed later.) If deficit financing of central government expenditure is used to pay for increased military spending inflation will result from an increase in the stock of money. On the other hand if deficits in the balance of payments are caused by arms spending in reserve currency countries, then the stock of money, and thus inflationary pressure, will grow in other countries. Secondly, arms industries are believed to be less resistant to wage increases and other input costs than most industries since they can more easily pass on such extra costs to the government. These cost increases spread to other sectors of the economy resulting in price rises there as well. Thirdly, long-term productivity growth is slowed and the economy made more vulnerable to inflation through the diversion of considerable R&D resources from the civilian to the military sector.[7]

In short, the 1977 report argued, a big cut in global military spending would help to bring inflation under control. This line of argument, though, has not been entirely convincing, as illustrated by a number of dissenting statements to a later UN report concerning in part this very issue of the impact of military spending on inflation.[8] Historical experience also does not fully support this argument: the big reductions in military spending in the USA and Western Europe after the Second World War led to a short-lived but rapid *increase* in the rate of inflation.[9] When the findings of peace researchers are evaluated the relevance of this point of disagreement and what, ultimately, can be said of the relationship between inflation and military expenditure will be clarified as far as possible.

The UN report went on to consider three factors which impinge directly on the rate of economic development and growth of Western market-based economies: the volume and structure of investment, the size and composition of the workforce, and the rate of technological change. On the first factor, the report recognised that the extent to which defence budgets would be transferred to investment would depend on the economic framework and on the willingness and ability of governments to redirect resources in this way. Even on the basis of the crude calculations in the 1977 UN report, economic growth rates might have been expected to increase by 1 or 2 per cent if the greater part of world military expenditure had been allocated to investment. This would have been equivalent to probably more than the growth rate of world output as a whole in the mid-1970s and, if higher levels of investment had been sustained, the effects would have been cumulative thereafter.[10] Further evidence, some contradictory to this, will be cited from peace researchers in the next section of this chapter.

As far as employment is concerned the job-creating potential of much military expenditure has been reduced because of its increasingly high technology content. The 1977 UN report pointed to growing evidence that high military expenditure adds to unemployment problems. It cited US government estimates that whilst one billion dollars of military expenditure creates 76 000 jobs the same amount spent on civilian programmes creates an average of over 100 000 jobs. If this same sum were released for private consumption (via tax cuts) 112 000 jobs would be created. Consequently reductions in military spending together with tax reductions could appreciably cut unemployment if both reductions and alternative programmes were selected to have the optimum impact on employment.[11] This general observation – though relevant in terms of demonstrating that arms spending creates fewer jobs than many civilian alternatives – does not answer the question of what happens to the military-related personnel who lose their jobs in defence spending reductions. Later in this chapter the importance of also distinguishing between different kinds of employment-generating activities, relating to military expenditure, will be illustrated.

Finally, on the factor of the rate of technological change in achieving economic development and growth, the 1977 UN report attacked the 'myth' that civilian spin-offs from military R&D have been very significant in relation to technological innovation. Although this did occur during the Second World War, military spin-off from civilian research has been very much larger, the report claimed, and what is remarkable is how little that is new has been developed from civilian spin-off.[12] Defence research has been mostly directed at product improvements relating to specifically military equipment, rather than basic research, with the result that defence and civil technologies have diverged and civilian spin-offs have become comparatively rare. Moreover, military technologies were focusing on areas largely irrelevant for the solution of the world's most pressing problems.

An earlier UN report added the point that, if only a small part of military R&D were used for a direct assault on some of these major global problems, one could expect much greater benefits in the peaceful uses of science than have come from the spin-off from military R&D, provided only that the correct motivation is generated and institutionalised techniques of organisation can be developed.[13]

Summarising these related factors, the 1977 report highlighted a tendency in post-war history for high economic growth and relatively low military expenditure to be correlated in the main industrialised countries. Apart from the fact that lower military expenditure meant that more investment and R&D funds were available in the civilian sector, countries in this situation had more opportunity to respond to growing world demand, particularly in dynamic sectors like electronics, so improving export position and thereby growth performance. Conversely, high military expenditure both diverted capital and skilled personnel from productive employment and also reduced the need to compete in world markets since such countries already had a secure and profitable domestic market for arms. This in turn led to lower productivity growth and balance of payments difficulties which could slow economic growth. However, as the report later pointed out, the production of weapons for export as opposed to weapons for a country's own armed forces is no different in economic terms to any other export production.

Indeed it may be of greater advantage since important sectors of the economy are stimulated as a result of the high technology content of weapons exports.[14] This helps to explain the case of countries like France, which the report did not discuss, in which high military spending and high growth rates were able, to an extent, to go together.[15] Clearly there is no simple cause and effect between high military spending and low rates of economic growth.

PEACE RESEARCH (AND OTHER) STUDIES

Turning now to the peace research field, a survey by Lindgren of the literature on the consequences of military expenditure in the industrialised market economies provides a useful entrance to the subject.[16] This reviewer's assessment will be supplemented, as required, by the observations of other experts on this topic.

Before beginning, though, a cautionary note is required. The extent to which research findings can be generalised across different Western industrialised countries appears limited. Another reviewer, Steve Chan, concluded that a point of diminishing returns had probably been reached as far as cross-national studies were concerned, in terms of their ability to improve understanding of the economic consequences of military expenditure. Although he favoured in-depth national studies instead, on the grounds that claims to generality frequently impose major costs in the sensitivity and specificity of data,[17] for the requirements of this book an assessment of how far the results of research can be generalised will be valuable in both revealing the complexity of the issue and the potential political strength (or weakness) of economic arguments against high military expenditure.

Lindgren's survey referred to a school of thought, beginning with Pryor in 1968, which has investigated the 'trade-offs' within a national economy or state budget, i.e. the reduced civilian components, when military expenditure is increased. He claimed that 'the results have not been conclusive'.[18] Five economic effects were examined, all of them being vital for the long-term development and structural change of the economy. They are investment, economic growth, employment, business cycles and electoral cycles. The question of business cycles relates directly

to the Marxist position which sees military expenditure as vital
to the survival of capitalism (and so will be dealt with in Chapter
4). Research into electoral cycles has so far produced only
contradictory results and will not be considered here.

Significantly, in relation to the criticism made of the UN view
on this matter, Lindgren did not go into detail about the effect of
military spending on inflation because '... the empirical evidence so far is quite meagre'.[19] Not all peace researchers would
agree with this. Apart from Melman, Huisken took the view
that:

> ... although it is not possible even approximately to quantify
> the extent to which military expenditures contribute to infla-
> tion there can be no doubt that these expenditures are among
> the factors at work on both sides of the inflation phenomena
> [i.e. the demand and the supply sides].[20]

His line of argument was similar to that in the UN reports and
need not be repeated here. Perhaps, though, Blackaby came
closest to the mark, for while accepting that in wartime shortages
of goods and labour have inflationary effects, which are normally
reduced by price and wage controls (yet still seen in the
movements of black market prices), he concluded:

> It is quite clear, therefore, that military expenditure can cause
> excess demand and lead to inflation in that way. However,
> given the high figure of unemployment in recent years in the
> Western industrial world, it is not easy to label the inflation of
> the late 1970s as an excess-demand inflation.[21]

Blackaby also stated that, even when unemployment is high
and the general level of demand low, 'bottleneck inflation' can be
caused by sudden increases in military spending. This kind of
inflation arises particularly in the procurement area when there
are specific shortages of skilled labour or material. However,
given a low level of demand in the civilian economy, these
bottlenecks are likely to be of short duration and, indeed, it is the
developing countries with a narrow productive base which tend
to be more prone to them.[22]

Government budget deficits, for which military expenditures
will be partly responsible, may also be a cause of inflation but, as
Blackaby pointed out, this is an area of controversy amongst

economists and '... if the economy is at less than full employment (however defined), it cannot be categorically stated that
the deficit is necessarily a cause of inflation.'[23]

Other authorities, like Mosley, agreed with Blackaby that the
acute inflation since the early 1970s was not caused primarily by
the high levels of military expenditure during this period.[24]
However, there have been few studies on the relationship
between defence spending and inflation that provide any clue as
to how significant a factor military expenditure has been in
generating inflation. A report from the Council on Economic
Priorities, published in 1982, anticipated a renewed bout of high
inflation, after the deep recession of 1981–82, in the wake of
President Reagan's massive arms build-up. Rising prices would
arise principally from bottlenecks in the military supply industries and soaring federal deficits. In the event Adams and Gould,
writing in 1986, were able to argue that such fears proved
unfounded as surplus manufacturing capacity and a large in-
flow of foreign funds to meet public and private borrowing
requirements helped obviate any new inflationary spiral.[25] An
important empirical study by Starr and his colleagues, using
data between 1956 and 1979, found that no significant relationship between defence spending and inflation existed in the USA
or UK but that these variables were mutually related in France
and the FRG.[26] The possible explanations for these different
effects are very complex and do not resolve the issue of causation
since, in the case of France and the FRG, a two-way relationship
between defence spending and inflation is posited.

So it can be concluded that although, in some circumstances
(especially in wartime), military spending may induce inflation
this need not always be the case and there is '... no widespread
agreement about the existence and form of the relationship
between defence spending and inflation'.[27]

Returning to Lindgren's survey, the one area in which an
almost clear-cut consensus has been reached regarding the
effects of military expenditure is on investment. In large measure
this is due to the work of R. Smith whose considerable research
into this question has largely stood the test of time and criticism.
His perspective is a Marxist one although his empirical investigations, using econometric models, are based on Keynesian
categories. Hence his findings can be related to those of
non-Marxists whilst, at the same time, they have formed the

basis for a powerful critique of those Marxists whose economic determinism will be a matter for discussion in the next chapter.

R. Smith used data for fifteen countries over the period 1960–70 and found a significant negative correlation between military expenditure and investment, that is as military expenditure increased investment decreased. Investigating this further, investment was made a function of military spending and the rate of growth and then a regression equation was computed. Military expenditure and the growth rate accounted for 55 per cent of the variation in investment. R. Smith explained these findings by arguing that as workers resist cuts in private consumption and public welfare the remainder of national output will be divided between investment and military expenditure, with a given balance of payments and rate of utilisation (of productive capacity). Higher military expenditure thus leads to lower investment.[28] This negative correlation between investment and military expenditure has been found in studies by other experts as well.[29] Only one did not obtain this result and his investigation was limited to private investment.[30]

Since higher investment is required to achieve a higher rate of economic growth, and as military spending has a negative impact on investment, it would be expected that higher levels of military spending would also have a negative effect on economic growth. Indeed most researchers have found, as Szymanski and Lee did in independent studies undertaken in 1973, that military spending does harm economic growth. Some, like R. Smith, have concluded that this negative effect on growth is the consequence of reduced investments.[31] Yet R. Smith, in particular, is not emphatic on this point for in his introductory remarks on the economic consequences of military expenditure he pointed out:

> Given the character of the industries that supply military procurement, an expansion in military demand may create supply bottlenecks that reduce investment and exports ... but there is no reason to suppose that supply could not adjust subsequently, through the expansion of these industries, were resources available. Over time, extra resources can be generated for military expenditure through growth, though this depends on the extent to which military expenditure helps or hinders the growth process. It may increase the growth rate because it maintains demand and confidence, and aids tech-

nical progress through spin-off. Alternatively, it may reduce growth by diverting resources from investment and exports, causing balance of payments and capacity constraints, while increasing inefficiency in industry through the provision of 'soft' government contracts. At different times, either effect may be dominant.[32]

Lindgren, too, emphasised that one would expect substantial differences in the impact of military spending on growth depending on the extent of excess capacity in the economy. Military expenditure would be expected to stimulate inadequate demand when there was idle production capacity. A study by Brown and Kelleher in 1971 gave support to this deduction in that they found that military expenditure was less of a drain on most components of GNP in a situation of excess capacity. This view rather goes against that expressed in the 1977 UN report, discussed previously.[33] Another danger in looking too crudely at military spending is that sectoral differences (between industries) are not taken into account.

Several studies have been unable to find any correlation between higher military expenditure and growth[34] and one or two have even claimed to find a positive association.[35] Lindgren concluded that the studies of economic growth are not as clear-cut as those of investment. However, almost all the studies agree that higher military spending is not associated with growth (and many found that it tended to hinder growth) but more research was needed to take into account the impact of military expenditure at different phases in the business cycle (in conditions of full or under-utilised capacity).[36]

When it comes to the relationship between military expenditure and employment the position is, if anything, even more complex. However, it can be said that existing studies do not support the argument that disarmament will create unemployment.[37] One problem in investigating the economic effects of military expenditures on employment is, yet again, an inadequate data base which, in particular, does not elaborate sufficiently, if at all, on the levels of national funding over time for different kinds of employment-generating activities, for instance in the armed forces, in the armaments industry and the various defence departments.

R. Smith initially found evidence of a significant correlation between defence expenditure as a proportion of GDP and unemployment but, in a later study, found no convincing evidence of a direct link between military expenditure and unemployment. Data on unemployment was a problem in these studies, too, as they are not standardised for inter-country comparisons. A study by Szymanski in 1973, mentioned previously, found that the level of military spending was negatively associated (with significant exceptions) to unemployment. However, a further conclusion of his appears to be entirely contrary to many other studies which have been done, namely that military spending, whether on personnel or equipment, necessarily creates more jobs per unit of expenditure than most non-military expenditure, which is usually for welfare expenses.[38]

Investigations by Albrecht, Lindroos and DeGrasse all found that, as the UN study cited earlier also demonstrated, military spending creates fewer jobs per $billion spent than almost any other kind of public expenditure.[39] As the actual figures quoted vary widely between sources, depending on the methodology employed, they are not repeated here but this conclusion, for what it is worth, does seem firm. An important exception to this result, though, arose from a Congressional Budget Office (CBO) study which found that an additional $10 billion of either defence or non-defence spending in fiscal year 1983 each created about 250 000 jobs.[40] Clearly, though, in this case non-defence spending was not concentrated only in the more labour intensive service industries but spread across manufacturing as well. It is only when military procurement is replaced by civilian expenditure in the service sector that the differences in employment generation between defence and non-defence spending are evident.

This debate over military expenditure and jobs has been taken further to try to demonstrate that military spending causes unemployment because of the numbers of jobs foregone. Marion Anderson attempted this in *The Empty Pork Barrel: Unemployment and the Pentagon Budget* (1975) and stimulated a lively controversy in which the methodology employed and the empirical data were challenged.[41]

Like R. Smith in 1978, DeGrasse found no association between military expenditure and unemployment.[42] Lindgren again stressed the need to distinguish between different phases of the business cycle. When there is excess capacity, increased military expenditure can create jobs without excluding other types of employment, even if fewer jobs are generated by military spending than by the same amount of public expenditure elsewhere in the economy. However, in the long run, as both Fontanel (in 1980) and Huisken (in 1982) have argued, military expenditure reduces the potential for activities which are more crucial to economic growth.[43] It seems, though, that econometric models are currently unable to provide any definite findings on the relationship between military spending and employment.

Lastly, on the topic of the rate of technological change and the role of spin-offs from military R&D, opinion is divided. On the one hand Kaldor and her colleagues took a very similar view to that expressed in the UN study, cited previously in this chapter. They believed that technological spin-offs from the military sector are comparatively rare and represent a poor return on R&D, as opposed to equivalent civilian R&D expenditure. In their view the qualitative differences between military and civilian technologies have been increased because of the special nature of the post-war defence market.[44] However, on the other hand, the opposite point of view was expressed by a Council for Science and Society report with respect to the perceived convergence of civil and military developments in the microelectronics field. A study by Greenwood on European involvement in the USA's Strategic Defense Initiative also took the view that the relevant technologies include almost all those recognised as potentially vital for civil economies in the 1990s.[45] Clearly the role of spin-offs in the development of the civilian economy remains problematic but there is little doubt that the bulk of military R&D spending, which goes on development rather than basic research, has little or no relevance to the civil sector.

4 The Impact of High Military Expenditures (II)

MELMAN'S STUDIES

Amongst peace researchers Melman's work looms large in this field of study yet in the preceding chapter it has received scarcely a mention. This is not so much by design as simply a reflection of the distinctive approach he has taken, in a series of books written over nearly thirty years, explaining the economic and social consequences of high levels of military spending. Melman himself does not use econometric techniques to test or help elaborate his theory of the 'permanent war economy' (though he does sometimes cite such work undertaken by others). His findings relate to the US economy in particular and, indeed, in his main work on the subject *The Permanent War Economy: American Capitalism in Decline* (1974) he stated that other major capitalist states do not follow the American pattern.[1] However, as in an earlier book, Melman has more recently emphasised the applicability of his ideas to other industrialised countries, particularly the USSR and the UK.[2] Unlike some of the hypotheses and theories adopted by peace researchers which have just been discussed, his theory cannot easily be refuted on empirical grounds. It has not been disproved because it cannot be tested. And it cannot be tested because Melman's theory does not abstract economic relationships from their political context but, on the contrary, attempts to explain the multi-faceted and complex events of American post-war economic history in terms of a military economy dominated by politicians and institutions that believe in, and sustain, an ideology derived from the premise that war brings prosperity. This is its strength and its weakness. Its strength because it takes a holistic approach that is specific to one country, instead of trying to generalise about many. Its weakness, on the other hand, is due to the fact that, precisely because the theory cannot be refuted by the facts alone, it has to stand or fall by the extent to which its assumptions are convincing. The thesis of the permanent war economy becomes, more or less, an article of faith.

None of this in any way invalidates it. Its value to conversion theory and practice has, as will be illustrated in due course, proved inestimable. Its influence on both the UN reports and peace research studies on the economics of arms spending has been, directly or indirectly, significant. Yet the preceding discussion of the findings of peace research clearly indicates the severe limitations, in most aspects of the subject, to formulating testable hypotheses let alone ones which stand up to repeated investigations by various authorities. Thus while scientific studies do appear to demonstrate a trade-off between military expenditure and investment, which strengthens our confidence in the original hypothesis, similar studies on the relationship between military expenditure and employment do not provide confirmation of any comparable trade-off, which must in turn sow some seeds of doubt about the frequently voiced contention that military spending causes unemployment. It *may*, nevertheless, be true yet other theories, themselves perhaps not capable of refutation, may prove more convincing in explaining unemployment simply because they take account of more factors than the theory of permanent war economy, for instance liberal theories of business cycles or the Marxian paradigm of the capitalist system.

Melman's ideas on an alternative to the arms race were first elaborated in 1962.[3]. This led, a few years later, to a major work documenting what he argued was the economic and social damage in the USA, and abroad, caused by two decades of cold war. In this book he gave numerous examples of depletion, that is the process of technical, industrial and human deterioration within American society as a result of excessive military spending.[4] Then, in 1970, Melman addressed himself to what he saw as the cause of this depletion: the unprecedented concentration of political and industrial power as a result of Secretary for Defense McNamara's centralised control system over the operations of military industry.[5] He termed this 'Pentagon capitalism' because of the way the Pentagon treated defence firms as divisions of its own firm.

Although not his most recent book,[6] Melman's main work on the war economy (cited at the start of this chapter) represented the fullest expression of his ideas on this subject. In essence it challenged the thesis that the war economy brings prosperity. The first part of the book, the one that concerns us here, examined how the notion that war brings prosperity arose and analyses both the way in which the military economy works and its unforeseen effects on industrial efficiency and society. Finally Melman considered how the ideology of war economy is sustained in the face of realities which contradict it.

The conclusion that war brings prosperity was the result of American experience in the Second World War which brought to an end the Great Depression. What President Roosevelt's civilian New Deal policy had not achieved, war had: military spending boosted the economy; war work created full employment. And despite some doubts about using military spending as the road to prosperity:

> ... these shared perceptions among Americans spurred the development of an ideological consensus about war economy that has permeated the thinking especially of intellectuals and political leaders since the end of World War II. The ideological consensus that evolved from World War II transformed the justification for military spending from a time-limited economic effort to achieve a political goal (winning World War II) to a sustaining means for governmental control of the economy. It is a central thesis of this book that this consensus on the economic benefits of military spending has played a vital role in marshalling the commitment of the American people to a permanent war economy.[7]

Hardly had the war ended than the confrontations with the Soviet system began and became known as the cold war. Melman argued that the concept of permanent war economy then became a reality as military industry was expanded and put into action to win an arms race that could go on indefinitely.

The support of the American people was necessary to ensure the operation of a war economy. This was forthcoming, in fact strongly so, as people were convinced that large military budgets meant prosperity and jobs. So by the 1950s a broad political consensus had emerged involving industrialists, workers, civil servants and intellectuals all convinced that the war economy was sustainable and, indeed, desirable.[8]

Melman, in looking at the way this war economy worked, started with the military–industrial firm. He defined its central characteristics as cost-maximisation, and maximisation of subsidy payments from the federal government. The economic forces behind these operating features of the military–industrial firm, as well as the state management that controlled it, were contrasted with those of the civilian-product firm. Managers of civilian-product firms, seeking the maximum profit, are restrained from just increasing prices by the existence of competing firms, who may not follow suit, and by customers who may not buy a given product any more or who may buy an alternative. Instead these managers can try to minimise their costs, particularly their costs of production. One of the principal mechanisms for achieving this is by improving internal efficiency and so raising the average productivity of the labour force. However, in the case of military industry big contracts are often arranged by negotiation between the Pentagon and one chosen supplier, so no competition exists. Additionally the Pentagon is usually prepared to pay many times the negotiated price for a product because it usually wants it – for military or political reasons. From the perspective of the military–industrial firm there is no incentive to reduce costs through internal effectiveness, especially considering that if costs go up so do prices and, in consequence, profits. This is true for most defence contracts whether or not they are officially described as cost-plus arrangements. As far as the Pentagon itself is concerned, rising prices are normally met by obtaining further funds from Congress. This extra money paid to military–industrial firms is felt to be good for the economy and provides the logic of subsidy-maximisation.[9]

Melman did not claim that all military–industrial firms have these features. He acknowledged that some do practise a degree of cost-minimisation and many smaller firms, which do some military work, persist in efficient operating procedures. However, the main features described above are the dominant ones.

These and other central operating features of military–industrial firms, including their control by state management, have, according to Melman, imposed special characteristics on the American economy and society as a whole (as well as having important consequences for conversion, which will be investigated in Chapter 7). First, he claimed that because military goods and services have no economic value,[10] whole industries and regions of the USA which specialise in the military economy are put in a 'parasitic' relationship to the civilian economy, since they rely upon it for sustenance but give nothing of economic value in return. This can have serious effects on civilian industry when, for instance, more than half the national research and development effort is concentrated on military activities to the detriment of the civilian sector, which is left at a competitive disadvantage. Secondly, the dynamic of state capitalist managers to extend their control is given unrivalled capability in terms of their ability to draw upon large resources from national income and to avoid or oppose any actions taken to prepare for a peace economy. In this they are supported by employees and communities dependent on the military economy. Thirdly, the economic consequences of the war economy are a mixture of civilian goods and services foregone (the opportunity cost concept discussed in the last chapter) and the major damage inflicted on the economically productive economy. This latter aspect, in the form of depleted industries and a flight of capital from the USA, will be elaborated upon shortly. Fourthly (and perhaps most controversially), the military economy comes to dominate the traditional civilian economy. In relation to three chosen criteria to test this proposition, Melman argued that the military economy has primary control over capital, research and development and the direction taken by educational institutions responsible for new technical talent.[11] He did not imply that the managers of private capitalism had left the scene and ceased to exert influence but that the new economic and social conditions are dominated by the managers of the state capitalist economy.

Melman underlined the fact that two essential requirements for industrial efficiency are better equipment and more effective management. Previously America had excelled in these areas and as a result could afford to pay its workers far more than foreign competitors whose workers received lower wages but were less productive. Now as a result of the permanent war economy a whole series of industries have emerged lacking in both technical and economic capability to meet the requirements of some or all domestic or foreign markets. The capital and technical talent, which the military economy has in abundance, are lacking in these industries as are the managerial and technical methods essential to industrial efficiency. In consequence:

By the 1960s the American war economy had come full circle: from being welcomed as a solution to problems of capital and labor surplus to becoming a prime generator of surplus capital

and surplus labor. The long concentration of talent and
money on nonproductive economic growth had made the
growth prospects for American civilian industry look plainly
unattractive. Technically and economically, American firms
became less competitive and hence uninviting to investors.
But holders of investment capital in the United States, un-
impressed with the growth of domestic opportunity, had
attractive options abroad, especially in Western Europe and
Canada. The capital made surplus by conditions 'at home'
was swiftly converted into profitable investments abroad.[12]

The consequence of this export of capital abroad, and the closure
of factories at home, was the loss of many jobs in the USA.

A comparison between the USA and Japan, a country with a
low level of military expenditure, led Melman to the conclusion
that: '*The Japanese attended to productive economic growth while
the United States built and operated a permanent war economy.*'[13]

Melman argued that the directorate of state capitalism has no
institutional or ideological commitment to ensure a productive
future for American society.[14] He then detailed what he saw as
the many other consequences of reliance on defence spending
including the collapse of the dollar in August 1971, increasing
inflationary pressures and the much needed public expenditures
which have had to be foregone to maintain the military effort.

Finally Melman tried to explain why the war economy
ideology is sustained in the face of so many events which
contradict it. He suggested three reasons for this: the layman's
need to rely on experts for forming opinions on complicated
matters; the 'cultural lag' that exists in teaching and research on
economics which means that the harmful effects of military
spending are largely ignored; and the ideological controls operated by those experts who guard and sustain conventional beliefs
and policies.[15]

Melman's work is, arguably, the most comprehensive economic case against the arms race. A discussion of what emphasis
economic factors (as opposed to strategic, political and military
ones) ought to be given will follow shortly, in the conclusion to
this chapter. Melman's work does raise all the issues relating to
the economic and social consequences of high military spending
without divorcing them from a political context. So even if one
cannot accept every aspect of his case, and this writer does not

accept it in its full rigour, nevertheless it is a most useful analysis against which to set the findings of the other peace researchers discussed beforehand. The main criticism that has to be made is that he overstates his case, perhaps unconsciously to compensate for the neglect of war economy by conventional economists, and tends to blame virtually every social and economic ill on excessive military spending. This is a little too much to digest given an awareness of a multitude of other factors to account for any one of these misfortunes. That said Melman's thesis of permanent war economy forms the basis for a most illuminating and valuable contribution to the economics of disarmament and conversion which will be discussed at length in Chapter 7.

A MARXIST CRITIQUE

This exposition on Melman's work brings to a close what has, of necessity, been a highly condensed assessment of views, within the United Nations and amongst peace researchers, on the harmful effects of high levels of military spending. Before summarising the conclusions which may be drawn from this review it is necessary to consider a Marxist view, touched on previously, that high military expenditures are vital to the continued functioning of the Western capitalist system. Although various versions of this perspective exist, perhaps the best known, and most influential, was that formulated by Baran and Sweezy in the mid-1960s. The main line of argument, as well as a Marxist critique of their position, will be briefly outlined in order to demonstrate why this writer does not accept the necessity of high military expenditures in a modern capitalist economy. However, this will not involve a complete repudiation since the attention Baran and Sweezy and others have drawn to political constraints on economic change is accepted as a valid criticism of some liberal approaches to conversion matters.

Baran and Sweezy analysed the nature of the American capitalist system in their day and emphasised the extent to which many industries were dominated by huge corporations. Under this 'monopoly capitalism', as the system was described, '... owing to the nature of the price and cost policies of the giant corporations, there is a strong and systematic tendency for surplus to rise, both absolutely and as a share of total output'.[16]

By 'surplus' was meant, in briefest terms, the difference between what a society produces and the costs of producing it.[17] For the sake of argument this contention, concerning the tendency for economic surplus to rise, can simply be accepted without explaining in detail the process by which it occurs.

The problem Baran and Sweezy highlighted is how this growing surplus is to be absorbed. One method is capitalists' consumption and investment, but this is insufficient on its own. Another is through the sales effort. The third method of absorbing the growing surplus is by government spending. This role of government is very important:

> The structure of the monopoly capitalist economy is such that a continually mounting volume of surplus simply could not be absorbed through private channels; if no other outlets were available it would not be produced at all. What government absorbs is in addition to, not subtracted from, private surplus. Even more: since a larger volume of government spending pushes the economy nearer to capacity operation, and since up to this point surplus grows more rapidly than effective demand as a whole, it follows that both the government and the private segments of surplus can and indeed typically do grow simultaneously. It is only when government absorption continues to expand even after full utilization has been reached, as during the later years of the Second World War, that private surplus is encroached upon.[18]

Baran and Sweezy illustrated these relationships by reference to corporate profits before and after taxes in recent decades. Increased levels of corporate taxation had not prevented after-tax profits growing as the economy expanded during the 1950s.[19] Baran and Sweezy rejected the view that there were massive private interests opposed to increased government spending and taxes. (The situation did, of course, change in the 1970s and 1980s.) However, by examining modalities of political power in American capitalist society, they came to the conclusion that defence spending was greatly preferred by the private interests which control the big corporations in preference to other non-defence spending:

> It is of course in the area of defence purchases that most expansion has taken place ... This massive absorption of

surplus in military preparations has been the key fact of postwar American economic history ... If military spending were reduced once again to pre-Second World War proportions the nation's economy would return to a state of profound depression, characterized by unemployment rates of 15 per cent and up, such as prevailed during the 1930s.[20]

So high levels of military spending were seen as an essential prop to the capitalist economy to absorb economic surpluses and maintain economic growth. Defence spending is more politically acceptable because, whereas in most cases spending on civilian projects by governments stands in opposition to the private interests of the oligarchy who control the major corporations, spending on defence involves no competition with private enterprise and provides a virtually risk-free means of making large profits. Added to this is the need of the American oligarchy to have a large military machine to contain, and eventually destroy, the rival socialist system in the world today. Baran and Sweezy did point out the economic and military limitations of arms spending as an instrument of economic control, and even suggested that big military outlays may have reached the point of contributing substantially to an increase in unemployment.[21] However, this only related to the efficacy of military spending and did not alter their judgement as to its necessity.

This theory has been attacked by radical liberals, notably Melman himself.[22] Melman claimed that the economic need for war economy is related only to the state-capitalist parts of the US economy but is not intrinsic to the civilian part.

However, the most interesting rebuttal of the monopoly capitalism thesis was that provided by R. Smith. Taking a Marxist perspective, but using econometric techniques, he criticised the 'underconsumption' theories of Baran and Sweezy as well as Mandel and Kidron.[23] He argued that this theory presupposed that the state responded to increases in unemployment with increases in military expenditure.

To document the argument that military expenditure is used for stabilisation purposes requires evidence not of a negative multiplier relation between military expenditure and unemployment, but of a positive state reaction function (a state response to actual or expected increases in unemployment with increases in military expenditure). Time-series evidence for the US or UK does not indicate any systematic positive reaction function of this sort.[24]

In fact it is war, not military expenditure, which has generated full employment – in the USA the unemployment rate was below 4 per cent only during the Second World War through to 1948, the Korean War period 1951–53 and the Vietnam War period 1966–69 – so economic determinism, R. Smith maintained, would lead one to conclude that the wars were generated by the need to legitimise the defence spending required to maintain full employment! But it is not clear that this was the case in, say, the escalation of the Vietnam War. An alternative explanation of the data is that American capitalism prefers high unemployment so as to keep workers quiescent, and only sacrifices that objective when war is deemed necessary to maintain its international domination. Also R. Smith asked, quite pertinently, what reason capitalism would have in maintaining full employment especially as such a situation undermines labour discipline and so endangers profits and leads to instability.[25]

R. Smith rejected the view that high military expenditure was caused by the need to maintain demand. He pointed out, as Melman had done, that some capitalist states had maintained demand without military spending levels comparable to those in the USA. He posited an alternative view:

> ... that the functions of military expenditure were not primarily to maintain demand, and that its economic consequences may have been contradictory – expenditure necessary for strategic reasons had economic consequences which, in fact, undermined the system it was intended to support.[26]

These economic consequences have already been investigated. On the other hand, the strategic requirements of capitalism involve a need to create a political and military superstructure to defend the economic system. There are three aspects to this: the defence of the 'free world' from the threat of communism; influence amongst capitalist states and the ability of the dominant Western power (the USA) to organise the system, which depend on relative military strength; and, within each state, the military power to meet threats arising internally to the existing order.[27] So R. Smith contended that while the underconsumption argument is inadequate, military expenditure is essential to maintain capitalism as an international system.

One final point merits consideration before leaving the Marxist view on military spending. Granted that, as Melman and R. Smith have argued, military spending is not economically necessary to the functioning of capitalism might it not still have some role in stabilising the system? Lindgren's review suggested there is some evidence for military expenditure as a counter-cyclical instrument in the USA.

Lindgren cited the work of Cypher in 1974 which concluded that, in various post-war recessions, military expenditures were used as counter-cyclical devices in order to end these recessions. However, Lindgren questioned this conclusion and stressed the importance of distinguishing between military spending which is used as a deliberate instrument of economic policy and that which has the unintended consequence of stabilising the system. He stated that while Nincic and Cusack (in 1979) referred to some anecdotal evidence from the Nixon administration to support the former proposition, the work of Krell (in 1981), based on both an analysis of quantitative data and the Economic Reports of the President, concluded that military expenditure is only one of many possible instruments of economic or fiscal policy and, in fact, its relative weight has declined. Nevertheless other studies, including one by R. Smith and Georgiou in 1983, provided some support for the view that US military expenditure is used to regulate the economic system.[28] So while military spending cannot be regarded as economically essential to the maintenance of capitalism – and it is worth noting that official Soviet thinking on this matter was brought into line with this view, in the early 1960s, in order to allow for the possibility of reaching arms control agreements[29] – there does seem to be some evidence, at least in the USA, for the view that military spending can be used to help regulate the economy.

SUMMARY AND CONCLUSIONS

As the preceding discourse over the last two chapters will have amply illustrated, this subject is a complex and difficult one in which various, sometimes conflicting theories have been propounded and for which conclusive, supporting evidence is frequently, if unavoidably, lacking. Yet it is no more possible to circumvent these difficulties or the topic itself than it is to have a coin with only one side to it. The economics of disarmament is the other side of the coin from the economics of the armaments build-up and the two are, therefore, inextricably linked. What has been learnt from the latter, and how it affects the former, in the Western market economies?

Within the liberal perspective, the extent to which the United Nations studies have been influenced by the findings of peace research is quite marked, particularly from the 1977 report onwards. These reports, especially the more recent ones, have in many respects reflected the more radical peace research theories on the economic consequences of the arms race,[30] which as the foregoing review has shown, are only partially supported by empirical studies. This is encouraging, in one sense, as it allows the United Nations to use its modest influence on public opinion continually to lay stress on the harmful effects of high levels of military spending, but in another way perhaps it illustrates the political impotence of the United Nations in that Western (and Eastern) governments have, on the whole, been able to sanction these reports without feeling that any political action on their part is necessary to reduce levels of military expenditure. More importantly, it throws into sharp relief the difficulties of generating sufficient political support for the economic case against high levels of military spending when governments, supported by a substantial section of their publics, continue to regard, rightly or wrongly, political and military factors as being of overriding importance.

The peace research (and other) studies have, unsurprisingly, not reached a consensus on the economics of high military spending. Most, though, would agree with Blackaby, that it is the opportunity costs of defence expenditure that represent the most powerful part of the economic case against the arms race:

> The main economic point to make about military expenditure is a very simple one: it uses up resources which might alternatively be employed to provide consumer satisfactions – either in the provision of private or collective goods and services. In particular, if the skill and ingenuity devoted to weapons development were diverted to civil objectives, the process of technological advance in the civil field could be appreciably accelerated.[31]

Additionally, most researchers appear to concur with the view
that there is a trade-off between military expenditure and investment.[32] When it comes to economic growth, though, the
picture becomes much less clear. Almost all the studies showed
that higher military spending was not linked to growth, and
some found that it tended to hinder growth, yet the precise
impact depended on various factors, not least of which was the
existence of excess productive capacity. The relationship between military spending and employment (and unemployment)
is not at all clear except that existing studies do not support the
argument that disarmament will lead to unemployment. Indeed
one of the few points on which studies do largely concur is that as
a mechanism for creating jobs military spending is not as
suitable as almost any other kind of public expenditure. The
contention that military spending is a significant cause of
inflation, except in wartime conditions or bottleneck situations,
remains unproven.

Yet the more radical theories on the economic and social
consequences of military spending, notably that of Melman,
have had considerable influence not only on the United Nations
studies but the Western peace movements and, more recently,
some parts of the labour and union movements. Even though the
evidence so far corroborates only a part of those theories they
remain sufficiently convincing, in theoretical terms, to retain the
support of those who, for various reasons, oppose the arms race
and high levels of military expenditure. Yet the question remains
as to the relative weight to be attached to economic (as opposed
to political, military or moral) factors in reversing the seemingly
unstoppable tide of global spending on armaments and in
convincing the public of the need for disarmament.

Returning to the earlier analysis of the arms race, the 1977
UN report pointed out that removing one of the forces behind
the arms race will be insufficient to reverse its course.[33] Even if
the economic case against high military expenditures was a clear
and simple one – which, in some aspects, it is not – and even if
the empirical data to support it were incontrovertible – which,
again, is not often so – and, finally, even if everyone were in
agreement with it – which is also not so[34] – it would not
necessarily have a great effect on the intensity of the arms race.
For whatever the arguments about the domestic causes of the
arms race, the 'follow-on' imperative in industry, and so on, the

ideological justification for high levels of military spending, as R. Smith rightly observed, rests on perceived strategic require-ments for the defence of Western capitalism. (A similar point could be made for the Eastern state socialist countries.) In short, the economic case against the arms race is bound to remain subordinate to wider strategic arguments, whatever the real reasons for the armaments build-up in any particular case, and the prospects for convincing the public otherwise must remain limited, especially given the complexity and difficulty of some parts of the theories involved.

So the economic case against the arms race, important as it is, ought to be part of a wider disarmament strategy which takes into account these other political and military factors. Neverthe-less, in relation to the economics of disarmament, what it does do is to provide the basis for showing, in economic terms, both the desirability and feasibility of converting military industries. The economics of disarmament will have similar limitations to the economics of the arms race, as will be seen, but this is an inevitable constraint on any essentially economic approach to conversion. The Marxist perspective of Baran and Sweezy and others did at least have one redeeming feature to an economic determinism which is largely unconvincing, even to a Marxist like R. Smith. It took into account the political constraints on economic choices and this is a theme which will be taken up again in Chapter 8.

One of the dangers, which Lindgren emphasised, in the debate on the economic and social consequences of the arms race is that over-generalisations will be made which obscure more than they reveal. To avoid this, and set the context for the discussion of the economics of disarmament and conversion, the next step is to examine the features of the main Western defence industries.

5 The Major Western Defence Industries

The defence industries[1] are the focus of conversion efforts. Yet until comparatively recently very little by way of in-depth research had been done into the economic parameters of those industries. A great deal of theorising about conversion had been undertaken on the basis of a very limited data base. The publication of *The Structure of the Defense Industry: An International Survey*, edited by Nicole Ball and Milton Leitenberg (1983), represented therefore an important step forward in that it provided a comparative assessment of the economic parameters of the defence industries of several countries, including all the major Western industrialised states except the United Kingdom. (The latter was confined to a statistical appendix.)[2] As the authors of this study themselves claimed:

> Any realistic assessment of the effects of reductions in defence industries – that is, the conversion of military industries to civilian uses – must take as its starting point the role played by these industries in present-day national economies.[3]

By comparing and contrasting the main features of the major Western defence industries it will be possible to determine how far the basic findings of conversion literature are generalisable from one country to another. The countries with which this book is concerned are the United States of America, the United Kingdom, France, the Federal Republic of Germany, Italy and Sweden.[4] All except Sweden are members of NATO, although France does not belong to its military structure. Each country attempts to maintain an indigenous defence industry although, as will be seen, Italy and Sweden have had the greatest difficulty in sustaining self-sufficiency in all major types of equipment for their armed forces. Indeed only the USA has the capacity for almost complete self-reliance and even that superpower has chosen to encourage some limited arms imports from its NATO partners.

Since most conversion literature relates to the USA it seems appropriate to discuss its defence industry in some depth. The structure of the defence industries of the other countries can then be compared with that in the USA and also between themselves.

One particular problem, which has already been referred to in Chapter 2, needs to be highlighted in the context of this comparative study, namely the incomplete if not fragmentary nature of the data available. The barriers of state and commercial secrecy are formidable, although the extent to which this is so varies immensely from the United States and Sweden, where freedom of information is greatest, to the European continental states, where sometimes hardly any official data is available.[5] The UK comes somewhere in between, but probably closer to her European partners than the USA or Sweden. Consequently care must be taken, particularly in interpreting quantitative measurements of different defence industries, since not only are figures more reliable from some countries than others, but the basis on which statistics are collected often varies between these countries. Certain categories of information, like the capital value and profitability of the defence industries, are so difficult to obtain or interpret accurately that for the purposes of this exercise they have been left out of the reckoning (though they are discussed in Ball and Leitenberg, where possible).

THE US DEFENCE INDUSTRY

As already noted, a full-scale defence industry only emerged in the USA after the end of the Second World War. This industry was sustained by comparatively high levels of peacetime defence spending, illustrated in Table 5.1. Of special note is the high level of expenditure on research, development, testing and evaluation (RDT&E) which in some years has reached up to 40 per cent of total funds for investment in new military equipment (RDT&E plus procurement). It should also be borne in mind that military-related spending within the Department of Energy, tied to the development and production of warheads, and within the National Aeronautics and Space Agency, relating to the military's space programme, are not included in the figures in Table 5.1.[6] Moreover since 1980 the proportion of the Federal budget, and GNP, devoted to defence increased under President Reagan's big rearmament programme.

It is the monopsonistic power of the US Department of

Table 5.1   US Department of Defense budget, selected years

Financial year	Total obligational authority ($ million)			Budget as percentage of	
	Total	Procurement	RDT&E[1]	Federal budget	GNP
1950	14 337	4 176	553	27.4	4.4
1955	33 790	8 917	2 621	51.3	9.2
1960	40 257	11 137	5 476	45.0	8.3
1965	49 561	14 112	6 433	38.7	7.0
1968	74 965	22 528	7 263	43.2	9.3
1970	75 517	19 161	7 399	39.2	8.0
1972	76 502	18 526	7 584	32.4	6.7
1975	86 176	17 320	8 632	26.0	5.8
1978	116 494	30 346	11 474	22.9	5.0
1980	139 343	35 792	13 517	22.6	5.1

[1] Research, development, testing and evaluation.

Source: Judith Reppy, 'The United States', in *The Structure of the Defense Industry: An International Survey*, edited by Nicole Ball and Milton Leitenberg (Beckenham, 1983), p. 24.

Defense (DoD) which, above all else, defines the principal features of the defence industry. While the private defence firms have influence they exercise it within constraints laid down by the government's ability to determine the rules of market-place transactions.[7] The most significant features of this defence market, which emanate from the role of governmental demand, are:

- an emphasis on the performance of high technology weaponry rather than the cost;
- risk is borne principally by the government, which supplies most of the R&D funding;
- elaborate rules and regulations for contracts, progress reports and final audits so as to ensure public accountability;
- a complex, well developed budget process within both the DoD and Congress;
- close personal relationships between major defence contractors and the DoD, ensured by regular exchanges of people and information between these enterprises.[8]

These features favour firms which have specialised in defence rather than commercial work.

The military stress on advanced technology results in hundreds of weapons development programmes which are keenly sought by the defence firms as the best means of obtaining the subsequent production contracts. These development programmes are characterised by 'buy-ins', whereby firms understate the problems of technological risk and costs in order to win the initial contract; by 'gold-plating', which results in continuous technological elaborations during the lifetime of the projects in order to keep pace with the latest technical breakthroughs or meet perceived threats arising from a potential aggressor's own weapons development programmes; by 'cost-overruns', which are a consequence of both the previous two characteristics as well as the general tendency of those defence markets which are largely uncompetitive.[9]

There tends to be a mutual interest between defence firms and military customers resulting from the advantage that both gain from ensuring the continuance of the various weapons programmes. Defence firms themselves, through their trade associations, lobby for large defence budgets.

The defence industry is characterised by stability, at least amongst the top contractors. Turnover rates have been low for over twenty years.[10] This is partly due to impediments to new entry arising from the need for very high technical capabilities coupled with mastery of complex government regulations. Also of consequence – and highly relevant to conversion issues – is the difficulty of leaving the defence market as a result of different attitudes to cost control and different marketing skills required to operate successfully in civilian markets.

Competition tends to be very limited in defence markets. In financial year 1980, 64 per cent of all prime contracts were let on a sole-source basis involving no competition whatever. Only rarely does a major firm lose out completely in obtaining prime contracts. The industry is highly concentrated, too, for in financial year 1980 the top ten contractors received 30 per cent of all prime contract awards.[11] There has been some diversification within the main defence firms, though, so that as technological trends have changed these companies have entered new technological areas either through acquisition or developing new capabilities.

Amongst the top defence firms there is a wide variation in the degree of defence dependence, measured in terms of sales.

However, within the firms themselves, defence and civilian oriented subsidiaries are usually kept separate (and the defence dependency of the former may be very much higher than that of the parent company). Civilian oriented subsidiaries can provide a financial buffer against the uncertainties of the defence market,[12] particularly for those parent companies that are most defence dependent.

Defence work is concentrated in those industrial sectors which contribute most to major items of military hardware since 61 per cent of all DoD prime contract awards in financial year 1980 related to such hardware. Aircraft, missile and space systems, electronics and communications accounted for 75 per cent of this amount while shipbuilding for another 9 per cent. Contract awards for RDT&E follow a similar pattern although shipbuilding itself (as opposed to the equipment used in warships) involves very little R&D. This concentration of domestic defence work in just a few industries results from the emphasis placed on advanced technology, in performing military activities, and the development of aerospace and missile systems in private industry. As regards the latter point, it should also be noted that in 1980 eight out of the top ten defence companies were in the aerospace industry.[13]

The aerospace industry is dominated by the DoD. It has faced increasing difficulties over the years in coping with the problem of excess capacity due to a decline in the numbers of aircraft produced each year. This itself is partly a function of their rising cost due to increased technological sophistication. As a result the aerospace industry adopted strategies during the 1970s involving increased foreign military sales and diversification.[14]

Likewise shipbuilding programmes have been dominated by the US Navy, although instability in the ordering of new vessels has created further difficulties for the industry to add to the acute problems in the world-wide merchant shipbuilding market. Other industries, such as missiles and ordnance, are largely dependent on the DoD, although the latter is comparatively small in size. At the other extreme the petroleum refining and electronic computing industries have large sales to the DoD but these are only a very small proportion of total sales. In between these two extremes, of heavy and minimal dependence on the DoD, is the electronics industry which is dependent on the DoD only in specialised product lines. Since the military market is too small compared to civilian markets, which are of prime concern to leading semiconductor firms, the DoD has to cultivate a select group of manufacturers who will produce to exacting military specifications.[15]

A huge number of subcontractors lie behind the big prime contractors. About half of all prime contracts are subcontracted to the divisions of other prime contractors or to smaller firms, each group taking roughly equal shares.[16] However, the lack of comprehensive data in this area makes analysis difficult, even in the United States.

At the beginning of the 1980s military R&D accounted for about one quarter of total spending on R&D in the USA, although in the 1950s and 1960s it was very much more. This miltary R&D has accelerated the development of certain technologies in the civilian field, e.g. computers, jet engines and integrated circuits. However, Reppy took the view that, in the case of the USA, as military technology has become more specialised it has increasingly diverged from the common technology base shared with civilian users and, on balance, the opportunity costs of military R&D are probably more significant than the recognisable spin-off benefits to the civilian economy.[17] This view is similar to that expressed in the UN study discussed in Chapter 3.

Turning to an examination of the geographical distribution of DoD contracts it is very noticeable that these are concentrated in the regions where the main defence industries, described previously, are based. The pattern of defence contracts does not, therefore, follow that of manufacturing activity in general. California was found to be the most defence dependent region in the USA with 21 per cent of the total value of military prime contracts in financial year 1979.[18]

Unsurprisingly, defence employment follows this pattern of regional and industrial concentration of military spending. Altogether 5 058 000 people were engaged in defence-related employment in the USA in 1980. This represented 4.7 per cent of the labour force or 5.1 per cent of total employment. Of this total 3 036 000 were DoD Civil Service employees and military personnel and 2 022 000 were in defence-related industry, including indirect employment in supplier industries but not the multiplier effect on the economy of DoD purchases of goods and services.[19]

An occupational analysis of defence industry employment in financial year 1970 revealed that there was a lower level of service workers but a higher level of blue-collar workers in the defence economy compared to the economy as a whole. The employment of scientists and engineers in defence work closely follows the percentage of national R&D funds spent on defence, that is about 25 per cent[20] – though this does not allow for substantial cyclical variations.

Finally a brief word is called for on the role played by foreign military sales which in financial year 1978 accounted for 4.7 per cent of total US exports and produced a weapons trade surplus of $6.7 billion. Only $120 million was spent on arms imports in that year. The value which aerospace firms place on export orders for military equipment has already been touched upon but US governments themselves have, during the 1970s and 1980s, tended to place greater emphasis on selling weapons rather than simply transferring them to client countries as military assistance. Although President Carter did attempt to reverse this policy change he did not have much success. In financial year 1971 weapons exports totalled only $1.4 billion but by financial year 1980 they had reached $15.3 billion.[21] Inflation could be held only partly responsible for this increase. One of the most important factors, assisting this growth of military exports was the rapid increase in sales to the oil-producing Middle Eastern countries with large, newly-acquired cash surpluses to dispose of. On the other hand, sales to industrialised countries have often required production sharing arrangements, particularly in the case of NATO countries determined to protect their own defence industries, and it is agreements like these, rather than military sales to developing countries, which could have a significant impact on the US defence industry in terms of technology transfer and employment.

US VERSUS WESTERN EUROPEAN DEFENCE INDUSTRIES

How does the US defence industry compare with the major Western European industries? To answer this question a comparison of the principal characteristics of the defence economies of all the countries involved is required. This is intended to bring out the main points of similarity and difference between the structure of each national defence industry.

The arms industries of France, Germany and Italy lay in ruins after the Second World War because of wartime devastation. In the case of Germany in particular, the Allied powers destroyed the remaining arms production facilities after hostilities had ceased.[22] Apart from the USA, only the UK and Sweden survived with their defence industries largely or wholly intact: the former as it had not been occupied and had, with American assistance, largely recovered from the bombing raids of earlier years, and the latter in consequence of its neutral status. So both the USA and UK had a head start on the other major Western powers in building up their weapons development and production facilities under the joint influences of the cold war and the increased rate of technological change.

Rearmament in the FRG could only begin in 1951 when arms production was legalised once again. In 1955 the West German government took over control of armaments manufacture from the Allies except for certain categories, like atomic weapons, which were prohibited by the Western European Union. Imports of arms accounted for 60 per cent of procurement in the late 1950s and it was only in the early 1960s that the first steps were taken to establish independent aerospace and tank industries in the FRG. Later, projects in the aerospace sector suffered a setback with the cancellation of various military and civilian projects in the later 1960s and early 1970s. Some of these deficiencies were made good in the later 1970s but German military technology has continued to suffer severe limitations, particularly in electronics and aero-engine design and manufacture, so technology has had to be borrowed from partners in various collaborative projects, notably the Tornado combat aircraft.[23]

The history of Italy's post-war development of its arms industry showed a similar reliance on imported technology, especially manufacture under licence from the Americans, which enabled the country to build up a technological base for creating new indigenous weapons systems.[24] Collaborative projects also became more important in the later years and, again, the Tornado features prominently amongst these.

American aid was important in the reconstruction of the French defence industry bewteen 1948–58 at the same time as

France attempted to rebuild its civilian industries and fight a number of expensive colonial wars. However, in 1959 it exploded its own nuclear device and from 1960 on, under an increasingly independent foreign policy, its arms production plans were developed through a series of five-year programme-laws.[25]

As Tables 5.2 and 5.3 illustrate, the main difference between the USA and the major Western European countries is in the absolute size of its defence spending which is also significantly greater in relation to Gross Domestic Product (GDP).

In relative terms the UK led the other European powers in defence spending during the period 1978–87. The Conservative government, which took office in May 1979, increased military expenditure rapidly until 1985, so much so that it almost drew level with France which, in absolute terms, has had the largest defence budget in Western Europe. The greater defence burdens of these two states are due to historical reasons, already advanced, as well as matters of policy concerning national security and the maintenance of a defence-industrial base which could offer as high a degree of self-sufficiency in armaments manufacture as possible.

It is worth noting, too, that Sweden has had to carry a heavier defence burden than Italy, in percentage terms, as the price for maintaining a considerable domestic defence industry. This in turn has been necessary in order to enhance Swedish credibility over its neutral foreign policy stance, which could scarcely be sustained if Swedish defence policy were seen to be over-dependent on imported military technology from West or East.

When military R&D is examined on its own, given the exceptional importance it has in a technological arms race, the disparities between the major Western powers become even more striking. Table 5.4 sets out the recent position.

The contrast between the high levels of R&D expenditure for weapons production in the USA, UK and France, on the one hand, and the much lower levels in FRG and Italy, on the other hand, is quite marked. Moreover, in the USA and UK in particular, military R&D accounted for a high proportion of all government-funded R&D: approximately 60 per cent and 49 per cent, respectively, based on average figures for the period 1981–84.[26] The opportunity costs are especially severe for the much smaller and weaker UK economy and the lack of sufficient civilian R&D funds has recently become a matter of increasing

Table 5.2 Military expenditure[1] for six Western powers, 1978–87

Country	1978	1979	1980	1981	1982	1983	1984	1985	1986	1987
USA	189 071	190 747	194 479	210 873	222 650	240 091	251 355	269 157	282 935	275 190
France	25 076	25 646	26 104	26 737	27 287	27 753	27 656	27 641	28 459	29 038
UK	21 371	22 027	23 497	23 076	25 142	26 408	27 583	27 603	27 304	27 019
FRG	20 974	21 255	21 550	21 808	21 527	21 707	21 485	21 529	22 127	22 447
Italy	10 104	10 744	11 241	11 316	12 103	12 372	12 737	13 196	13 463	13 885
Sweden	3 570	3 710	3 595	3 516	3 430	3 327	3 332	3 293	3 332	3 408

[1] Figures for military expenditure are in US $ million at 1986 prices and exchange rates.

Source: SIPRI, SIPRI Yearbook 1988: World Armaments and Disarmament (Oxford University Press, 1988), Table 6A.2, pp. 163–4.

Table 5.3 Military expenditure as a percentage of GDP for six Western powers, 1978–87

Country	1978	1979	1980	1981	1982	1983	1984	1985	1986	1987
USA	5.1	5.1	5.4	5.8	6.3	6.5	6.4	6.6	6.7	6.4
UK	4.6	4.6	4.9	4.8	5.2	5.3	5.4	5.3	5.0	4.9
France	3.9	3.9	4.0	4.1	4.1	4.1	4.0	4.0	3.9	4.0
FRG	3.3	3.3	3.3	3.4	3.4	3.4	3.3	3.2	3.1	3.1
Sweden	3.0	2.9	2.9	2.9	2.8	2.6	2.6	2.5	2.5	2.4
Italy	2.4	2.4	2.1	2.1	2.3	2.3	2.3	2.3	2.2	2.2

Source: SIPRI, *SIPRI Yearbook 1988: World Armaments and Disarmament* (Oxford University Press, 1988), Table 6A.3, pp. 168–9.

Table 5.4 Military R&D[1] for six Western powers, 1977–85

Country	1977	1978	1979	1980	1981	1982	1983	1984	1985
USA	16 363.6	16 206.8	15 850.5	15 766.5	17 125.2	19 386.4	21 050.5	23 673.7	27 796.7[3]
UK	2 936.8[4]	3 181.8[4]	3 503.9[4]	3 718.7[4]	3 583.3[4]	3 354.0	3 514.1	3 695.2[3,4]	3 814.2[3,4]
France	1 982.8	2 235.2	2 517.1	2 685.8	3 276.1	3 116.5	3 081.3	3 303.0	3 152.1
FRG	991.1	1 047.0	1 072.3	951.8	813.7	809.6	873.1	899.9	1 139.8
Sweden	[2]	323.0	281.0	228.6	210.6	246.4	311.3	358.9	387.1
Italy	58.1	59.5	46.4	48.7[5]	166.6	121.4	160.3	259.4	325.2

[1] Figures for military R&D are in US $ million at 1980 prices and exchange rates.
[2] Information not available.
[3] Provisional figure.
[4] SIPRI estimate.
[5] Break in series.

Source: SIPRI, *SIPRI Yearbook 1987: World Armaments and Disarmament* (Oxford University Press, 1987), Table 6.10, p. 156, citing M. Acland-Hood, SIPRI, *Military R&D Resource Use and Arms Control* (Oxford, forthcoming), appendix 1.

public concern.[27] In France, where military R&D represented
about 36 per cent of government R&D between 1981 and 1984,
there has instead been public concern over a perceived lag in
military R&D spending. This threatens the quality of French
arms, and hence affects the country's independent military
posture while also reducing the economic competitiveness of the
French arms industry, whose strategic importance will be elaborated upon later. Kolodziej pointed out, in 1983, that since the
1960s France has, in fact, been a net importer of technology. In
sharp contradistinction neither the FRG nor Italy devote a large
share of government R&D resources to military ends: around 8
per cent and 6 per cent respectively over the period 1981–84. In
the FRG military R&D has declined since the 1960s as a part of
total R&D mainly because the federal authorities now finance a
much larger share of all R&D resources. The level of R&D funds
for military purposes in Italy has, according to the defence
companies in aerospace and electronics, been brought up to
minimum requirements through using their own resources. The
low priority of R&D in the Italian defence budget is partly due
to the fact that sizeable R&D is included in particular weapons
programmes.[28] However, Table 5.4 suggests that, in absolute
terms, Italian military R&D has virtually doubled in size since
1981, in real terms. Nevertheless the continuing dependence of
the FRG and Italy on imported technology for many military
procurement programmes remains quite clear. Finally, Sweden
has to bear a burden of military R&D spending which, at about
19 per cent of government R&D between 1981 and 1984 almost
puts it into the ranks of the Great Powers.

The defence market itself is structured along very similar lines
in all six Western countries. In each country the government
alone can purchase military hardware for national defence
purposes. Likewise the government determines the rules under
which contracts are negotiated and agreed between its ministry
of defence and the defence firms, whether private or public. All
but one of the principal features of the US defence market are
mirrored by its European counterparts: the emphasis on
weapons' performance rather than cost; elaborate rules and
regulations to ensure public accountability (though much more
is kept secret from the public itself in Europe than the USA,
except perhaps in Sweden); a complicated budget process in
defence ministries if not in parliaments; close personal relation-

ships between major defence contractors and the ministries of defence. There are, no doubt, differences of degree between the countries involved but none of substance. The additional feature of the defence market in which these differences appear to be most pronounced concerns the risk borne by the government through its funding of R&D. In the case of the FRG and Italy the risk is substantially reduced through dependence on imported technology and, in the latter country, reliance on the defence companies funding some of the R&D costs themselves.

Following from these characteristics of the defence market arms manufacturers have emerged in all six countries whose specialist knowledge and experience give them a substantial, if not overwhelming, advantage over civilian firms in winning defence contracts. Problems of waste and inefficiency in defence procurement seem to plague the European arms industries as they do the USA's, despite persistent efforts by various governments to control costs and increase efficiency. And, no doubt, the tendency to mutual interest between military customers and defence firms is no less likely in Western Europe than the USA since the reasons for wishing to ensure continuance of the various weapons programmes obviously arise from very similar pressures.

Although the evidence in Europe is much more patchy it does appear that, allowing for mergers and takeovers, turnover rates amongst the top contractors have, in most cases, been on the low side, i.e. few major firms have entered or left the various national defence markets over the last twenty-five years. This is what would be expected, given the same kind of structural obstacles to new entry or exit from the defence market, whether a European or an American context is being considered.

The pattern of competition and concentration within US military industries is largely repeated, as far as the evidence allows a judgement to be made, in the European counterparts. Taking competition first, in the UK 62 per cent of contracts (by value) were awarded non-competitively in 1983–84 (though the government's declared objective to increase competition between defence firms has reduced this proportion to 51 per cent in 1987–88) while in the FRG the BWB (the Federal Office of Military Technology and Procurement) contracted 88 per cent of its orders in the late 1970s without any tenders at all.[29] Regarding the concentration of the top ten defence firms, the figures show an even higher proportion of defence output accounted for by the top ten in the UK, where they took 70 per cent of domestic military expenditure in 1983–84; in the FRG, where they had 37 per cent of defence sales in 1977; in Italy, where they obtained 42.5 per cent of total domestic arms sales in 1980; and in Sweden, where they gained an overwhelming 80 per cent of all domestically produced equipment orders in 1983–84.[30] It appears that the smaller size of the European defence markets makes the degree of industry concentration even greater than in the USA.

Until recently only the FRG and Sweden were similar to the USA in terms of most defence firms being in private hands. In the FRG the majority of arms producers remain privately owned concerns, rather than going 'public' (to obtain wider share ownership), while in the electronics sector there are a large number of foreign-owned subsidiaries which seem to reflect the technological gap in the area of advanced military electronics.[31] As for Sweden, most defence firms, except the warship yards which are state-controlled, are in the private sector. Previously the state sector was dominant in the UK as far as its aerospace, shipbuilding and munitions sectors were concerned but under the current government's privatisation programme the major arms companies in all these industries have been returned to the private sector. Electronics was always a private sector concern and its main defence companies are British not foreign. France had a substantial private sector until 1981 but the socialist government then nationalised nine industrial groups including a number of important defence firms. This factor, coupled with pre-existing government control of an arsenal and shipbuilding complex and the military part of the output of semi-public firms, has meant that the public sector dominated all major parts of the defence industry including electronics, airframe and missile development, where the private sector had previously played a substantial role. However, some defence firms were again privatised after the Socialists lost power in 1986. In Italy, too, state control has been prevalent in aircraft and shipbuilding firms as well as in the 'defence industrial area' – a complex of 30 plants and arsenals and, additionally, several technical, research and maintenance centres. However, the private sector dominates the electronics industry.[32]

The defence industry in the USA was characterised by widely

varying degrees of dependency on military work amongst the arms manufacturers themselves, but a high degree of concentration of those firms within a few key industrial sectors. Where evidence is available in the UK, the FRG and Sweden, the European position follows a very similar pattern. It is hard to generalise about the defence dependency of the arms companies in these countries since they vary considerably, even for firms in the same industrial sector. One author stated that the official policy of the FRG's BWB of limiting individual firms' dependence on arms production so as not to mix procurement with employment decisions, while not being entirely successful, may have resulted in top arms producers being less reliant on weapons contracts than other Western European counterparts.[33] The way in which weapons production is concentrated in military orientated subsidiaries in the major defence firms is clear both in the UK and Sweden, though evidence from the other countries is insufficiently disaggregated to be able to confirm this in their cases.

As in the USA, it tends to be, broadly speaking, the aerospace, electronics and shipbuilding industries of Western Europe which account, in varying degrees, for the bulk of procurement expenditure.[34] On the whole aerospace is the most dependent on military work and electronics the least, but it is hard to quantify the variations between countries as different countries use different standard industrial classifications. It is reasonable to assume, though, that these differences will be significant in some cases considering the wide gap between the technological bases of, say, the USA and Italy in the field of advanced military electronics.

Some degree of regional concentration of the defence industry is to be found in each Western European country under examination, though the evidence is, in most cases, much more sparse than for the USA. In France the greatest number of defence staff are located in the Paris area, although arsenal work for the army and navy is heavily concentrated in the west of France, while the south east and south west also have concentrations of personnel which in the latter case, especially near Toulouse, is devoted to air and navy production and repair facilities. In the UK the sites of the main defence contractors are especially numerous in the south east, south west and north west of England. The FRG has one main regional centre of arms production around Munich while at county level defence work is centred around a few areas in the larger states. In Italy regional concentration is very pronounced given that in 1980 over 80 per cent of defence industry employment was absorbed by only five out of the country's twenty regions: Campania, Lombardy, Piedmont, Liguria and Lazio. Liguria has the highest degree of defence dependency measured in terms of industrial employment. Even this, though, involves only 3.4 per cent of regional employment in industry or 10.2 per cent of all manufacturing employment. Swedish arms production is concentrated in its traditional engineering belt from the Lake Malaren region towards western Sweden and to Gothenburg in the south west. Normally the arms industry has no significant role in the employment situation in different regions though there are exceptional cases.[35]

A comparison of the absolute levels of defence industrial employment is not easy since the basis of the calculations, for each country, varies as does the reliability of the estimates. However Table 5.5 summarises the available data as far as

Table 5.5 Military-related employment in the defence industries of six Western powers

Country	Year	Domestic military demand[1] (000s)		Arms exports[2] (000s)
USA	1980		2 022	
UK	1981	600		140
France	1981	341		110
FRG[3]	Early 1980s		290	
Italy[3]	Early 1980s		160	
Sweden[3]	1970s		54	

[1] Figures for the USA, UK, France and Sweden include direct and indirect employment.

[2] Figures for arms exports include direct and indirect employment.

[3] These figures should be treated as rough estimates only, due to uncertainty concerning their accuracy and also their consistency with employment estimates from other countries.

Sources: Jacques Aben and Ron Smith, 'Defence and Employment in the UK and France: A Comparative Study of Existing Results' in *Peace, Defence and Economic Analysis*, edited by Christian Schmidt and Frank Blackaby (London, 1987), pp. 384–98; *The Structure of the Defense Industry: An International Survey*, edited by Nicole Ball and Milton Leitenberg (London, 1983), pp. 37, 119–20, 165, 220–1; P. Wilke and H. Wulf, *Manpower Conversion in Defense-Related Industry*, Disarmament and Employment Programme, Working Paper No. 4 (Geneva, June 1986), Table 1, p. 6.

possible. The most interesting point to note is that despite very similar levels of expenditure on military goods and services the defence-related employment is much less in France than the UK. According to Aben and R. Smith, the British Ministry of Defence (MoD) employs 1.7 times the number of workers in industry as the French ministry, for a given expenditure. The reasons for this are unclear but appear to relate, at least in part, to the higher productivity (in terms of value added per employee) achieved in key defence sectors of France, as compared to the UK.[36]

Virtually no information is available on the occupational profiles of the Western European defence industries so almost all the data in this area, for conversion purposes, has to come from US sources. It can, though, probably be assumed in general terms that similar occupational profiles will tend to recur in the European defence industries, given the many ways in which they follow the US pattern.

Lastly, the role of arms exports and, to a lesser extent, imports deserves some consideration. Nowhere in the West, outside of the USA, has a defence industry been more export-driven than in France. French arms exports became a key component of France's trade structure and helped maintain the balance of payments position and politically acceptable levels of domestic economic growth and employment. Various factors enabled the French defence industry to achieve a strong global position: American preoccupation with the Indo-China War in the 1960s; government encouragement of arms manufacturers to fill the world demand for arms; and other potential competitors were either unable or unwilling to fill the void. Further considerations encouraged this policy including the success of French conventional weaponry, the weakness of non-military exports and the employment opportunities created by arms sales. By 1977 arms transfers accounted for 4.6 per cent of overall exports (compared to 3 per cent in 1972).[37] However, by the mid-1980s France was struggling to maintain its position in the global arms market in the face of growing international competition. On the other hand the UK, which lost a dominant position in world arms markets in the 1960s, has seen something of a revival in the mid 1980s. According to SIPRI, the UK was the third largest Western exporter of major weapons in 1987, after the USA and France.[38]

By way of comparison, arms exports accounted for only 1 per

cent of all exports in the FRG, and about the same proportion in Sweden during the late 1970s. Italy, however, despite the comparatively small size of its domestic arms industry had military weapons exports representing 2.8–3.1 per cent of total exports in 1980.[39] During the 1980s, though, Italian arms exports have declined rapidly.

Italy's dependence on licensed production anyway acts as a constraint on exports, and its dependence on foreign weapons technology is illustrated by the fact that in 1977 its arms imports were not much less than the value of its exports. During 1974–82 between 20 and 30 per cent of Italian government arms contracts were placed with foreign firms (the share having increased towards the end of that period), while in Sweden it seems that during the 1970s more than 33 per cent of government arms procurement was imported. In the FRG only 18 per cent of the domestic demand for arms production in 1978 went to foreign firms. The figure in the UK was a mere 5 per cent (over 1980–84).[40]

That completes the comparative review of the six major Western defence industries. It remains to summarise the findings to date in relation to the implications for conversion and the extent to which these countries can draw upon each other's knowledge and experience in this field.

SUMMARY AND CONCLUSIONS

The structural similarities between the major Western defence industries are close on most of the main points of comparison. This does not mean, of course, that there can be any substitute for a full examination of any given national defence industry in order to discuss as many as possible of the factors relevant for conversion purposes in that country. Yet it does strongly suggest that the lessons from conversion studies and experience, such as it is, have a wider applicability than the Western country from which they are derived. So, at least as regards the fundamental aspects of conversion, the studies and experience from, for instance, the USA and Sweden have relevance to the UK and vice versa. But at the same time the significant differences between the structures of the major Western defence industries have also to be kept in mind.

⌐Looking first at the points of *similarity*,⌐ all the defence industries are sustained primarily by the arms procurement share of
the national defence budgets. In all cases these budgets absorb
more than 2 per cent and less than 7 per cent of GDP – a
significant but not overwhelming share of domestic resources. ⌐
Each country attempts, with varying degrees of success, to
maintain an indigenous defence capacity. This has led, since the
end of the Second World War, to a defence market in each major
Western country that follows similar lines and encourages the
growth of specialist defence firms. The characteristics of these
defence markets act as strong barriers to the entry of new firms
and the exit of existing defence firms. So while the overall size of
the defence sector is not too much of a problem, in terms of
achieving conversion in the event of disarmament or major arms
reductions, the nature of the defence markets themselves poses
significant obstacles. These are exacerbated by state and commercial secrecy over defence data vital for conversion planning.
Moreover, the existence of a mutual interest between the military, the state bureaucracy and the defence firms in ensuring the
continuation of weapons programmes forms the basis for a
powerful pressure group – a 'military-industrial complex' –
resisting efforts to convert the defence industries. On the other
hand, governments' monopsonistic power in the defence markets
could be used to counteract this influence within the Western
democracies and support a smooth transition from military to
civilian activities.

⌐The major defence firms themselves share common features in
all the Western countries examined here: turnover appears low
amongst the top contractors (allowing for takeovers and mergers); the extent of competition for domestic procurement orders
is limited, though some governments are attempting to encourage greater use of competitive tendering; and the degree of
concentration of procurement awards within the top contractors
is high. All these factors serve to intensify resistance to change
and make more difficult any efforts to move into more commercial markets. Additionally it means that cut-backs in defence
spending or the cancellation of individual projects has a severe
effect on particular companies which, without assistance, the
firms are usually ill-prepared to cope with. The extent of the
economic damage, related to cut-backs or cancellations, is also
linked to the defence dependency of the companies concerned, in

terms of sales and employment in particular. This defence dependency has been seen to vary widely between companies in all the Western countries considered here. The further concentration of defence work in particular industrial sectors, like aerospace and electronics, and particular regions is again common to all the countries and makes the conversion issue potentially much more significant for those defence companies in these sectors and regions. This, in turn, affects employment much more intensely in these areas than in the economy as a whole.

A historical perspective is needed to appreciate the *differences* between the defence industries. Those of the USA and UK, which emerged intact from the war, became the dominant ones in terms of size and scope. In absolute terms, though, the US arms industry dwarfs not only the UK's but all European defence industries together. The USA and UK also spent a much larger proportion of their respective government's R&D resources on military work than any of the others. France did, though, largely recover from the setback of the last world war and the difficulties of the 1950s. It did this partly through reducing the dependence of its defence industry on domestic procurement by encouraging arms exports, which were also linked to its national economic strategy. Like Britain it developed its own nuclear strike force and built up its own military R&D resources. However, for France, this was principally a means of ensuring political independence and an independent foreign policy. The other continental European powers, the FRG and especially Italy, were only able to start rebuilding their defence industries later and were much more reliant on imported technology and weapons collaboration in order to establish their own technology base. They spent a much smaller proportion of their own governmental R&D resources on military projects than the USA, the UK or France. Indeed Sweden, in its objective of remaining non-aligned to either of the major power blocks in the world, has had to spend a great deal more than the FRG or Italy, in relative terms, on R&D and over the last few years has had to rely increasingly on arms imports to ease the economic strain of maintaining an indigenous defence industry. Collaboration has been largely ruled out for political reasons.

These factors point to the greater challenge of converting R&D resources from military to civilian purposes in the UK and USA (and to a much lesser extent, Sweden) than the FRG and

Italy. In the case of France, the integration of their arms industry into the national strategy for economic growth and the emphasis given to an independent foreign policy and political freedom of action make it very difficult for conversion planning in general, let alone R&D conversion in particular, to be seriously considered. Furthermore, the growth of collaborative weapons programmes, not only amongst those countries dependent on them for much of their technology, but also amongst countries like France, the UK and the USA which perceive economic advantages, will add a further dimension to conversion planning since those programmes are politically difficult for a country, once committed, to withdraw from, and to deal with this contingency conversion policies may need to take on an international dimension.

The ownership of defence firms varies from one country to another with either the state or the private sector tending to be dominant. In conversion terms the importance is simply that direct government control of production makes it politically easier, at least in theory, to intervene to cope with the restructuring of defence firms made necessary by arms reductions, and to prevent redundancies through redeployment and retraining of personnel. Differences in the size of the workforces of the various national defence industries are hard to quantify but clearly reflect the proportion of domestic resources devoted to defence, and procurement in particular, as well as the size of arms exports. Arms imports remain relatively small in most of the Western countries considered, except Italy and Sweden, which have been under most pressure in maintaining independent defence industries. Any change of policy regarding either arms imports or exports has implications for defence employment and, therefore, conversion policy and planning.

The foregoing discussion has concentrated principally on the economic boundaries of the major Western defence industries. This is in keeping with the economic approach to conversion. Yet, as this discourse moves on to an assessment of the related literature, it would be as well to keep in mind the political constraints on each of the countries involved as far as the scope for conversion in recent circumstances is concerned. For while many of the studies in Ball and Leitenberg, like the one on the USA, demonstrate that '. . . this list of obstacles to conversion would not form a serious barrier to disarmament if political conditions were suitable...',[41] several also emphasise that conditions have not been, or are not yet, conducive to conversion. In the case of France:

> The economic benefits associated with producing arms, inextricably tied to a tenacious policy of national independence in defence, make it difficult for any regime in France, whether of the right or left, to change the existing pattern of dependency of the French economy and France's export position on arms production and sales ... for the foreseeable future, and for compelling strategic, economic and political reasons, the French arms industry is here to stay.[42]

In Germany:

> The most sensible alternative – to reduce arms production capacity and to finance alternative employment schemes – does not seem to be politically feasible in the short run...[43]

While in Italy:

> With respect to the conversion question, informed opinion in Italy holds that the conversion of military production facilities to civilian uses is not likely to be given serious consideration in the near future. This assessment arises primarily out of the general economic crisis and the potential social consequences of a quick conversion of the military sector, that is, still higher unemployment. Only significant changes in the current stagnant state of the world economy and a movement towards a more stable politico-strategic system internationally, particularly in those areas which directly affect Italy's national security, could alter or even reverse this conclusion.[44]

And, finally, Sweden:

> It is rarely the case that a firm specializing in arms production faces the need of a dramatic 'conversion' into civilian production.[45]

These political constraints should not be overlooked in reflecting upon the conversion question.

6 The Economic Approach to Conversion (I)

Of all the approaches to conversion (see Figure 1.1) that which deals with the economics of disarmament has received by far the most attention. Beginning in the late 1950s and reaching a peak of interest in the mid-1960s, the publication of fresh studies fell away sharply with the onset of the Indo-China War, only to rise once more as the Americans began to withdraw, then continuing to the present day on a more infrequent basis.

This does, however, leave the analyst – intent on understanding what has been learnt about conversion and, in particular, conversion as a dynamic process – with a difficulty. For most of the studies on the economics of disarmament and related conversion proposals were done in the period before the oil price crisis of 1973 which, by bringing to a head those pre-existing structural problems in the world economy, led to the latest period of recession and high unemployment. As the earlier review of the literature on the economic and social consequences of the arms race has shown, this changed the whole context of the conversion debate, and it might be expected to nullify some of the more optimistic assessments for transforming military to civilian industries and increase the difficulties in implementing conversion plans. In recognition of these factors greater emphasis will be given, in the ensuing review, to the more recent literature though it is much less extensive than that pertaining to the era of low unemployment which existed 25–30 years ago when the bulk of conversion studies were undertaken.

There have been a number of significant earlier reviews of conversion literature[1] as well as several valuable bibliographies.[2] The intention here is that the relevant portion of this literature will be assessed historically and analytically, within and between the various sources of knowledge on the economic approach to conversion, with heavy reliance on US empirical studies and policy proposals which dominate those from all other Western countries.

ECONOMIC MODELS OF DISARMAMENT OR ARMS CONTROL

The economic approach to conversion is so called because it is normally primarily concerned with the economic consequences of disarmament based on certain political assumptions about the degree of reduction in armaments involved. Sometimes, though, the economic case against high military spending is used, as in Melman's work, to try to achieve political change in the direction of disarmament. The economic models used have examined the effects of all kinds of changes in the levels of military expenditure from a 'freeze' on the development of new, particularly nuclear, weapons to 'general and complete disarmament'. In very general terms it may be said that in the 1960s the emphasis was more on the latter assumption while, more recently, the former has tended to be of greater interest. That is not to say that economists in the 1960s personally believed that full disarmament was just around the corner, whilst today that goal is seen as being too remote to bear detailed investigation. However, it may well reflect the extent to which economists have been influenced by a climate of world opinion that, until very recently, was much less optimistic about the prospects for disarmament after two decades in which very little progress had been made. Arms control, rather than disarmament, has tended to be the focus of attention for policy-makers, hence it is necessary to distinguish between the two since the implications for conversion will be different.

As Thorsson stated, these two terms are commonly defined as follows:

> *Disarmament* is both a goal and a process. It means that the number of arms would be sharply reduced or totally eliminated. It also means the adoption of measures which will contribute to the attainment of this goal. Disarmament can, for example, involve deep cuts in arsenals. The abolition of certain categories of weapons or their removal from particular geographic areas are also disarmament measures.

> *Arms control/arms limitation measures* signify actions designed to control, slow down or limit the armament process. They can involve numerical limitations (setting of ceilings), smaller reductions in numbers of weapons, or other measures which have as their purpose reducing the risk of war.[3]

The material in this section is arranged according to the various sources of knowledge which have made noteworthy contributions. The United Nations studies are examined first, followed by government-sponsored projects, especially those undertaken in the USA and Sweden. Then the findings of peace research will be investigated together with a few works from orthodox economic or radical labour sources.

The perspective adopted, and the economic models used, mostly reflect the national basis of all defence establishments and industries. Nevertheless the United Nations has advanced most of its thinking on conversion matters within the context of the link between disarmament and development, so providing an international framework for conversion planning. However, the wider literature on the whole question of linking disarmament and development cannot be dealt with here.[4] The focus in this book must remain firmly on conversion itself.

This chapter deals with the more general studies on the economics of disarmament and conversion. In addition the bibliography provides details on some of the more specialised works which have been published on the following subjects: conversion of defence industries, conversion of research and development resources, occupational conversion, regional and local economic impact and base conversions.

UNITED NATIONS REPORTS

The very first United Nations report in 1962 dealt primarily with the economics of disarmament, not the economic and social consequences of the arms race. The Secretary-General's Consultative Group made the assumptions that, once disarmament was agreed upon, it would be both general and complete and accomplished rapidly.[5] This *modus operandi* also had the advantage of making the benefits and difficulties of disarmament most clear and reduced the danger of underestimating the risks involved.

The report argued that while the resources released by disarmament could be used for any of a great variety of peaceful purposes over the long term because any advanced market economy is highly adaptable, in the very short run the choices are likely to be more limited. The labour and equipment no longer required for military use was much more suited to producing consumer durables and industrial equipment than the building of houses, production of food or clothing or any other items implied by public investment or social welfare programmes. While it might have been of advantage, therefore, to try to match patterns of expenditure in the transition period to the particular military resources being released, some major powers had excess industrial capacity already so that any new demands generated by disarmament could be largely met from available civilian sources.[6]

In terms of national production and employment, disarmament raises two main questions:

● how to maintain the level of overall economic activity;
● how to cope with the specific problems concerning manpower or productive capacity in transferring to civilian purposes.

The UN report stated that careful planning is required in both cases and that successful handling of each aspect will ease the problems of the other. The assumption that disarmament will occur over a few years only would raise special problems which will be made easier the higher the rate of economic growth.[7]

The former of the two main questions – on how to maintain aggregate demand – was to be dealt with using the standard Keynesian fiscal and monetary policies of the time. It is the latter question, though, relating to the structural problems of conversion that is the main source of interest since these difficulties refer to the specific sectors and areas of the economy in which defence work is concentrated.

Defence industry resources could, in some cases, be transferred to peaceful purposes by changing the product while using the same productive equipment. The report cited the examples of shifting from tanks to tractors, military to civilian aircraft, naval to merchant vessels, electronic equipment to television sets. It is poignant that all these illustrations of potential shifts within industries and plants would be very difficult in the West today, given the severe crisis which all the named civilian industries came through during the 1980s. Although the civilian aircraft industry was, in the late 1980s, enjoying a boom after a very difficult period, it could not hope to absorb more than a very small fraction of the much larger, military aerospace sector. So, whilst there may well be other possibilities for conversion or diversification, it is well worth bearing in mind how much conditions have changed since the 1960s and that now such a change, within industries and plants, might not be '... a relatively easy procedure'.[8]

The second way of dealing with the structural problems of conversion is through shifts between industries. In a few cases, like that of the ordnance sector, production would have to be heavily cut back, or even ended altogether, while in other cases expansion would be possible. Such shifts between industries would mean workers learning new skills and would require investment in new plant and equipment. This process would take longer than shifts within industries but comparability of resource contents (particularly technologies, skills and equipment) would shorten the time taken.[9]

The 1962 UN report maintained that net shifts in employment and output would be relatively small. However, special problems would arise because of the concentration of military work in particular industries and areas, namely changing skills from military to peaceful tasks, assistance to companies, industries and areas heavily dependent on military use, and reorientation of R&D to civilian activities.[10]

The overall conclusion of the report is worth quoting in full:

> The Consultative Group is unanimously of the opinion that all the problems and difficulties of transition connected with disarmament could be met by appropriate national and international measures. There should thus be no doubt that the diversion to peaceful purposes of the resources now in military use could be accomplished to the benefit of all countries and lead to the improvement of world economic and social conditions. The achievement of general and complete disarmament would be an unqualified blessing to all mankind.[11]

This was one of the first, if not the first, of the major reports on the economics of disarmament in the 1960s and the later reports, from peace research and other sources, followed similar lines of argument and came to much the same conclusions, even if their models and project methodology varied. It will not, therefore, be necessary to discuss the other works covering the pre-1973 period in similar depth.

Both the 1971 and 1977 UN reports endorsed the findings of

this 1962 report, while the 1982 report in its turn cited the earlier reports in stressing the technological and economic feasibility of disarmament.[12] All these reports were unanimously agreed by their authors and formally accepted by the United Nations General Assembly.

The 1977 report did suggest a number of measures to facilitate conversion and urged that plans and legislation to support those initiatives be drawn up and adopted as soon as possible. Defence industries might be required to limit their reliance on military orders to some given percentage of total production or, where this is impossible for technical reasons, might be made to locate in areas which could best absorb their workforce if it were made redundant. Sometimes military production might be dispersed around the country and, additionally, arms producing factories could be obliged to draw up alternative plans for civilian production. These measures would not only assist the process of disarmament but help to break up powerful political interests in the defence industry by reducing both their dependence on military orders and also the pressure for follow-on contracts, which might prove irresistible in the absence of concrete alternatives.[13]

Whilst these latter observations are of interest it is to the UN's reports on the link between disarmament and development that attention must be turned for the most detailed discussion of the UN attitude to conversion. In the earlier and shorter study in 1972 the Group of Experts were asked how to establish a link between the Disarmament Decade and the Second United Nations Development Decade (the 1970s) and to propose measures for mobilising public opinion accordingly. Their report stated that the objectives of disarmament and development stood separately from each other, and that the UN had determined that it would pursue both strongly in their own right, irrespective of the pace of progress in either.[14] In this way neither goal would be held back by delays, from whatever cause, in the other.

The 1972 UN report stated that the employment of resources released by disarmament would not be likely to be spontaneously applied for development purposes. It argued that to achieve this would require the governments of both developed and developing countries to act in concert since the objectives of reduced military expenditure and of furthering economic and social development are mostly a matter of political will and international cooperation. Once again the findings of the 1962 UN report were endorsed concerning the technical feasibility of conversion. However, the UN study also included an analysis which suggested that replacing a 20 per cent reduction in military expenditure, with a proportionate or greater increase in assistance to developing countries, would result in fewer industries suffering negative consequences than if domestic personal consumption was raised instead.[15]

The UN report urged all countries to consider the best ways of redeploying resources from military to civil use in terms of potential contributions to development and, in particular, what specialised resources could be appropriately used as aid from developed to developing countries. Advance planning of the links with development might also have avoided some of the unemployment amongst scientists and engineers caused by changes in the composition of military programmes. Problems of conversion of R&D resources were especially noted in the report and examples of the peaceful uses of military R&D were provided.[16] These resources, it was argued, could have a large impact on development. The recommendations of the 1972 UN report were, like almost all the other UN reports, made unanimously.

However, it was the 1981 UN report which provided the most comprehensive analysis ever undertaken by that organisation of the range of relationships between the prospects for, on the one hand, balanced and sustainable global economic and social development and, on the other hand, disarmament through redeployment of real resources.[17]

Initially the report reviewed the traditional way of linking disarmament and development by contrasting the existence of a great deal of poverty and deprivation in the underdeveloped countries with the comparative affluence of the developed states. The enormous resources devoted to military purposes throughout the world was then described which, by implication, could be used to reorder global priorities and, especially, to meet the pressing needs of the developing countries. The authors of the report concluded that, although the share of GNP going to the military had declined in many countries in recent years while social expenditures as a share of national government budgets had risen, the arms race had continued virtually unabated and that, therefore, this broadly moral and political argument for

disarmament and development had not outweighed concern
with military security. Although there was a potential relationship between disarmament and development in economic terms
the fact remained that no automatic mechanism existed by
which unmet human needs could be transformed into a claim on
resources within the armaments sector.[18]

So the 1981 report, while completely supporting the moral
argument, suggested a different approach to the subject which
has as its basis a wider definition of the concept of security. This
wider definition includes economic and social aspects which, together with the military factor, are subject to continual evolutionary change. In this context the central political task, nationally
and internationally, is to determine whether available human
and material resources are being disposed of rationally, given
current and expected threats to security.[19] The report concentrated on a number of themes which cover the principal,
interrelated challenges to international security in the future:

> The first of these is the arms race itself ... the capacity of
> armaments to fulfil their purpose of providing for security is
> seen as increasingly open to question. In addition, however, it
> is beginning to be recognized that prevailing notions of what
> constitutes security are overly narrow and that armaments
> are, at best, impotent against many of the factors that
> challenge security if the latter is more broadly and realistically
> defined. When viewed in this broader perspective, the experi-
> ence of the past decade has dramatized the fact that inter-
> national peace and security are no longer threatened exclu-
> sively by the competition between East and West although
> their competition in armaments can be considered the greatest
> threat to peace and security. Rather, it has become apparent
> that the future security for all nations is and will be challenged
> by such factors as declining prospects for economic growth, by
> a variety of physical limitations and by the tensions arising
> from the increasingly inequitable distribution of the world's
> wealth.[20]

This alternative security concept is an important development
and will be discussed more fully in Chapter 8. Suffice it is to say
that the 1981 UN report discussed conversion within this framework, in which a strong conceptual relationship between disarmament and development was said to exist in terms of this

broader definition of security, embracing military and non-military factors. It stressed the need for states to recognise that important goals relating to their security and national interests can only be accomplished through cooperation and mutual accommodation. Moreover, since economic growth is a pre-condition for development and economic prospects are greatly influenced by states' interdependence, one with another, increasing such interdependence and international economic cooperation would be in the economic interests of all states. However, as long as the arms race continues the 'cooperative management of interdependence' in all its facets – political, economic and physical – remains a rather unrealistic prospect. To this extent the report argued that disarmament and development are fundamentally and closely linked.[21] The economic and social consequences of the arms race, discussed previously, simply reinforce this point concerning the incompatibility of pursuing the armaments build-up on the one hand, and global development on the other.

The 1981 report identified one main purpose of planning conversion as that of minimising opposition to disarmament measures from those groups who currently specialise in the development and production of modern weapons, and fear the uncertainties of transferring to the civilian sector. Another aim of conversion, given the very high opportunity costs of the arms race, is to form part of a more balanced and realistic approach to national and international security where, as just described, military security is not overstressed to the detriment of economic security. Also the report pointed out that conversion is only one aspect of a much more general process of economic conversion[22] going on all the time and that, if it were developed in the context of major structural adjustments of both national economies and the international economic system, then conversion could be usefully integrated with these wider changes. The 1981 report was based on the assumption of gradual disarmament in which case there should be no difficulty in gearing the pace of disarmament to that at which resources could be moved smoothly from military to civilian activities.[23]

This UN report emphasised the need for planning at all levels, so that a comprehensive strategy for conversion is developed which would allay the fears of the groups affected and give responsibility for different stages of the process in the most

efficient manner. While central government would have primary
responsibility for conversion, and should take the lead in initiating preparations for this process, detailed arrangements would
be a joint effort between industry, trade unions and officials in
the most defence dependent regions and communities. The
extent to which the process is decentralised will vary, with each
state taking maximum advantage of the resource allocation
mechanisms available, from central planning to open markets.[24]

Disarmament would present governments with a strategic
opportunity to tackle major economic and social problems by
ensuring that the conversion process contributes, as much as
possible, to meeting national and international priorities in these
areas. In similar vein to the 1962 UN report, this 1981 report
argued that, in the medium to long term, governments in the
market economies can be fairly confident about maintaining
aggregate demand through a variety of fiscal and monetary
mechanisms. The timing of such adjustment measures with
disarmament measures to ensure maximum beneficial effect
would be important. Also the mix of such measures will be
significant in the short run owing to the differing time-lags
associated with different measures.[25]

Transferring human and material resources from military to
civilian purposes presents no problem at all, according to the
1981 report, in terms of identifying economic and social alternatives to which these resources could be applied. Rather, as with
the 1962 report, the difficulty would be one of choice since even
disarmament would not eliminate the overall global scarcity of
resources relative to demand. While recognising that '... it is not
practicable to reduce a 45 year-old aeronautical engineer to a
high-school graduate or a missile assembly plant to scrap metal
and refashion them in the desired manner...'[26] there is an
overwhelming consensus that resources in the military sector
can, over a period of up to two years, be adapted to work in the
civilian sector. As with the 1962 and 1972 UN reports, the
nature of this alternative work was discussed in some detail
including in particular renewable energy sources, efforts to
arrest environmental degradation and repair the damage
already caused, and new transportation systems. Additionally
resources now devoted to developing and producing chemical
weapons can apparently be converted to civilian production of
pesticides, plasticisers and fire retardants.[27] Further proposals

on alternative work in the developing countries, or in the context of a new international economic order, lie outside the scope of this book.

The 1981 UN report, in its recommendations relating to conversion, stated that conversion presented 'no insurmountable problem' given that the disarmament process would, most likely, be a gradual one. However, it went on to argue that, while conversion would be the final step in the implementation of any disarmament agreement, the preparation for conversion should be among the first steps on the road to disarmament. The Expert Group recommended

> ... *that Governments create the necessary prerequisites, including preparations and, where appropriate, planning, to facilitate the conversion of resources freed by disarmament measures to civilian purposes, especially to meet urgent economic and social needs, in particular, in the developing countries.*[28] (Emphasis in the original.)

The Group suggested the creation of a core of experts on conversion issues in each country with a major defence sector, the development of contingency conversion plans by plants involved in specialised military production, and the involvement of all parties affected by conversion planning.

These preparations would help to foster international confidence since they would help to make disarmament measures more credible. In consequence of this the Group recommended governments to consider making the results of their experiences and preparations for conversion available by submitting reports at intervals to the General Assembly on possible solutions to conversion difficulties.[29] All these recommendations were made unanimously, despite some reservations in the report on other matters,[30] and adopted by the United Nations General Assembly.

The 1981 UN report clearly represented a synthesis of all previous discussions of conversion issues within earlier UN reports. The emphasis on planning and the central role of government, with full involvement by other interested parties, are the key planks of UN policy set in the context of a sophisticated analysis linking disarmament and development to a broader definition of security, one involving economic rather than purely military dimensions. Moreover, the more difficult economic and political environment of the post-1973 era, which one might expect to make conversion more problematic, is at least partly countered by the discussion of the damaging economic and social consequences of the arms race which might be reversed, to some extent, in the event of disarmament creating the opportunity to tackle existing social and economic problems, nationally and internationally. This position will, though, require further elucidation at a later stage, after the research findings from other sources of knowledge on conversion have been evaluated, since it goes back to, amongst other matters, the question of the extent to which the present global economic difficulties can be blamed on excessive military spending.

GOVERNMENT-SPONSORED REPORTS: THE USA

Governments have themselves sponsored a number of studies into the economics of disarmament and conversion, though as Ball pointed out:

> There is no government which has as yet accepted that it has a special role to play in assisting defence producers and workers to adjust to lower levels of military expenditure.[31]

During the 1960s and early 1970s the USA was virtually the only government in the world which made any really significant contributions to sponsoring research into conversion-related matters, and most of these were under the aegis of the US Arms Control and Disarmament Agency (ACDA). It should be noted that the findings of the research work which ACDA funded did not necessarily reflect the views either of that body or the US government itself. Nevertheless some assessment of this literature would be of interest and relevant to this review.

It is well worth bearing in mind the historical context which provided the impetus for US governmental consideration of defence conversion potential. The first, and probably major, influence was the anticipation that between 1960 and 1965 a series of weapons programmes would come to an end which would be likely to result in important shifts within the arms production sector. Allied with this, Secretary of Defense McNamara had, by March 1961, started a whole series of military base closures with pronounced effects on local economies. Of still greater significance, several senior administration officials thought there might be sizeable cuts in the total defence budget as the major US missile procurement programmes neared completion in 1965 or 1966. Secondly, the USSR was seeking agreements with the USA on the limitation of military expenditure, which actually resulted in unilateral cuts in military expenditure being announced by both governments after summit meetings in August–September 1963. A direct consequence of this was the formal establishment of a Presidential Committee on the Economic Impact of Defense and Disarmament known subsequently as the 'Ackley Committee'. Thirdly, defence contractors were said to be indicating their willingness to convert defence production facilities, in response to investigations conducted by a subcommittee of the US Senate on the economic impact of arms control agreements. However, they expected to see the federal government taking a lead in determining priorities for civilian programmes. This led directly to Senator McGovern's legislative proposals which, together with subsequent conversion initiatives, will be discussed in Chapter 13. Finally, it may be that the 1962 UN report helped to stimulate serious thinking on conversion amongst US government officials.[32] Soon after his inauguration in 1961 President Kennedy set up the ACDA and mandated it to carry out, amongst other tasks, studies on the economic consequences of arms control and disarmament.

Here the implications of cut-backs in military spending for the national economy is the central topic for examination. The ACDA-sponsored research (between 1963 and 1971) concluded that:

> ... while arms control and disarmament measures involving a major reduction in military expenditures may bring significant transitional problems for the economy, the proper use of federal tax, expenditure, and monetary policy can sustain total output and employment.

The point is that there is nothing unique in the challenge to the economy posed by reduced military expenditures. The economy is constantly undergoing evolutionary changes in the patterns of resource use. Shifts in the composition of defense procurement and between defense and civilian production have occurred frequently. The problem at the national level is the familiar one of maintaining aggregate demand at high employment levels without exerting too much pressure on prices.[33]

Public and private policies would be needed to assist workers, firms and communities who would otherwise face difficulties in the transition period. The research proposed that the federal government should outline its role in a public statement so that state and local governments, as well as the private sector, would know what the central authority was willing to do. The desirability of advance planning for economic adjustment, which the federal government should encourage at state and local levels, was also highlighted.[34]

The vital time-lag problem was the object of a special study, on the assumption that there would be increased government spending on civilian programmes to offset reduced defence expenditure. 'Inside lag' – the time elapsing between commencement of government policy action and actual commitment of funds – was distinguished from 'outside lag' – the time between obligation of funds and actual expenditures or employment. Inside lag could take up to two and a half years, constituting a major delay for any compensatory programme, which might reduce its effectiveness. These lengthy delays, arising from cumbersome federal–state procedures, could be reduced by simplification of intra-governmental procedures, improved efficiency in funding federal aid projects and greater use of 'off-the-shelf' pre-approved programmes ready for such contingencies as reduced military spending. Outside lag is a less significant problem. Usually the delay would be expected to be less than one year.[35]

So, apart from a more insightful view of the time-lag problem, the ACDA-sponsored research at national level differed little from the 1962 UN report in terms of its conclusions. It is worth noting, though, that one of the ACDA's principal studies, which considered the impact of reduced military spending on the assumption of an agreement limiting strategic weapons and a withdrawal of American troops from the Indo-China War, was rather more sophisticated than some of the many investigations of the economics of disarmament in the early 1960s. The editor himself contrasted this study with these previous ones:

> The inclusion of material on the long-term structural shifts in the American economy that are possibly traceable to the

secular rise in military spending, and the explicit treatment of the organizational and administrative issues influencing the government's ability to smoothly shift resources ... differentiate it from most other treatments of the impact of changes in military spending.[36]

To this list should be added an interesting theoretical treatment on 'societal turnability' which explored the social and political factors involved in a major shift from war-making capacity to domestic missions in the USA.[37] It considered the role of consensus-building, in gaining support for this new course of action, before turning to the constraints on implementing such a policy caused by the limitations of existing control structures. This essay, taken together with the others previously mentioned on the long-term consequences of military spending and the organisational and administrative factors affecting shifts in defence expenditures, all pointed to the beginnings of a new approach to conversion: one based on reduced, if more realistic, expectations of disarmament or arms control and one in which the economic aspects would be set in a much broader context.

Since 1972 official US government-sponsored research on the economics of disarmament has dwindled. In the 1980s, though, policy-related research on conversion has resulted in some noteworthy publications. One report on conversion, this time by the Congressional Budget Office (CBO), warrants special attention.[38] Its interest here is derived from its primary purpose, which is to consider what the role of government should be in economic conversion. (In this context the term – economic conversion – is synonymous with the broad non-military meaning given in Chapter 1. On the other hand, peace researchers, and the peace movement generally, in the USA normally use the term in a way that is similar to that in which conversion is used here. This terminological confusion will be clarified, as far as possible, when Melman's work is appraised in the next chapter.)

Even though defence conversion is only one of many possible examples of economic conversion, the CBO discussion papers are relevant in two respects: firstly, in delineating the conflicting arguments relating to the need for conversion assistance; and secondly, in assessing what form, if any, that assistance should take.

The CBO report contrasted the 'free market' view with the

'political case' for conversion assistance. The former argument can be put in a nutshell:

> If the free market systems work well, economic activities subject to frequent dislocation will also benefit from disproportionately large rewards – higher profits to capital, higher wages to labour. These compensate for the greater risks of change. The more smoothly the market system works to absorb resources freed up by contraction of an activity, the smaller these premiums need be. Observers who believe that the free market system works well will therefore question the need for conversion assistance.[39]

Moreover, the CBO report continued, proponents of the free market would claim that there are certain dangers inherent in a conversion scheme: conversion aid could tempt firms, individuals and communities into making unwise choices through ensuring relief from the damaging consequences of risky decisions involving, for example, uneconomical investments or the failure of firms to diversify their activities as an insurance against sudden shocks; also extended benefits to the victims of change may slow the process of adjustment since workers with guaranteed incomes may not pursue new jobs very vigorously or move to other areas where more jobs are available.[40]

As against this perspective, the political case for conversion assistance rests in major part on the blocking action which the losers from a given action may otherwise succeed in imposing. Mechanisms to compensate these losers are especially significant when the federal government itself is responsible for the gains and losses. In these cases, since the effects are usually more far-reaching, so many groups and individuals may be affected that a successful coalition to oppose the change may be more easily organised. This view effectively turns the free market argument on its head:

> Moreover, changes in government policy may be much harder for economic actors to foresee than changes in private policies. If so, cautious individuals and firms may demand much higher premiums for participation in activities that are affected by government policy changes and this could undermine the efficient workings of the free market system. For example, firms may be reluctant to invest where the future course of government regulation is particularly uncertain.[41]

The political case for conversion can also be supplemented by a moral motivation to help those injured by government actions (though the CBO added that such assistance should presumably take account of compensation which market forces have already provided).[42]

From these two perspectives it follows that the advocates of *laissez-faire* would question the need for conversion assistance, while the proponents of economic conversion would be likely to favour either various *ad hoc* approaches or a general economic conversion programme. The *ad hoc* approach is effectively the one followed by federal government at the present time. It permits aid programmes to be shaped for specific situations. Also it allows for innovative solutions to be tried in a small way at low cost. If they work they can be applied more widely; if they fail they can be dropped.[43]

The case for a general economic conversion programme arises from 'economic friction', whereby the victims of change are more likely to try to attack the cause of dislocation than to accept the need to adjust to changed circumstances. Such efforts can be costly to the rest of society. The CBO suggested two approaches to a general programme: an economic planning framework, or a series of general income support schemes. Significantly it found the former unconvincing on the grounds that past experience did not suggest that governments are able to forecast accurately, or know how to influence resources to move to appropiate new activities.[44] The problem then becomes one of suggesting how best to target income support schemes to workers, firms and communities in order to encourage change without subsidising inefficient firms.

The CBO report provided a brief but poignant reminder of the powerful ideological and political opposition in the USA to a major government role in the process of economic adjustment, of which conversion of military industries is only a part. This stance is made most transparent, even from such a source of supposedly objective and impartial information, in the CBO's attitude to economic planning which is virtually dismissed out of hand. While it may be argued that the extent of planning required is debatable, the difficulty in implementing conversion programmes in the USA is clearly not unconnected with wider questions relating to the role of government in the economy and the long-standing debate over the need for an industrial policy

– itself far short of a commitment to economic planning. These themes, it will be readily apparent, are also relevant, in varying degrees, to the main Western European states.

Since the CBO report one further US government-sponsored study has been published which, in a backhanded way, testified to the recent renewed interest in conversion. This study, into the feasibility of establishing an office of conversion in the Pentagon, was carried out by the DoD at the instigation of a House–Senate Conference Report on the 1985 Defense Authorization Bill.[45] Although this procedure might seem extraordinary, given the known antipathy of the former Reagan Administration and the DoD to conversion, it did at least signify the political impact that conversion activists were starting to have in the USA (which will be discussed in Chapter 13). Moreover, while the negative response of the DoD was predictable, the resulting voluminous report contained a number of useful analyses carried out by independent experts on various aspects of conversion policy and practice.

The terms of reference for the feasibility study emphasised the community/worker economic adjustment problems following defence programme changes, rather than the national macro-economic issues in the event of disarmament or reductions in military spending. Additionally the DoD report limited the meaning of the term 'conversion' to dealing with the effects of contract cancellation on the *individual firm* by changing to alternative civilian products. It presumed (wrongly, as it turns out) that conversion implied using the same buildings and equipment to produce the new products, as well as the same labour force.[46] The DoD study contrasted this approach – which will be described as 'factory-based' conversion in this book – with adjustment mechanisms, already in existence, which provide assistance to workers and their communities when military bases close down or contracts are curtailed, but not usually to the firms themselves. These mechanisms include the facilitating role of the Office of Economic Adjustment (and the President's Economic Adjustment Committee).[47] Thus, at the stroke of a pen, conversion had been defined in the most limited way possible, and then put in a strait-jacket by precluding the possibility of new investment. Having set up this 'man of straw' it was not difficult to marshal the evidence needed to knock him down!

In fact the juxtaposition of factory-based with what the DoD portrayed as 'community-based' conversion in no way implies that they are mutually exclusive. Moreover, the acknowledged lack of success in the former approach cannot be cited as proof that it does not work, since conversion advocates have long argued that it is precisely the absence of the necessary pre-conditions for success – advance planning and central government intervention in particular – which have made conversion initiatives so rare and, when they do occur, so often unsuccessful. However, discussion of the diversification and conversion of individual military contractors and the US government's own initiatives at economic adjustment or community-based conversion will be deferred until Chapters 10 and 13.

At the policy level the DoD report criticised the conversion approach for treating defence impacts as inherently different from other major dislocations in the economy, meriting extraordinary treatment over and above existing federal and state assistance programmes. The difficulty of distinguishing defence workers from other workers in the economy, apart from those within a military-specific core of firms, was given as an added reason for Congress to evaluate carefully the extent to which it would wish federal government to intervene in a market economy. In short, how could an industrial policy for defence-related industry be separated from all other economic policies for the economy in general?[48]

These observations, like those of the 1980 CBO report, bring the conversion issue back to ideological and political considerations. For while it can certainly be argued, on the basis of the analysis of Western defence industries conducted in Chapter 5, that defence impacts do have special characteristics different from most other major dislocations in the economy, the need to integrate conversion policies with wider economic policies clearly remains if political opposition is to be reduced. Also it should be recognised that the special characteristics of the defence industry environment, as a barrier to conversion, are likely to prove greater in the case of factory-based than community-based conversion. This is so because, in the latter case, workers are dispersed to new, mostly civilian environments where adaptation can take place without the dead weight of a given military firm's past acting directly upon them.

GOVERNMENT-SPONSORED REPORTS: SWEDEN

Sweden has a long-standing commitment to peace and disarmament and, particularly in recent years, has built up an international reputation for peace research, most notably through the government-funded Stockholm International Peace Research Institute (SIPRI). The country's most significant contribution to conversion literature was, however, made only a few years ago when on 14 July 1983 the Swedish government decided, as a direct response to the 1981 UN report, to commission a study of the relationship between disarmament and development from a national perspective. It was conducted by Inga Thorsson, appointed as the Special Expert. She had also chaired the Group of Governmental Experts which had prepared the earlier UN report. As with the US studies, it is primarily the economics of disarmament and conversion that constitute the focus of attention here.

The Thorsson study assumed various global disarmament scenarios which could lead to a reduction in the level of Swedish defence expenditure without jeopardising the country's security policy goals, namely the maintenance of independence and security. These security policies were not themselves the object of any discussion though the report followed the UN in pointing to the need to broaden the definition of security to include its non-military aspects. The Thorsson study recognised that the then current international tension and inflexibility between the superpowers made any major breakthrough in the disarmament field over the next few years appear slight. Hence its global disarmament scenarios were based on a gradual reduction in force levels over a twenty-five year period, beginning in 1990 and continuing until 2015. These scenarios also presumed a much improved negotiating climate than that which existed when the report was written. The Special Expert examined two disarmament scenarios both envisaging a 50 per cent reduction in conventional forces of NATO and WTO. In one scenario the forces of the two military blocs would be halved so that offensive units would be reduced far more than other conventional forces. In the other it was simply assumed that all conventional forces were cut by 50 per cent. Under the first scenario Thorsson argued for, and assumed, a similar reduction in Swedish defence forces over the same twenty-five year time period. However, so as not to be placed in an unfavourable position, Sweden was assumed to reduce its defence forces by only 40 per cent under the second disarmament scenario.[49] For conversion purposes, it was the former scenario, based on a 50 per cent cut in Swedish defence expenditure over twenty-five years between 1990 and 2015, which was used by Thorsson.

Swedish disarmament along these lines would necessitate at least 20 000 military and civilian employees of the armed forces and 14 000 defence industry employees changing their jobs over a twenty-five year period. Accounting for retirements and new recruitments within the armed forces, about 1430 people would be required to leave the Swedish armed forces and defence industry each year as a result of disarmament. The Thorsson study stated:

> From a macroeconomic point of view, this would mean that over the 25-year period in question less than 1 percent of the total Swedish work force would have to find new jobs because of disarmament. From this perspective, conversion can hardly be considered a large problem.[50]

Nevertheless the employment issue was still deemed to be a significant one given the pressure it can put on government either to oppose demobilisation of military forces or to place further orders for military equipment. Thorsson argued that those people whose work in the defence sector was no longer required should not have to carry the whole burden of disarmament alone when such a process would benefit all Swedes.[51] (These and further reasons for treating the defence sector differently to other parts of the economy were discussed by her at some length and will be outlined in more detail in Chapter 14.)

So despite the modest employment changes in the Swedish economy, which disarmament would imply, Thorsson argued that the effects of military expenditure reductions on society must be considered. There would be a number of beneficial consequences: budgetary savings for the government; and economic benefits to society arising from alternative uses of the released resources.[52]

The social costs of defence – basically the alternative value of production lost through devoting resources to defence – would be reduced though by what proportion would depend on decisions taken on the stockpiling of essential items and changes in the conscript system. There would also be a fall in the social cost of defence because of the gain in the growth of civilian production attendant upon disarmament.[53] (Some attempt was made to measure the latter element in the social cost–benefit analysis of the defence sector.)

The study accepted that budgetary savings would probably exceed real savings as money would have to be allocated from the budget to support the conversion process. Increased government support to companies, defence workers and communities would be required during the transition period. Even if all budgetary savings had to be committed to this process – which the study did not consider necessary – the economy would probably still perform better than before.[54]

Thorsson argued strongly for greater government involvement in defence industry efforts to diversify and so increase its proportion of civilian production. Many defence firms lack venture capital because of heavy reliance on defence orders and pre-payments from the Swedish procurement agency. Government funding could act as a stimulus to civil sector innovation. A further factor is the interdependence of government and defence companies which makes it vital for cooperative conversion planning to take place.[55] Hitherto only *ad hoc* contacts had occurred which Thorsson regarded as inadequate for an active conversion process.

The Thorsson study came to the conclusion that the initiation of conversion planning would be a logical step for Sweden to take, in line both with its UN activity and its conviction that it would be politically and economically advantageous to lower the defence industry's reliance on military orders. Provided that this defence sector conversion is well planned and carried out gradually the effects of disarmament ought to be manageable. It would be important, though, that the conversion process should involve government, defence producers and unions, adopting a long-term perspective. On these conditions the disarmament scenarios in the report would not lead to increased unemployment. However, in the event of defence industry conversion proving unfeasible, some defence workers might be affected and these people would have to draw on existing unemployment measures. The economy as a whole would undoubtedly benefit from disarmament.[56]

Thorsson proposed that the government implement the following measures to facilitate the conversion process:

● establish a *Council for Disarmament and Conversion.* Its tasks would include being informed on the disarmament–development relationship, examining the possibilities for increasing civil sector employment, and developing a programme of action with defence producers and unions to resolve conversion problems;
● set up a *central conversion fund,* linked to this Council;
● promote the creation of *local conversion funds* within each defence company.[57]

These proposals were designed for implementation even *before* any disarmament agreement so that by encouraging arms producers to reduce their reliance on military orders the government would favourably influence efforts to ease the way for the process of disarmament.[58] In this respect the Thorsson study goes beyond the 1981 UN report. So far, though, only a small conversion office within the Ministry for Foreign Affairs has been under any consideration by the Swedish government, and it appeared likely to be oriented to conversion-related issues, not to providing special assistance to defence companies or workers confronted by reduced domestic demand for armaments.[59]

7 The Economic Approach to Conversion (II)

The last and most numerous group of contributors to the literature on the economics of disarmament and conversion are the peace researchers, although eminent economists and writers with a radical labour perspective are also included. The material will be arranged in the following manner: titles prior to 1973 will be assessed first, then Melman's work which straddles both periods will be examined, finally the remainder of the literature from 1973 onwards will be considered in detail. The objective will be to compare the results of these studies with those from the UN and those produced under government sponsorship and, in particular, to identify what new insights the peace research and other studies have been able to provide.

PEACE RESEARCH (AND OTHER) STUDIES: PRE-1973

In the 1950s economic studies on military spending tended to emphasise a supposed link between comparatively high levels of expenditure on defence and economic prosperity.[1] Real fears were expressed in various quarters about the consequences of disarmament;[2] the Great Depression of the 1930s was still too vivid in many people's memories for such fears to be lightly dismissed. Moreover, as previously recounted in Chapter 4, Melman had laid stress on the way in which the notion that war brings prosperity had helped to forge an ideological commitment on the part of the American people to a permanent war economy. Consequently when Boulding claimed in 1960 that 'We are ... totally unprepared for peace'[3] he was one of the first to draw attention to the lack of formal or academic studies on the economic implications of peace and disarmament.

Saltman's definitive review of the studies produced in the 1960s and early 1970s spares reader and author alike from what might otherwise have been a lengthy and tedious diversion.[4] Her summaries of the findings of these researches, including those from UN and government-sponsored sources, showed a virtual unanimity on all the main points arising. As previously cited in the 1962 UN report, the economic problems of disarmament were found to be of two kinds: maintaining the level of aggregate demand in the economy, and dealing with structural problems affecting particular areas and industries. Advance planning of the measures to offset the fall in military expenditure, through detailed analysis of inter-industry effects on output and employment[5] and of unmet social needs, was also highlighted as an important requirement in the studies examined by Saltman. The unmet social needs referred to cover not only domestic concerns but aid to underdeveloped countries as well. There was an overwhelming consensus amongst the authors of these studies that disarmament would not result in economic depression but, on the contrary, would improve productivity and growth for all economies. Indeed, the threat of nuclear war makes economic and human disaster likely in the absence of disarmament.

Nevertheless, despite this optimistic note on the economics of disarmament, Saltman pointed to the main difficulty:

> The chronological analysis of these studies of the economic impact of disarmament reveals that economic feasibility as a focal concern has gradually come to be replaced by a deep and pervading recognition of political feasibility as the prime problem.[6]

This problem – a perennial one in the conversion debate – raises the question of how decision-makers in each country can be persuaded to proceed to convert the economy from production of war-making materiel to civilian production for peaceful purposes. Baran and Sweezy implied that it could not be done in a capitalist society[7] and others, whose views will be considered in the next chapter, have also expressed doubts for related reasons.

Most of the studies reviewed by Saltman do not require any special attention here though one of them did investigate the economic effects of disarmament in the UK. This study, conducted by the Economist Intelligence Unit, differed only in comparatively minor ways from the general consensus summarised above. In particular the report took a more optimistic view of the time-scale required to effect a transition to a peaceful economy believing that it was both possible and desirable to achieve this within two years.[8] Most other studies proposed a longer transition to disarmament of up to five years.

However, one major work, edited by Benoit and Boulding, demands some comment as it provides a number of insights into the problems of economic adjustment in the event of disarmament which remain relevant to this day.[9] More than this the study is not inattentive to the political difficulties in achieving disarmament, for which much of the literature on the economics of disarmament in the 1960s has been more or less justifiably criticised. For the editors themselves put their research project in this perspective:

> We are under no illusions that disarmament is easy or close, or that the economic adjustments are the major problem involved. The political problems of disarmament are the most difficult and the most important, and the economic problems will rise in importance only as the political problems are solved. It is essential, however, to know that we *can* solve the economic problems concerned; otherwise, our fears in this regard, even though they are below the surface, may operate as a serious handicap in our efforts to solve the political problem.[10] (Emphasis in the original.)

The economic model used was based on general and complete disarmament as it would affect the USA.

In the conclusion to the study Benoit highlighted the greater structural immobility of the resources employed in defence activity, compared to defence production in the Second World War or even the Korean War, in consequence of its entrenchment as an enduring component of the US economy. Those persons involved in defence are, therefore, more likely to resist a shift to civilian activities if no satisfactory alternative opportunities are provided. This much covered familiar territory, but Benoit then explored the critical area of the relationship between the two main kinds of problem in the economics of disarmament:

> While structural problems, therefore, possess an independent importance, they are, nevertheless, of clearly subordinate significance when compared to the fundamental problem of maintaining adequate demand. If demand remains slack there is little point in worrying about structural problems. What is the advantage in turning a discharged Marine sergeant into an unemployed laboratory assistant – or even

into an employed laboratory assistant, if this is attained only by keeping an existing laboratory assistant out of a job? Does it really help to transfer an unemployed airplane worker from Wichita to Chicago, thereby bringing the average unemployment rates of the two cities closer together, if both those cities have unemployment well above the acceptable minimum?[11]

So if disarmament began at a time when the national unemployment rate was 'still' 5.5 per cent, then displaced defence workers would have a bitter struggle to find work. These conditions would sap both the will and resources to deal effectively with the structural problems. Moreover, Benoit argued that the long-term unemployed would appear to have at least as good a claim for extended unemployment benefits, retraining and relocation assistance as the defence workers who, until recently, were working on excellent wages. Structural adjustment programmes would, under these conditions, be no more than palliatives – quite incapable of curing the real evil.[12]

While Thorsson, as related previously, put forward an argument for making defence workers a special case in the event of disarmament, Benoit's general point remains and is very relevant to economic conditions at the start of the 1990s and the prospects for successfully coping with the economic consequences of disarmament, and with conversion.

It is only under conditions of substantially full employment and full utilization of capacity that policy on structural adaptation suddenly assumes importance. For, under these conditions, a reduction in structural immobility may actually increase the use of resources; and any reduction in the difficulty of making transitions does not merely benefit one individual or firm, or community, in favour of another, but reduces the delays and costs of the changeovers, and makes possible a more exact and appropriate matching of desires, capabilities and opportunities.[13]

This whole area of the implementation of appropriate economic policies to deal with the transition to civilian production, and the extent to which such policies can in fact be applied, will be examined again at the end of this chapter, in the context of more recent economic and social conditions.

PEACE RESEARCH: MELMAN'S STUDIES, 1962–84

During the whole of this period Seymour Melman was developing his own ideas on the economics of disarmament and
conversion. This process, which by the mid-1960s was elaborated within the context of the depleting consequences of high
levels of military spending on the US civilian economy, continued right into the 1980s, so his conversion strategy, though
born in the boom years, foresees and reaches its full stature in
the worsening economic climate of the post-1973 era. Melman's
theoretical framework was outlined in detail during the earlier
discussion on the economic and social consequences of the arms
race, and need not be repeated here.[14] Its main consequence is to
emphasise the role of conversion in moving from a military to a
civilian economy in order to help reverse the arms race and
restore the civilian economy to health. The term used by
Melman and other peace researchers in the USA is 'economic
conversion' which more closely relates to conversion, as defined
in Chapter 1, than to economic conversion, in the broader and
non-military sense in which that phrase is applied either in this
work or by economists generally. Hence the words conversion or
defence conversion will be used here, rather than economic
conversion, although the reader should bear in mind that,
strictly speaking, economic conversion – in the US peace
research sense – has a somewhat wider connotation in that it is
also consciously related to a corresponding programme for
reconstruction of the civilian economy.

By 1965 Melman had located his conversion strategy within
an ambitious set of objectives aimed at halting the depletion
process in the US economy, beginning to reconstruct American
society and eliminating poverty by applying the principle of
useful work for all who are capable. This principle was to be the
primary means for planning and implementing alternatives to
the depleted society. Secondly, planning by government and
private agencies working together was necessary if useful work
was to be provided for everyone. Thirdly, private and public
organisations, including federal, state and local governments,
were to be motivated to devise specific plans for new, productive
investments. Fourthly, conversion from military to civilian economy would enable people to work on these new productive
activities, developing any additional skills required in the

process. Finally the 'war against poverty' would have to be rapid enough to obviate any further loss of morale and work abilities, particularly amongst the young. In Melman's frame of reference conversion does not need to wait upon disarmament; as defence is not, inevitably, a growth industry planning for conversion to civilian work is both reasonable and necessary.[15]

Although the vital question of how to effect this economic reconstruction without creating a centralised bureaucracy was discussed by Melman in 1965, his main work in the 1970s provided a more complete assessment of the problem. Moreover, unlike most of the other studies examined in this section, Melman's analysis of economic reconstruction and conversion prospects was set in an explicitly political framework which made his judgements that much more relevant and interesting:

> There will be a chance for a new opening in American public life if the belief system that supports the war economy is sufficiently eroded and if people who are trusted by wide publics seek out and proclaim new orientations in economy and society. But new public policies do not spring from the earth spontaneously. Given the characteristic human distrust of unfamiliar economic and social forms, one task for intellectuals is to formulate proposals for political-economic change that have some roots in American experience and that will thus have a chance of being accepted. Alternative political-economic ideas must be at once practical solutions to the serious problems created by the war economy and also culturally congenial to a majority of the population.[16]

In Chapter 13 there will be an opportunity to briefly consider whether Melman has succeeded in this task of postulating credible political-economic ideas to deal with the problems posed by the war economy. He himself argued the need for a major alteration in the composition of Congress, given the current militaristic emphasis in federal government policies, which would require the election of representatives from a non-militaristic tradition. Melman associated militaristic policies with centralised forms of organisation, of which the Pentagon is the supreme example, and he pointed out that a national decision to dismantle the war economy would not only necessitate new economic priorities but alternatives to centralist organisation to carry out this new productive work on a large scale.[17]

Looking first at the issue of new economic priorities, Melman stated that even rough blueprints of alternative projects would be useful for the time when widespread support for reducing the size of the military economy exists. Indeed, these plans would encourage a sense of realism about the alternatives and so help to allay some of the fears induced by long reliance on the military economy. Various programmes for civilian investments to improve public facilities were investigated so as both to illustrate the possibilities for large-scale projects to replace military spending and also to show that such work need not be competitive with private firms. Programmes involving water-supply systems, urban transit and other such facilities are not generally undertaken by private firms which would normally act as suppliers. Moreover the size of the programmes was of an order which compared with the savings Melman adduced from a massively reduced defence budget – one which recognised the limits of military power, disposed of unnecessary 'overkill' capacity and eliminated the role of US armed forces in achieving world hegemony.[18] In this manner Melman attacked the ideological consensus that there is no real alternative to military spending.

Taking the problem of centralist organisational forms, he then questioned the reliance on centralism in American economic and political development since 1945. It has meant that only those issues which seem amenable to central government control are emphasised. In turn this has led to an even greater concentration of tax revenue in the hands of federal government to enable it to pursue foreign political and military objectives. Another consequence of centralism is the alienation it produces in the populace who feel remote from those whose decisions affect their lives. Melman countered the argument that this kind of effect is justified by the greater efficiency of centralised organisation by challenging, with relevant data, the belief that the intensity of managerial control is related to industrial efficiency. Instead he advocated decentralised and regional approaches which would give local people more control over the alternatives to military activities in national policy, particularly in the matter of detailed implementation. Increasing the taxing powers of state and local governments, at the expense of federal government, would also be essential but the success of this policy would depend on genuine democratic participation and an improvement in competence for economic planning and administration.[19]

Melman's assessment of the prospects for pursuing this new direction in economic reconstruction without centralism was sober:

> I am not optimistic about the likelihood of readily overcoming the weight of ideology and administrative vested interest in centralism in government and in industry. So much energy has been poured into ways of concentrating power and so little has been done to fashion ideas for new institutions of local control. But these gaps can also be seen as constructive opportunities for all who are willing to break with the ideologies of centralism-at-all-costs and participate in some innovative thinking for defining the limits of centralism, and the characteristics of alternative ways of organizing, wielding and controlling economic and political power.[20]

As far as conversion itself is concerned Melman was under no illusions about the difficulties of motivating workers and managers to move to civilian work, even if jobs were available. He thought that there would have to be a widespread revulsion against the war economy to move defence dependent personnel into civilian activities.[21]

To this end Melman saw the need for a national political and economic movement with conversion to civilian work as its goal. In tandem with this political mobilisation would be a progamme of new economic investment on the lines discussed previously. Without this there would be no market opportunities against which conversion planning could be carried forward with any prospect of success.[22] It is of interest to note that despite some encouraging signs in the earlier 1980s no such movement has yet emerged in the USA or elsewhere.

Since most of those involved in the military economy have a stake in maintaining the status quo Melman believed that any initiative for conversion to civilian economy would have to come from outside. Nevertheless defence personnel can be expected to participate in the conversion process provided that society shows that this is what it wants and makes available such economic and social assistance as will ease the transition process.[23] In this manner the costs of change would not be borne solely by those whose defence work was, anyway, partly at the behest of society itself.

Melman has continued and consolidated his work on conversion in the 1980s. If anything his confidence in its importance and, most significantly, its characteristic as an autonomous activity has increased. Melman considered that conversion – i.e. economic conversion in US terms – has a role to play in reversing the arms race:

> The absence of economic conversion planning promises that any shift from the present course of policy would automatically penalize the employees of the military economy. As this threat is replaced by the promise of an alternative economic future, there is bound to be a greater inclination to consider ways of improving security by reversing the arms race. I believe that a lowering of resistance towards a reversal of the arms race would be a reasonable consequence of competent conversion planning.
>
> A society that has prepared conversion plans is, automatically, a more credible proponent of measures to reverse an arms race.[24]

Melman re-emphasised the point that the research and industrial planning for conversion can be carried out without any international agreement. Moreover, the damaging effects of a military economy are a political factor which can be used now (though the summary given at the end of Chapter 4 on the evidence relating to this point suggested the results were, in various aspects, somewhat inconclusive and questioned how much political weight they would actually carry). Finally, Melman distinguished between the political commitment required for disarmament and that needed for conversion, claiming that the latter involves a lesser degree of support.

Clearly some crucial issues are raised here: the extent to which conversion is an autonomous activity; the degree to which conversion would improve current economic conditions rather than be slowed down or halted as a consequence of them; the role of conversion, not simply in dealing with the economic effects of disarmament or removing a potential impediment to an agreement on disarmament, but in contributing significantly to a reversal of the arms race; and, finally, the extent of political commitment required for conversion and in what way it differs from that required for disarmament. These questions, implicit also in the Thorsson study and the 1981 UN report, will be addressed again in the conclusion to this chapter, since the answers to them largely determine the nature of any theory of defence conversion.

PEACE RESEARCH (AND OTHER) STUDIES: POST-1973

It only remains to review the contributions, comparatively few as they are, from other authors on the economics of disarmament and conversion in the period from 1973 onwards. This can best be done by taking, first, the writers from the USA before summarising, briefly, some significant works from the UK and FRG.

The most significant departure in the economic approach to conversion in recent years, within the *USA*, was as a direct result of the emergence of the Nuclear Weapons Freeze Campaign in the early 1980s. This attracted widespread support not only in the American peace movement but more widely amongst the US public. It led to two studies, the first by McFadden and Wake and the second by Hartung, which examined the economic consequences of a nuclear freeze.[25] This reflected not so much a switch in emphasis, within the US peace movement, from disarmament to arms control – at least not as an end in itself – but a move to a more gradualist approach to disarmament best expounded by Forsberg.[26] The way in which the American Nuclear Freeze Campaign, an essentially political phenomenon, brought together the twin issues of military and economic security and linked them with conversion as a significant part of a broader disarmament strategy, following similar lines to that envisaged by the 1981 UN report and the Thorsson study, makes this an extremely interesting and practical example of the kind of role which conversion could fill.

Although both the McFadden and Wake and the Hartung studies adopted similar approaches and reached similar conclusions, albeit with some variations in the quantitative assessments of budget savings and jobs displaced by a nuclear freeze, only the latter study will be summarised here since it is the more recent and academic of the two. Hartung examined how a halt in the production of new nuclear warheads and their delivery vehicles would affect the US economy, assuming that a bilateral US–USSR nuclear weapons freeze were to be agreed. It should be borne in mind that this investigation was carried out in the context of the biggest military build-up in American peacetime history since 1945, which has been outlined in detail elsewhere.[27]

Over a period of five years about $98 billion in budget savings could have been realised as a result of a nuclear freeze (assuming it had taken effect from financial year 1984). A freeze could displace between 250 000–350 000 workers in the US defence industry depending on the timing of an agreement, the impact on research funds and various other areas of uncertainty. Under worst case assumptions less than 0.4 per cent of the total US workforce would be affected. However, the study claimed that a freeze need not lead to an increase in unemployment since applying the budget savings to civilian programmes, or to tax cuts, could result in an overall increase in employment. (This did not, of course, take into account the effect of applying some portion of budget savings to a conversion programme, aimed at assisting those workers whose jobs are lost in consequence of a nuclear freeze.) Various civilian programmes were proposed in order to highlight the opportunity costs of the nuclear weapons build-up: restoring basic human services relating to social security benefits, health and education facilities; public investment and employment programmes; and cutting the federal deficit.[28] The study stressed that the net economic effect of a freeze would be heavily dependent on how released resources would be applied, in particular, their employment-generating capability would vary widely with deficit reductions having the least impact.

The economic transition from nuclear weapons production would be made easier, according to Hartung, by applying freeze savings to civilian programmes or by returning these savings to people in the form of tax cuts. Additionally job losses in the defence industry would be heavily oriented to scientific and technical staff whose job categories have unemployment rates of less than one half the national average. Moreover, most states in the USA will face few, if any, damaging economic consequences from a freeze since nuclear weapons production is heavily concentrated in a handful of states. Nevertheless, even under the most favourable conditions, special readjustment measures would be needed to aid communities most affected by a freeze. Hartung maintained that a nationally coordinated approach to conversion was required to minimise local economic hardship. He rejected the view that comprehensive conversion planning would be unnecessarily bureaucratic, arguing instead that it would offer some public control over existing bureaucracies like the Pentagon. Also, since defence contracting is not an open market activity, it did not make sense to leave the problems arising from a nuclear freeze to the normal operations of the labour market.[29] Hartung's arguments against the *laissez-faire* opponents of conversion planning represent a useful supplement to the points made in the CBO report, cited previously.[30] He outlined various mechanisms for carrying out conversion planning, to be discussed in Chapter 13, including the Weiss and Mavroules economic conversion bills before Congress, a number of state initiatives and local alternative use planning by defence workers.

The Hartung study throws light on two questions about conversion which have been raised earlier in this review of the literature. First, there is the long-standing issue of the political feasibility of conversion. Hartung took the view that the popularity of the freeze proposal itself would improve the prospects for successful reintroduction of conversion legislation in Congress, if it had the backing of the freeze campaign, the major unions and other organisations opposed to nuclear weapons production. Second, Hartung at least partially answered the criticism of conversion planning, namely that it offers assistance to one group of workers, many of whom are on better conditions of service, at the expense of workers in declining civilian industries and those who are unemployed. He supported the view (indistinguishable from Melman's thesis discussed earlier) that conversion should be seen as part of a process of democratic reconstruction of the whole economy. Thus the resources released by a nuclear weapons freeze would provide an opportunity to solve some of the country's most pressing economic problems, even though no arms control measures alone could be expected to cure all its economic ills.[31]

It still appears, though, that there is an unresolved tension between using the budget savings to benefit the economy as a whole and applying an unspecified proportion to a conversion programme, which might well be expected to reduce the overall net gain to the economy. For the costs of conversion would presumably be expected to be paid for from these budget savings and, given the difficulties and complexities of reorientating and retooling defence firms and retraining individuals for civilian work, as compared to simply making tax cuts or initiating public investment programmes geared to employment generation, the more that is spent on the conversion programme the less will the remainder create new employment in the rest of the economy. More than this – and recalling Benoit's admonitions from his 1963 study – how far will any conversion programme be possible, or even acceptable, in the context of recession and high unemployment? For if the savings from an arms control agreement cannot resolve US economic and social problems, which clearly they cannot, then will a conversion programme prove to be no more than a palliative, as Benoit suggested? And this question takes us right back to the heart of the conversion issue in the period following the 1973 oil price crisis: to what extent do conditions of economic recession and high unemployment represent *a barrier* to any conversion programme, resulting from changes in the level or type of military spending of whatever degree, or to what extent does a conversion programme represent *an opportunity* to improve the economic climate either in its own right or as part of a broader reconstruction of the economy? This, and other related matters, will form part of the summary at the end of this chapter when an initial hypothesis will be formulated on the scope and nature of conversion in the major Western industrialised countries.

The *UK* has produced few major, academic studies of the economics of disarmament and conversion since 1963.[32] However, in the mid-1970s various influences including the then Labour government's plans to reduce defence spending, some highly innovative proposals on alternative products from a group of defence workers at Lucas Aerospace[33] and the work of various academics on the defence industry and the harmful consequences of high levels of military spending, all combined to increase interest in conversion again. The Richardson Institute for Conflict and Peace Research published *Alternative Work for Military Industries: Military Spending and Arms Cuts – Economic and Industrial Implication,* edited by Dan Smith (1977), while the Labour Party Defence Study Group's work led to the publication of *Sense About Defence* (1977).[34] The latter publication involved an examination of the economic consequences of any future implementation of the Labour Party's 1974 manifesto commitment to reduce the proportion of GNP spent on defence in order to bring it into line with Britain's main European allies. As a result of the debate on this question – the Study Group's report was not acted upon by the then Labour government although they did carry out some reduction in defence expenditure – Niven proposed an arms conversion policy in 1983 which borrowed heavily on American ideas.[35] Suffice it is to say that these British contributions advanced knowledge on conversion matters only in one respect that is of general interest to all major Western industrialised countries. This was in the matter of a new industrial, worker-oriented approach to conversion which will be described in detail in Chapter 11.

Studies by *West German* authors on conversion increased in number in the late 1970s and early 1980s. Wulf, for instance, presented a paper to an international scientific symposium which showed '. . . that the conversion of the war industry in the Federal Republic is basically feasible without having serious economic and social consequences'.[36]

Another study, by Brzoska, explored the parameters of arms production in the UK, France, the FRG and Italy whilst also estimating current and projected levels of overcapacity. He considered several ways in which this overcapacity could be handled including a conversion programme. In considering this option he concluded that in France, the UK and Italy conversion would be an attractive option, because of the long-term economic benefits from reduced military spending, yet it would be most difficult to achieve in these countries because of short-term economic problems. In the case of the FRG conversion would, on the other hand, be less necessary but easier to accomplish. This conclusion led Brzoska to recommend a joint conversion fund on a West European scale, financed primarily by the savings achieved through reduced defence spending and conversion in the FRG. A portion of these savings could then be applied to dealing with the more difficult conversion problems in the three other major West European countries. The short-term adjustment burden would thus be shared amongst all four partners and, in so doing, political and economic opposition to conversion in the UK, France and Italy could be weakened. In the long term the benefits of the programme could be directed to the Third World to help the fight against poverty. Brzoska also believed the idea of a joint conversion fund should be considered within the European Community (EC).[37]

Brzoska's West European proposal was certainly innovative although politically the obstacles would appear considerable (not least, perhaps, from within the FRG). Another point to consider – in relation to his EC proposal – is the controversy surrounding the question of how far the Treaty of Rome precludes discussion of military and defence-industrial matters.[38] This might hamper EC involvement in conversion programmes by complicating, or even disallowing, the integration of defence procurement and industrial policy questions. Nevertheless the EC has done work on the defence industries and arms procurement so some initiative may be possible.[39]

That brings to an end this lengthy discourse on the economics of disarmament and conversion in so far as the general issues are concerned. The summary which follows attempts to draw together the diverse strands of this debate within the economic approach to conversion, and reach some initial conclusions.

SUMMARY AND CONCLUSIONS

The extensive literature on this subject has been reviewed historically in relation to the six main Western industrialised countries, especially the USA. During the 1960s research tended to be based on more optimistic assumptions about disarmament whilst in the 1970s and 1980s arms control, including a proposed superpower agreement on a nuclear freeze, has increasingly become the focus of attention. At the same time the economic climate has dramatically worsened, so that recession and high unemployment have dominated much of the period from the oil price crisis of 1973 – the very period during which far fewer studies on the economics of disarmament have been undertaken. Fortunately the quality and sophistication of the analysis evidenced in the works reviewed here largely, if not wholly, compensates for their paucity.

The United Nations contribution to the development of ideas on the economics of disarmament and conversion has been highly significant in its own right. Its relationship with peace research can best be described as symbiotic. The UN produced one of the first major studies on the economic effects of disarmament in 1962 while, most recently, its 1981 report contains a theoretical framework for conversion unrivalled by any other save that of Melman. What distinguishes the UN model from Melman's is the central place given to the link between disarmament and development, within which conversion preparations are to take place. Although Melman did, in his earlier works, also make such a connection this was rather lost sight of in his main book on conversion.[40]

The 1981 UN model of conversion identified three main purposes in preparations for a transfer of resources from military to civilian production: to reduce opposition to disarmament and foster a climate of international confidence; to assist in a more balanced approach to the question of international security; and to foster, and be integrated with, wider economic changes both nationally and globally. The context for these preparations involved not only linking disarmament with development but each of these to a broader definition of international security in which economic factors, too, would be taken into account. The incompatibility of the arms race with economic development and economic security was reinforced by the harmful economic and social consequences of high levels of military spending.

The key requirements for successful conversion have been highlighted in various UN reports since 1962. Likewise every report since 1962 has agreed that disarmament and conversion are economically and technically feasible on a world-wide scale. National governments have a central role to play, during the transition period, in maintaining aggregate demand in the economy and dealing with structural problems in the industries and regions where the defence industry is concentrated. Advance planning of, and the involvement of all parties affected by, conversion have been repeatedly emphasised.

Conversion can take place within or between industries, the problem being one not of finding alternatives but of deciding how to choose between many competing claims on the resources released by disarmament. In recent years the UN has proposed many ways of encouraging conversion preparations and, where appropriate, planning which were given in detail earlier in this review.

While no government has given a high priority to conversion, government-funded bodies in the USA have, particularly in the 1960s and early 1970s and again in the early 1980s, sponsored studies on conversion issues. The ACDA-funded research reports, prior to 1973, reached conclusions on the feasibility of conversion which were generally similar to those of the UN and some encouraged state and local government roles in advance planning. One study reviewed here also suggested that the time-lag problem was more significant for conversion planning than some studies seem to have appreciated. More recently a CBO report and a separate DoD report both highlighted the 'planning' problem in the USA with its ideology of *laissez-faire* in civilian economic matters. The DoD feasibility study also drew attention to the difference between factory-based and community-based conversion (or economic adjustment) and rejected the former in favour of the latter.

The only other Western state to have made a notable contribution to the study of conversion is that of Sweden whose government commissioned a report from the Special Expert, Thorsson, in 1984. This report went further than the 1981 UN report (in which Thorsson had also played a leading role) in proposing that conversion programmes be initiated in advance of any disarmament agreement. The Thorsson study also proposed a detailed policy framework for conversion in Sweden. So far, though, no Western government has accepted that it has a role to play in defence industry conversion. The Office of Economic Adjustment in the USA (to be discussed in Chapter 13) does, though, give assistance to workers and communities forced to adjust to the impact of military base closures and contract cancellations.

Turning to the peace researchers and other writers on the economics of disarmament and conversion, the volume of published material was greatest in the pre-1973 period. During this time there was, at first, little or no linkage made between the economic and social consequences of high levels of military spending and the economics of disarmament. Indeed where this link was discussed at all it was generally assumed that defence spending had a positive impact on the economy – a reflection, no doubt, of the view prevalent in the 1950s in the literature on this subject. Melman was one of the first in post-war history to question the benefits of high military spending, and by the early 1970s this theme was beginning to gain wider currency and affect the debate on the economics of disarmament. In the period since 1973 it can be claimed that the economics of disarmament has only rarely been discussed on its own, for it has been largely subsumed within a wider context encompassing international security, disarmament (or arms control) and development, in addition to the damaging economic consequences of the arms race.

Saltman's review of the literature in the 1960s noted the nearly unanimous view of researchers on the economic feasibility of conversion whilst, at the same time, spotlighting the lack of political will. Most of these researchers thought a longer transition to disarmament (up to five years) was preferable to a shorter period (two years being the minimum required).[41] The views expressed on conversion were, again, similar to those contained in the 1962 UN report. One major study, though, by Benoit and Boulding in 1963 stressed the prior importance of maintaining aggregate demand, in order to ensure full employment and utilisation of capacity, if the structural problems in the economy were to be dealt with during the transition period. Under conditions of low growth and high unemployment structural adjustment programmes would be no more than palliatives.

One of the best of the recent studies on conversion is that by Hartung in 1984. It is a good example of the more sophisticated analysis of conversion issues which has characterised recent studies on the subject from various quarters. The economic consequences of a nuclear freeze were analysed both within the context of the harmful economic and social consequences of high levels of US military spending, and also as the basis for a discussion of the role of conversion in minimising the job losses for defence personnel and in defence dependent communities. Additionally, by linking conversion to the American Nuclear Freeze Campaign, which gained widespread popular support in the early 1980s, the study made conversion appear more credible in political terms than a largely academic research project into the economics of disarmament would have done. Many of the 1960s conversion reports would fall into this latter category. Hartung argued that a nuclear freeze need not lead to an increase in unemployment in the USA and, as far as conversion was concerned, it formed part of a democratic reconstruction of the economy which would, he thought, provide an opportunity to solve some of the country's economic problems.

In the USA a legislative framework for conversion has been sought in vain for over twenty years, by almost all the proponents of conversion planning. This aim was taken up in the

UK by Niven during the early 1980s. Other recent ideas on conversion policy include that of Brzoska who has suggested a West European or EC conversion fund to assist defence companies, with substantial overcapacity, in turning to civilian activities. (Thorsson made a similar proposal of a conversion fund to assist Swedish defence firms.)

What then has been learnt from this review of the literature? The economic approach to conversion provides a good initial assessment of the scope and nature of conversion in terms of its purposes, the main problems involved and what is technically and economically required for a successful resolution of those difficulties and the realisation of the opportunities for new civilian production. However, a full answer to the question posed must be postponed until both the criticisms of this approach have been considered, and also the defence policy and industrial approaches to conversion have been discussed. Nevertheless there are a number of observations which can and should be made immediately.

The heart of the conversion issue in the period from 1973 was said to be whether current economic conditions represented a barrier to conversion or whether a conversion programme might represent an opportunity to improve the economic climate. Considering that the review of the literature on the economic and social consequences of the arms race did not lead to the conclusion that *all* Western economic ills at the present time could be blamed on excessive military spending, even if some of them were undoubtedly exacerbated by such spending, it is clear that at best a conversion programme could provide only partial relief, depending on its size and scale. Without government support, especially in creating new civilian markets as envisaged by Melman, the prospects for successful conversion planning, viewed from the perspective of an individual defence contractor, might look dim indeed.

Moreover, on its own, a conversion programme would, as Benoit maintained in 1963, surely be no more than a palliative, protecting defence workers' jobs at the expense of the long-term unemployed. This may or may not be justifiable in some circumstances but it could hardly avoid being highly controversial in political terms. If, as Melman proposed, conversion were part of a much broader programme of economic reconstruction such an objection might be overcome. Inescapably, though, this returns the debate to the political question – can the will be found to effect such a change in the West?

The political constraints in most Western countries have recently become as serious as the economic ones and inimical to the basic precepts of defence conversion. First, conversion emphasises the role of planning and government involvement whilst the dominant economic ideology calls for reduced state intervention in the economy and increased reliance on market forces. Secondly, conversion theory has always placed primary emphasis on maintaining aggregate demand during the transition period while, today, powerful political and financial pressures exist to curb government spending. Thirdly, recession and high unemployment have hit some regions much harder than others making structural adjustments politically more contentious where some defence industries are concentrated in more prosperous areas (as in the UK).

These economic and political obstacles are formidable. They do not obviate the possibility of conversion programmes being adopted and carried through but they help to explain why no government in the West has attempted, and few have seriously considered, such programmes so far. While the lack of political will in achieving disarmament partially explains the absence of conversion planning it cannot provide the whole explanation. There is no doubt that defence industry conversion could occur even without a disarmament agreement and if, as Melman maintains, the political commitment required for conversion is less than that for disarmament, so far it has not been found, though there are some encouraging signs in the UK[42] and Sweden in particular.

Conversion can, as yet, barely be described as an autonomous activity. Until it is its potential as an instrument in lowering resistance to the arms race must remain somewhat speculative. An economic approach to disarmament, one that either assumes that the political will can be mustered, or argues the case for reduced military spending on the grounds of the economic damage currently being imposed on the civilian economy, has so far proved unavailing in winning sufficient support for conversion. To this extent it faces the same shortcomings as the economic case against high military expenditures discussed previously: the justification for high levels of military spending rests primarily on perceived strategic needs in the defence of Western capitalism, not on any supposed economic benefits.

Studies like that of Hartung have, perhaps, provided a clue as to how the political will for conversion can best be established. The key appears to lie not in assuming a high degree of autonomy for conversion initiatives, or in relying principally on economic arguments to generate political commitment, but rather in linking conversion to a wider disarmament strategy, (or an arms control strategy as a prelude to disarmament). An initial hypothesis in this book would be that, in the short term, conversion has very little scope for independent application but may win sufficient political support to allow for some modest experimental schemes if it is skilfully linked to wider political as well as economic policies. What this might mean will be discussed in depth in Chapter 14 once the criticisms made of, and the alternatives to, the economic approach to conversion have been assessed.

8 Limitations of Economic Models

The economic approach to conversion, while being the mainstream of thinking on this subject from the late 1950s until the early 1970s, has not been without its detractors and critics. As one author expressed it:

> If radical critics like Michael Reich are correct, then the sophisticated analyses of U.S. Arms Control and Disarmament Agency economists and university economists may have little more relevance than well conceived plans for the colonization of the sun. However well conceived, they simply will never be put into practice.[1]

The underlying argument is that conversion advocates have underestimated both the dependency of countries like the USA on defence spending and also the power of the 'military–industrial complex'.

Albrecht, too, noted the high priority placed on the political problems of conversion by many econometric studies but added:

> Any further effort, to learn what is understood by 'political problems' in this tradition is bound to fail because of the paucity of evidence. This is a queer situation: the most formidable problem, in the view of elaborated studies – the political one – is scarcely dealt with in any detail.[2]

The review of conversion literature in the last two chapters largely confirms this latter observation but with one major exception: Melman's theoretical contribution to the debate may be regarded as over-optimistic in its assessment of the potential for conversion but he *has* considered the political problem in detail. So in discussing the critics of conversion his position will need to be given special attention.

This chapter examines critiques of conversion from two main perspectives. The first arises from the debate on the military–industrial complex in the 1960s and early 1970s and the second from the growing literature on alternative security concepts in

123

the 1970s and 1980s. The latter includes for the first time in this book since the concept was defined the notion of 'peace conversion'.[3] Having assessed the validity of these criticisms of traditional notions of defence conversion it will then be possible to proceed, in the succeeding chapters, to evaluate the defence policy and industrial approaches to conversion. These more recent approaches did not, however, emanate from the radical critiques to be discussed here though they were to modify the economic approach to conversion in most significant ways. Before finally attempting to synthesise the various findings of this review of conversion literature into a theoretical framework, the historical legacy of conversion initiatives up to the present time will be assessed. Thus the future prospects for conversion may be forecast on the basis of the best available knowledge and experience of its scope and nature in the major Western industrialised countries.

THE THEORY OF THE MILITARY–INDUSTRIAL COMPLEX

As discussed in Chapter 4, Baran and Sweezy had claimed that the US economy was dependent on high levels of military expenditure. This view, which if correct would have meant that conversion would be impossible while capitalism lasted, was rejected for different reasons by both R. Smith and Melman. Yet even though economic determinism proved an unsatisfactory explanation for high spending on defence it could still be claimed that various political forces, acting in concert, were a major underlying cause of this high military spending, particularly in the USA and USSR. These political forces, generally known as the military–industrial complex, militate against any attempt to reduce defence spending and implement a conversion programme. The seriousness of this opposition is certainly a key question for proponents of the conversion of military industries.

The theory of the military–industrial complex, in its modern form, dates back to C. Wright Mills' *The Power Elite* (1956) and the concept was used by President Eisenhower himself in his Farewell Address in 1961.[4] A review of the extensive literature on the subject, published in 1973, emphasised the enormous impact it had had:

In a mere fifteen years, Mills' theory, legitimized by Eisenhower, has come from relative obscurity to being one of the foremost analytical tools employed by laymen to explain events and tendencies, particularly unhappy ones, in American foreign and strategic policy. The theory is employed to explain the high cost of defense, the longevity of the Cold War, the persistence of anticommunist mythology, the 'perverted priorities' of the Federal budget, the interventionist proclivities of American foreign policy, and even the generation of cultural values giving rise to riots and assassinations. The theory is part of the consciousness of every attentive student of politics and society.[5]

However, the concept has remained highly controversial and, as will be seen later, there is some evidence that its influence has declined in recent years. Before outlining what is meant by the military–industrial complex it is important to note that the theory forms part of a wider, and long-running, historical debate on militarism which has been discussed elsewhere.[6]

Although there are many versions of the theory the main propositions put forward by its principal advocates can be summarised here.[7] The high levels of defence spending since 1945 in the world's major states, particularly the USA and USSR, have created strong domestic groups with a vested interest in continued military expenditures and international rivalry. These groups comprise professional soldiers, the managers and owners of defence industries, various government bureaucrats involved in military matters and legislators whose own constituencies benefit from contracts for defence equipment and supplies. Other less influential groups, like the trade unions in defence companies and scientists and engineers involved in military research, provide additional support to the main groups in the military–industrial complex.[8] The influence of all these groups is coordinated and directed to maintain high defence expenditures and to control the nation's strategic foreign and defence policies. As these groups occupy very powerful positions within their respective domestic political structures their influence exceeds that of any other coalition of interest groups, at least on matters of national security. The position of those in the complex is secured through an ideology of international conflict, notably the cold war, which most theorists view as an exaggerated

picture of external threats to the state. However, theorists differ
on the issue of whether this ideology is a deliberate deception,
in which case the complex is essentially a conspiracy protecting and advancing its own interests by misleading the public,
or whether it is a 'false consciousness' arising inevitably, but
without prior expectation, as a result of high military expenditures, in which case the complex is a coalition which wrongly
thinks it is acting in the public interest.

The end result of adopting this theory is to make the external
threat a rationalisation of armaments policies which really
emanate from the self-interest of the various military–industrial
complexes. This view contrasts starkly with the conventional one
which postulates that arms races are the consequence of a
combination of international conflict and mutual fear amongst
rival states. Taken to extremes the theory of the military–
industrial complex would blame the occurrence of wars on
profiteering armaments manufacturers and militarism. Indeed
such a view has dominated much of pacifist literature in the
twentieth century.[9]

Unlike the theory of the military–industrial complex, Melman
viewed the private arms manufacturers in the USA as wholly
subordinate to the new state management based in the Pentagon, rather than as partners with this bureaucracy. However,
Slater and Nardin, as part of the 1973 review and evaluation by
Rosen, did not regard this feature of Melman's political analysis
as being of primary theoretical importance. They argued that
in terms of 'the nature of power, motivation, causation, and
explanation' his theory, and others like it, did not differ substantially from those writers who explicitly referred to a military–
industrial complex.[10]

Slater and Nardin rejected the concept of the military–
industrial complex in the USA on the grounds that it has four
basic weaknesses which undermine its use in scientific work:
first, the concept relies on a conspiracy theory which drastically
oversimplifies the explanation of political and social events;
secondly, it relies on very narrow assumptions about political
motivation, especially that people are always motivated by
'interests' expressed in terms of direct political and economic
gains; thirdly, the criteria for membership of the complex are
inconsistent and changing, and where a broad section of the
society is said to support it then the theory loses much of its

force, since this is based on the view that the national security policy is the product of a small, unrepresentative elite; and fourthly, the theory rests on questionable assumptions about the power which the military–industrial complex is said to have.[11]

Before attempting to determine the validity of these arguments against Melman's thesis it is worth noting the immediate and longer-term impact of such criticisms of the theory of the military–industrial complex. Rosen himself, in assessing all the papers in his review, concluded that the essential propositions of C. Wright Mills' theory had been upheld though some of the more simplistic, conspiratorial versions should be discarded. He contradicted sceptics like Slater and Nardin by claiming that the theory had withstood critical examination well and remained a very useful analytical tool for research and policy evaluation purposes.[12] Nevertheless, some years later a UNESCO review claimed that the relative significance of military–industrial complex analysis was declining partly as a result of the criticism levelled at it from writers like Slater and Nardin.[13]

It is not hard to see why this has been so. Rosen identified a key point in the Slater and Nardin critique which leads to the likely cause of this decline in the importance attached to the military–industry complex. It related to the connection between a theorist's prior assumption about the weakness of the Soviet (or American) threat and the use made of the concept of the military–industrial complex. Those who accept the official strategic rationale for high military expenditure simply do not require such concepts to explain American (or Soviet) foreign policy. Only those who are already convinced that the external threat is being exaggerated find the concept plausible or useful.[14] Consequently, it can be argued, the strength behind the whole theory rests on how convincing it is in claiming that domestic factors, notably the military–industrial complex, are a *primary* cause of arms races. Once it is conceded that there are external threats which do have a decisive impact on the size of military budgets and the role of the military in government and the economy, the theory loses much of its force. The concept of the military–industrial complex can still be applied, and may usefully redress the imbalance in official accounts by stressing the domestic pressures behind the arms race, but it is then only one of a number of important factors to be taken into account in explaining the persistence of high military expenditures. While the evidence of a number of other writers will be cited briefly it remains true that, outside of the pacifist tradition, the significance of the complex has been somewhat downgraded in recent years.

First, however, the relevance of Slater and Nardin's criticisms to Melman's work must be assessed. It should be remembered that their analysis, in so far as it related to his work, was centred on one of Melman's earlier works[15] and not his later, more sophisticated writing.[16] In attempting to question the implicit theory of politics of virtually all the critics of the establishment viewpoint at one go Slater and Nardin have, in the case of Melman at least, presented a distorted picture of his position. This is even more obvious in relation to Melman's later work than that available at the time.

There is no hint of a crude conspiracy theory in Melman's thesis. The ideology of war economy arose from past experience (during the Second World War) and is, according to Melman, both sincerely believed in by the politicians themselves as well as being strongly supported by the American people who are convinced that large military budgets mean prosperity and jobs. In Melman's theory the civilian rulers are firmly in control of both the armed forces and military-related industry. While power is concentrated in the new state management, the President is at the pinnacle of this establishment and he and the entire legislature are accountable to the electorate. The official strategic rationale for high levels of military expenditure – the external threat – was not dismissed by Melman though the point was made that US military capabilities go well beyond those required for defence alone. And far from relying on economic determinism, as Slater and Nardin implied, Melman argued that the debilitating consequences of high military spending on civilian industry makes necessary, and possible, a political and economic movement to reverse this process. In short, there is no conspiracy theory because Melman took account of factors other than the actions and power of individuals or groups with an interest in particular events and policies; there is no crude economic determinism – indeed Melman strongly criticised Baran and Sweezy on precisely this point; there is no military–industrial complex since this implies a coalition of interests while Melman is emphatic that civilian political control, albeit one imbued with militaristic values, is dominant through the new state management; and, finally, this state management is not all-powerful but is, ultimately, capable of being successfully challenged by a democratic movement for conversion and economic regeneration.

In terms of Melman's thesis it is pertinent to ask what empirical evidence exists to support the theory of the military–industrial complex? Lieberson conducted a study which tested the theory against available data and concluded that a military–industrial complex does indeed exist with a vested interest in maintaining high levels of defence expenditure. Nevertheless he regarded it as only one of several special interest groups that are able to exercise most influence over their own subject area. Consequently, whilst the complex has great influence over policies affecting national security, other vested interests, in agriculture or education for instance, have special influence in their respective spheres. Moreover, his evidence did not lend weight to the view that either large defence companies or the economy as a whole require defence spending to maintain current levels of profitability and prosperity.[17]

Another interesting contribution to military–industrial complex theory came from Kurth who examined major aircraft, missile and anti-missile procurement decisions taken by the US government in the 1960s and 1970s. He found that these decisions could be explained in terms of the requirements of the eight major production lines of the top aerospace firms, without any recourse to the official strategic rationale. According to Kurth, the 'follow-on' imperative means that as one production line opens up it will receive a new defence contract usually of a similar nature to the one before. This contrasts with the official view that the most cost-effective design for a new weapons system will be chosen from amongst several competing firms. Additionally there is a 'bail-out imperative' whereby the government rescues defence companies in financial difficulty with new military contracts.[18] The findings from this study lend support to the theory of the military–industrial complex but, it should be said, form too narrow a data base to be anything like conclusive.

Yet even if there is undoubtedly substantial evidence to support the existence of a military–industrial complex, the crux of the matter is really the extent to which this militates against the feasibility of a conversion programme. This raises the issue of 'systemic compatibility' whose importance was explained by

Albrecht in the following terms: 'A fundamental premise of any conversion strategy is the compatibility of this policy with the degree of change acceptable to the social system.'[19]

Lieberson took a view on this question not substantially dissimilar to the conversion specialists whose findings were discussed at length in Chapters 6 and 7. At the opposite end of the spectrum, Reich reached a very different conclusion. Writing in a Marxist tradition, influenced by Baran and Sweezy amongst others, he argued

> ... that a major shift in social and economic priorities would require a fundamental transformation of the US capitalist economy. The growth and persistence of a high level of military spending is a natural outcome in an advanced capitalist society that both suffers from the problem of inadequate private aggregate demand, and plays a leading role in the preservation and expansion of the international capitalist system. In my view, barring a revolutionary change, militarism and military spending priorities are likely to persist for the foreseeable future.[20]

Reich attacked the conventional wisdom which stated that expenditure on social needs could easily substitute for military spending as long as aggregate demand is maintained by appropriate economic policies. Given the inadequacy of private demand in the US economy since the late 1940s some form of government expenditure has been necessary but, he said, military spending provided much the most convenient outlet. Such spending is easily increased because it does not compete with private demand and so does not confront any corporate opposition. Indeed military contracts are very attractive to firms which receive them. Reich also claimed that these contracts are more profitable than comparable civilian work, a view rejected by other writers at the time and one that has remained controversial ever since.[21]

Conversely, US government spending on civilian projects is not a feasible substitute. Reich argued that, unlike military investments, investments in social facilities generally endure, do not become rapidly obsolete and are not consumed very quickly. Moreover, the technology involved is usually **not** very elaborate and the scope for rapid and wasteful expansion of social spending is more limited. More importantly, vast increases in social expenditure would interfere with the very basis of capitalism:

for many sorts of social spending, including housing and transportation, the government would be competing with private firms and the private sector as a whole. This latter point arose from the general ideology that too much social expenditure and government interference is bad and would threaten the private ownership and control over production that is the very essence of capitalism. Additionally large increases in social spending would upset the labour market, making it more difficult for employers to obtain workers, and it would tend to undermine the class structure because of the 'public good' character of much social expenditure. Finally improved social services would satisfy human needs and reduce the likelihood of people being influenced by the market and the pressures of the commercial world.[22]

However, Reich did not claim that military spending is *necessary* to capitalism but:

A capitalist economy with inadequate aggregate demand is much more *likely* to turn to military than to social spending, because the former is more consistent with private profit and the social relations of production under capitalism. If this military outlet were cut off, say by massive public opposition, it is possible that a capitalist economy might accommodate and transform itself rather than commit suicide. But such reasoning misses the point. Military spending is favoured by capitalists and is likely to be defended with considerable vigor ... so long as there is profit to be made in military spending capitalists will turn to it.[23] (Emphasis in original.)

Bearing in mind that the percentage of the US federal budget devoted to defence fell from 45.0 per cent in 1960 to 22.6 per cent in 1980[24] it is by no means obvious that the barriers to increased social spending, or at least non-defence government expenditure, are quite as formidable as Reich maintained. Nevertheless it should be accepted that Reich was right to emphasise how closely political and economic questions are related. As DuBoff, following similar lines of thought, succinctly put it:

'Conversion' models that ignore the concrete facts of social advantage and political control can offer few worthwhile insights into the political economy of the military–industrial complex – or how to begin the awesome task of reducing its size and influence.[25]

This survey of the impact of the theory of the military–industrial complex on conversion must conclude that, by the early 1970s, it had added an important dimension to an understanding of the difficulties in implementing conversion programmes. For, apart from Melman, hardly any writer on conversion up to that time had considered these political issues in any depth. Since then the purely economic studies of disarmament and conversion have declined in number while there has been a corresponding increase in political analysis of the problems posed by conversion.

In so far as Melman's thesis can be criticised it would be for, perhaps, overstating the degree of control exercised by the new state management and over-emphasising its internal cohesiveness. Despite this there can be no doubt that he is well aware of the strength of the political obstacles to conversion but, unlike the Marxists, he believed they could be overcome without recourse to traditional class-based revolution.[26] That he eschewed the term military–industrial complex was entirely consistent with his analysis of power in US society and in no way diminished the significance he attributed to domestic forces behind the arms race – itself the most enduring legacy of the theory of the military–industrial complex.

ALTERNATIVE SECURITY CONCEPTS AND PEACE CONVERSION

Since the late 1970s various alternative security concepts, which challenge the conventional reliance on deterrence through armaments, have become increasingly prevalent. This book has already discussed in some detail the ideas contained in the 1981 UN report.[27] The Independent Commission on Disarmament and Security Issues, chaired by the late Olof Palme, advocated a doctrine of common security to replace the expedient of deterrence, insisting that '*International peace must rest on a commitment to joint survival rather than a threat of mutual destruction.*'[28]

Both the UN report and the Palme Commission stressed the need for economic security,[29] highlighted the harmful consequences of high levels of military expenditure and strongly supported the link between disarmament and development.

Conversion of military resources to civilian purposes was placed within this context.

These moderate or 'reformist' views of conversion were to be challenged, both directly and indirectly, by those who felt that conversion of this kind would do little or nothing to unravel the armaments process and help establish peace and disarmament. One example of a more radical approach to conversion is provided by Mary Kaldor in *The Baroque Arsenal* (1982). While it is beyond the scope of this book to discuss her argument in detail, a brief synopsis will provide the basis for a better understanding of her attitude to the appropriate context for conversion.

Kaldor regarded modern military technology as decadent (i.e. baroque) rather than advanced:

> Over the years, more and more resources have been spent on perfecting the military technology of a previous era. As a consequence, modern armaments have become remote from military and economic reality. They are immensely sophisticated and elaborate; they are feats of tremendous ingenuity, talent, and organisation; and they can inflict unimaginable destruction. But they are incapable of achieving limited military objectives, and they have successively eroded the economy of the United States and the economies of those countries that have followed in her wake. Further spending can only make things worse.[30]

Baroque armaments, according to Kaldor, are the product of, on the one hand, the competitive drive of arms manufacturers to win contracts, and on the other hand, the conservatism of the armed forces and weapons designers who have maintained a certain way of thinking on how, and with what weapons, wars should be fought in order to justify a given set of military roles, organisations and industrial capacities. The technological drive of the defence contractors is thus confined within certain established traditions themselves largely influenced by the experience of the Second World War. In time improvements to existing hardware are achieved only by huge increases in the unit cost of individual weapons, and the resulting complexity and sophistication of these weapons is not matched by increased military effectiveness. This baroque technology has spread from the USA to the Soviet Union and the Third World.[31]

The long waves in capitalist history, associated with different technologies in different locations, led to the era of automobiles and aircraft in the USA which then provided the industrial base for the modern armament sector during the Second World War. Thereafter this base was sustained, even increased, through military expenditure. While in the 1950s and 1960s this may have had a positive impact on investment, innovation and growth, baroque military technology now uses up resources which are required in newer, more dynamic industries. It distorts technical progress by concentrating on over-elaborate product improvements typical of declining industries, in place of simpler process improvements notable in growing industries. Consequently, reduced capital investment and productivity growth have been the result leading to a decline in the US economy.[32]

Kaldor's thesis is more concerned with the way states arm rather than why they arm. Following the theorists of the military–industrial complex, she argued that domestic influences tend to prevail over international factors in determining decisions on armaments in peacetime and she examined how these decisions affect the international context. She claimed that military technology is in crisis and this crisis is part of a wider breakdown in the international system evidenced by global economic instability, new conflicts within the West and the Soviet Union as well as social upheaval in the Third World.[33] Whilst this might lead to war:

... there is also a possibility that the disintegration of the military–industrial consensus, the new fluidity of international politics, and the tide of protest in favour of more humane values could lead to a change of direction: to a rejection of baroque arms and the calculus of terror that goes with it and to the recognition that peace between nations, like peace within nations, and human development in the fullest sense can ultimately be achieved only through a process of disarmament.[34]

Kaldor did not tackle in detail the question of how to unwind the armament process rather than simply modifying it, as moderate proposals tend to do. However, she did conclude from her analysis that baroque military technology does make unilateral disarmament measures possible precisely because modern weapons systems add so little to military effectiveness. Consequently a decline in military expenditure would not reduce, and might improve, a state's ability to protect itself. Moreover, new military technologies, like precision guided munitions, which have not been institutionalised (because they do not form part of the old industrial base) make multilateral disarmament possible because a common interest exists between disarmers and those who develop and use baroque military technology in halting the spread of these new technologies.[35]

While the acceptance of these latter observations depends, in large measure, on acceptance of Kaldor's main thesis – that modern military technology is decadent – it is the next point which is most relevant to conversion, whether or not her thesis is accepted. This final conclusion from her work is that any attempt to limit armaments must involve major institutional change.

To understand this point, reference has to be made to Kaldor's view of technical change. Since technology is developed within a particular institutional framework situated in a specific political and economic environment, it follows that there can be technical change only if there is also social change.

We have seen how nearly all attempts to create 'austere alternatives' to the baroque weapons system have foundered. This was because such attempts did not deal with the underlying nature of the armament process. An effective alternative to baroque military technology would entail institutional change at every level: within the armed forces, within the wider geopolitical system, within the defence industry, and within the economy as a whole.[36]

Industrial conversion would, therefore, be a central strand in any set of proposals to dismantle the armaments process, though ... not in the *technical* sense of converting swords into ploughshares but in the *social* sense of transforming the industrial basis of the armament sector'.[37] Kaldor suggested that such a conversion process might have as its objective a new mixture of contemporary social systems, which might overcome the rigidity of centralised planning and, also, the economic crises associated with reliance on market forces. She urged that practical aims in conversion be located in a wider context of the kind of future to which humanity aspires. Given the very destructive nature of modern armaments this should mean a society in which such armaments would not be needed.

These are ambitious goals, especially given the conclusion reached at the end of the last chapter that, at least in the short term, conversion has very little scope for independent application. Yet, however utopian these objectives sound, Kaldor's analysis reveals the inadequacy of most economic approaches to conversion, which stress the importance of the 'political will' of governments but neglect the social structures that might help to explain the lack of political will in the first place. It is now necessary to consider in more depth what transformation might be required for conversion purposes, and why it matters to study a question which appears so impractical.

In the last few years no peace researcher has done more to criticise the conventional, economistic approach to conversion and argue the case for an alternative perspective than Jan Oberg. His view of peace conversion has much in common with that of Kaldor, but in terms of peace research he has even more to offer. Oberg started from the position that national security policies based on armaments lead to insecurity and that for true human and social development, coupled with security, structural transformation is essential. To realise peace, development and security must be combined in a positive manner. This involves the idea of both transformation and alternative defence strategies:

> ... directed towards the deep social, structural features of society and the world system which contribute to the 'need' – real or imagined – for armament. It maintains that societies must change radically to get rid of the armament syndrome *and* that there must be some 'realistic Utopia' to switch to intellectually before decision-makers can be convinced not only about the counterproductivity of present trends but also about the viability of some constructive alternatives.[38]

Contrasting arms control and conversion measures with the transformation idea, Oberg said that whereas the former attempts to reduce what is wrong (excessive armaments), the latter tries to project a vision of what would be good (a new society) and work out the means to achieve it.

The traditional, economistic and UN approaches to conversion have resulted in the neglect of some of the most highly regarded conceptualisations and value commitments of peace research. Oberg pointed to the failure of conversion studies to change the general security thinking amongst decision-makers or encourage popular participation in security matters. Most importantly there is no study of how to convert the world from war to peace or transform those social and structural characteristics that fuel the arms race.[39]

So, for Oberg, conversion – or what is defined as peace conversion in this book – is a sub-category of a wider disarmament strategy which seeks a changed attitude to the concept of security, democratic control over the forces which impel the arms race on, and true human and social development through a fundamental alteration in those structures and conflictual relationships which cause wars.[40] Defence conversion, as defined in this work, does not threaten established militarism.

Although it must be said that Oberg's criticisms of conventional economic approaches to conversion are not always fair – particularly with regard to the 1981 UN report[41] – and he entirely neglects Melman's work, nevertheless it remains true that even the most ambitious conversion studies have not been as radical (or perhaps Utopian would be a better word) as Oberg advocated. Before discussing the significance of this point it will be useful to develop the theme of a 'realistic Utopia' in the context of peace research.

Oberg argued for a strong methodological orientation towards the 'constructive' dimension of the research process, proposed by Galtung, in order to take up the vital issues of disarmament, conversion and transformation. Constructivism involves the interplay of theories and values, which taken together with empiricism and criticism, lead to strategies for change in the direction of better future worlds. Oberg emphasised the importance, in peace research, of attractive but realistic visions of alternative security and defence in order to show that there are choices available other than simply relying on security based on armaments.[42]

At the heart of this vision is the security of the individual – free not only from direct violence but from structural violence through poverty or repression. More than that, security should embrace the majority, not simply the rulers; it should be comprehensible, openly debated and subject to democratic control; and it should be carried out through broad, popular participation

Table 8.1   Typology of defence strategies

1. Nuclear	*5. Political-psychological*	*10. Structural/constructive*
2. Modern conventional	*6. Economic*	*defence*
3. Guerilla/militia	*7. Ecological*	
4. Civil defence	*8. Social*	
	9. Non-violent struggle	
Violent/destructive	*Non-violent/constructive*	*Non-violent/constructive*
Built upon/on top of	*Built upon/on top of*	*Built into/from below*
social structures	*social structures*	
Military	*Non-military*	*Non-military*
Aggressive, threaten	*Non-aggressive*	*Non-aggressive*
others		
Status quo-oriented	*Status quo*	*Change-oriented*
(Arms control)	*(Conversion)*	*(Transformation)*

Source: Jan Oberg, 'Disarmament, Conversion and Transformation: Some Elements of a Strategy Towards Constructive Defence and Peaceful Development', *Bulletin of Peace Proposals*, 10, no. 3 (1979), p. 310.

in building up defence systems on a decentralised basis.[43] From this foundation Oberg outlined a typology of defence strategies, illustrated in Table 8.1.

The first category (1–4) is a purely military one as arms control deals mostly with these types of defence strategy. The second category (5–9) covers the concept of 'total defence' involving additional types of defence deployed during a war or at a time of crisis. (Type 9 – non-violent defence – could also be included under the next category.) Conversion deals with this category because it aims at lessening the consequences of the current structures and relationships which lead to conflict, rather than transforming them. The last category of defence (10), structural or constructive defence, aims to build into society those structures which '. . . remove the causes of wars and offer alternatives to war in situations where wars might occur'.[44] Obviously a mixture of these defence types is possible but Oberg's aim was to push towards the right of the table to a lower military level, especially excluding nuclear weapons but also any major commitment to modern, conventional weapons as well.

The essential elements of a constructive defence built into, rather than upon, social formations consist of a highly decentralised society which is much less vulnerable than a very centralised one; a less dependent society (in terms of trade, technology and resources) that is better able to resist foreign pressures; a society based on commitment and solidarity rather than one which is polarised and breaking apart; and a society which has the ability to resolve conflicts without recourse to violence and threats.[45] Oberg cited Sharp, the great exponent of non-violence, in supporting his claim that the capacity for resolving conflicts rationally and without recourse to force, together with a thorough change of conflict formations, should, if closely combined, reinforce each other.

> There are several reasons why widespread use of non-violent action in place of political violence tends to diffuse power among the subjects. These reasons have to do with *the greater self-reliance of the people* using the technique, as related to leadership, weapons, the more limited power of the post-struggle government, and *the reservoir capacity for non-violent struggle which has been built up* against future dangers.[46] (Emphasis added by Oberg.)

Oberg's ideas on what a future peaceful society would be like and how it would be organised were heavily influenced by Galtung and also by those like Gandhi, Schumacher and Illich who have inspired modern alternative development thinking. While Oberg admitted that it cannot be known whether his theoretical elaborations on the organisation of a more peaceful society would achieve the goals of rational conflict resolution and a non-aggressive posture to other societies, his perspective did suggest that the problems of alternative security and defence, as well as alternative social structures, must be tackled at the same time.[47]

Oberg justified his open discussion of future aspirations in terms of the power which a vision of a better society can bestow on those seeking democratic changes through popular involvement. Presenting Utopias is necessary in order to unmake and replace the war-making system which humanity created in the first place.

Whether the study of 'realistic' Utopias matters should be considered as part of the broader question of the relevance of peace conversion. Although it is far from obvious that these images of a future society, no matter how compelling in themselves, will be able to overcome the weight of inertia and conservatism that often frustrates radical proposals, it may still be that peace conversion is significant, though of little or no immediate, practical relevance.

There is, indeed, a case to be made for peace conversion. First, it links defence conversion to the wider peace research issues concerning the causes of the arms race and the factors which contribute to wars. As Oberg observed, these matters are largely ignored in most conversion studies or dealt with quite superficially. Secondly, peace conversion offers various insights into the limitations on the traditional economic approach to conversion. Both Kaldor and Oberg stressed the importance of setting conversion in a wider context of disarmament and transformation. Each writer has also highlighted the need to consider the social structures behind the armaments build-up, and how to bring about fundamental social change, rather than simply modify the consequences of reliance on security through armaments (as conversion does). And Oberg in particular has emphasised that the alternative security concept, which is fundamental to a true disarmament strategy, should be linked directly to alternative social structures if a more peaceful society is to be established.

The increased sophistication of conversion analysis in recent years, noted in the last chapter, illustrates that some of these criticisms have been implicitly recognised, at least by some writers: especially noteworthy is the linking of conversion to a wider disarmament strategy, by Hartung and others, which will also be discussed in the defence policy approach to conversion in the next chapter. Yet the direct impact of peace conversion ideas on defence conversion studies and initiatives is likely to be remote given the severe obstacles confronting even the traditional economic approach. Indeed these difficulties were deemed so insuperable by one author, Gordon Adams, that he wrote an article in 1986 which dismissed conversion as 'impossible' in its current form. (This critique will be briefly examined after actual conversion initiatives have been described in Chapter 13.) In a nutshell peace conversion helps to reveal the causes of the difficulties in implementing conversion programmes without itself offering a practical alternative.[48]

Finally, the insights derived from peace conversion are applicable to Melman's theory of conversion in a number of ways: in highlighting the absence of any alternative defence strategies or even a clearly articulated alternative security concept,[49] and in criticising Melman's emphasis on organisational or managerial problems rather than on inherent structural obstacles to conversion programmes.[50] The advocates of peace conversion might argue that his brand of conversion would be unlikely to play a part in reversing the arms race while the problems of alternative security and defence, on the one hand, and alternative social structures, on the other, remain unresolved. Yet given Melman's commitment to democratic and non-militaristic control of the military establishment, worker participation in conversion planning and a decentralised approach to economic reconstruction, the differences between the two would appear to be much less than between them and those with a more traditional, economistic approach to conversion.

CONCLUSIONS

It may be argued that both the theory of the military–industrial complex and the radical alternative security concepts have illuminated some of the shortcomings of the economic approach to conversion. The former injected some political analysis to explain the domestic influences behind the arms race and the difficulties of implementing conversion programmes. The latter, which also formed the basis for a peace conversion approach, took the analysis a stage further by investigating the significance of social structures and social transformation as part of a wider disarmament strategy, which would also include a changed concept of security and democratic control of the forces behind the arms race. However, at least in the short term, defence conversion appears to be the only practical option (compared to peace conversion), although there is a risk that it may be co-opted by the establishment in a way that ensures it does not threaten the underlying structures behind the arms race. In that case, as Oberg forecasted, articles may indeed appear in the 1990s entitled 'The Crisis of Conversion'![51] It would seem, though, that that danger cannot be avoided – at least the proponents of peace conversion have forewarned us.

It is now time to turn to the two other approaches to defence conversion which have come to prominence in recent years: first, the defence policy approach to conversion which is related to the alternative security concept; secondly, the industrial approach to conversion which is linked, in some aspects, to the notion of democratic control of the military–industrial establishment.

9 The Defence Policy Approach to Conversion

Although discussion of alternative approaches to Western defence policy can be traced back to the 1950s it is only since the late 1970s that criticism of orthodox reliance on nuclear strategy, in particular, mounted sharply and increased attention was focused on alternative defence policies. While the number of titles remains comparatively few the significance of this development requires analysis, especially as conversion has tended to form a small but distinct part of these new policy proposals. In part the perceived requirement for these alternative defence policies reflects a perhaps subconscious recognition within the peace movement and amongst radical academics that the hopes for general and complete disarmament in the 1960s, never that high anyway, had proved too optimistic. The formulation of these policies was an implicit acceptance of this fact, since the need for such alternatives would hardly arise if general and complete disarmament was felt to be just around the corner.

ALTERNATIVE DEFENCE POLICIES

In the USA a major contribution, if not the first, to discussion of an alternative defence policy was made by the Boston Study Group's *The Price of Defense* (1979), subsequently reprinted under the title *Winding Down: The Price of Defense* (1982). The Group argued that a large part of the US military establishment was not required for truly defensive purposes, but for military intervention in any corner of the world. Through relying too often on force in the conduct of foreign policy, the USA had encouraged militarisation in other states. To reverse the armaments build-up and because it is the most powerful country on earth, which sets the pace not only in the West but as leader of the arms race as well, the USA should unilaterally reduce its forces and military expenditure to a level required for defensive purposes and to counter Soviet military threats. This alternative military posture, according to the Boston Study Group, would

143

actually be safer than existing policies because it would represent a significant decrease in global and US militarisation while
still ensuring that the USA and her chief allies in NATO and
Japan could be defended.[1]

This important study in effect, took the observations of those
like Melman that US military spending went far beyond the
requirements for defence, and examined in depth what level of
military expenditure was necessary for alternative foreign and
defence policies. It also took into account, though not in a major
way, the economic arguments against high levels of military
spending discussed in Chapters 3 and 4, and produced an
outline of how the economic consequences of reduced military
expenditure could be handled with minimum large-scale, federal
intervention.

An article, also written in 1979, by one of the authors in the
Boston Study Group, Randall Forsberg, developed this theme of
confining the military to defence by proposing a step-by-step
approach to the ultimate goal of a disarmed peace.[2] Each step,
starting with a bilateral US–Soviet nuclear weapons freeze, is a
very attractive intermediate goal, desirable in its own right and
helping to build popular support strong enough to prevail over
the status quo. Forsberg's ideas appear to be closely linked to
Oberg's, discussed previously, in that the ultimate goal of
abolishing the institution of warfare is not lost sight of while each
step in the disarmament plan is geared to a changed concept of
security, altering the institutions of military policy and the
armed forces and gradual elimination of the most aggressive and
provocative aspects of those policies and forces which remain.
Between 1979 and 1981 a popular movement actually emerged
in the USA around the freeze proposal in the way Forsberg had
envisaged.[3] This in turn led to various conversion studies
discussed in Chapter 7.

Turning now to Europe, rather more has been written on
alternative defence policies since defence issues, especially concerning the role of nuclear weapons, became much more polit-
icised in countries like the UK, FRG, Netherlands, Belgium and
Denmark from the late 1970s on.[4] The decision by NATO in
1977 to deploy cruise and Pershing intermediate-range nuclear
missiles in Western Europe was a major catalyst in this respect,
although some countries like France and Italy continue to
maintain a virtual national consensus on nuclear defence.

Michael Clarke has provided a useful review of the literature and the major issues involved. This book, though, need only be concerned with what constitutes, in Western European terms, an alternative defence policy and how it relates to defence conversion or peace conversion. The first question, therefore, is what themes recur within alternative defence theories and how, therefore, do they differ from an establishment position? Clarke identified four such themes. First, alternative thinking begins with the question, what is security? This has led to an emphasis on territorial defence as the main requirement since protection of the homeland is of greatest significance. Secondly, alternative defence writings discuss how their country's relationship with NATO would need to be altered. Most reject neutralism but expect either a modification in the character of NATO, or a changed relationship with NATO, consequent upon the adoption of territorial defence as the basic principle of an alternative policy. Thirdly, there is an absolute commitment to a non-nuclear Western Europe, whatever the USA does with its own nuclear weapons. Fourthly, and this point was discussed at some length in the last chapter, there is a view that changes in defence strategy have to be linked to changes in the deeper structures of production and distribution in society.[5] Or, to put it another way, the problem of appropriate defence policies is tied into the problem of transforming a capitalist economy.

On this latter point, though, Clarke made some interesting observations, on the radical perspective adopted by Kaldor and others,[6] which are very relevant to the second question to be answered: what is the relationship between alternative defence policies and defence conversion or peace conversion? Clarke accepted their approach as being honest, in that it is genuinely alternative, but he went on to identify some serious difficulties:

> Practical objections to alternative defence concern the ability to make such a strategy politically acceptable and, ultimately, acceptable to the defence establishment. Deeper practical objections, however, lie in the degree to which defence infra-structures can be changed in the short or medium term. Since the 'defence system' does not arise as a consciously directed structure, it may be doubted how consciously it can be re-directed, regardless of the political willpower behind the desire for change. It may be more accurate to characterise the

'defence system' as a morass of incremental actions, under a series of different domestic and international pressures, which governments can rationalise and influence, but not control. Infrastructures are intangible, and it may well be that there is no practical alternative but to break into the structure at the top of the pyramid, at the establishment level – the level of defence planning.[7]

So it is all very well to speak of the need for deep structural change but frequently it is not at all clear what, if anything, this means in practical terms. To the extent, therefore, that alternative defence policies are related to conversion, the type of conversion envisaged appears to be the radical one of peace conversion. Clarke's arguments here about the impracticality of alternative defence policies linked to wider structural change (the fourth theme discussed above) reinforce the points made previously about the practical obstacles to peace conversion.

Nevertheless there is a case for claiming that Clarke has generalised too far in defining the main characteristics of alternative defence theories. Neither the Boston Study Group's alternative defence proosals, which are admittedly outside the Western European context, nor the recommendations of the Alternative Defence Commission, which are very much within that context, link their ideas to a radical transformation of the capitalist economy. In both cases the conversion envisaged is of the kind defined in this book as defence conversion.

The Alternative Defence Commission produced a major report entitled *Defence Without The Bomb* (1983).[8] It addressed itself to the question of what defence policy Britain should adopt if the country were to renounce the use of nuclear weapons. The individuals who served on the Commission, though they came from many different backgrounds and held varying views, all accepted that Britain should renounce the use, or deployment on its territory, of nuclear forces. This support for unilateral nuclear disarmament was coupled with a thorough and wide-ranging review of alternative non-nuclear defence policies for Britain. While the Commission's precise recommendations need not be spelled out here a word is necessary on the role given to conversion.

The Commission's recommendations fall clearly within the categories of 'purely military' and 'total defence' strategies posited by Oberg (in Table 8.1). They relate to arms control (disarmament) and conversion matters respectively, rather than to transformation. All the same both the main report of the Commission and a special supplementary paper on the economic consequences of non-nuclear defence[9] recognised the need for economic adjustment and redeployment of workers, the size of the task depending on which defence options are taken up and when they are implemented. As with the Boston Study Group, the economic arguments against high levels of military expenditure were put forward and some consideration was given as to how the economic consequences of a non-nuclear defence policy would be tackled. However, a significant difference also existed in that the Commission put a strong emphasis on the role of workers and their unions in implementing conversion programmes. This leads us directly on to the industrial approach to conversion, examined in the following chapters.

CONCLUSIONS

Briefly, though, the significance of the defence policy approach to conversion should first be assessed. It is clear that this approach has contributed nothing new to our understanding of the processes of conversion. What is new, and highly significant, is the way in which the more radical alternative defence strategies can be linked to peace conversion whilst other alternative defence strategies, which are not so explicitly tied to transforming social and economic structures, have been connected to defence conversion. By putting conversion of either kind in the context of defence policy – especially a disarmament-oriented defence policy – it is then possible, as several studies have done, to use the economic case against high military expenditures to supplement the primary strategic case for a new concept of security and a changed defence posture – very much along the lines envisaged in the conclusion to Chapter 7. So the defence policy approach to conversion makes the economic case against the arms race a part of a wider disarmament strategy which takes into account political and military factors relevant to the strategic requirements for the defence of the West. This, in turn, improves the prospects for some modest experimental conversion schemes since the conversion of military industries is tied into major political and economic policies rather than simply being left to its own devices.

In a word, the defence policy approach to conversion is an essential element of any credible conversion strategy.

10 Defence Industry Diversification and Conversion (I)

Whereas the two approaches to conversion, previously discussed, are both primarily macro-level studies, the industrial approach to conversion is concerned, first and foremost, with practical initiatives at the micro-level of the individual firm or industry. There have been some valuable academic studies of initiatives undertaken by the top managers of defence firms. These initiatives include examples of both diversification and conversion although the former is, understandably, more common. The studies to be evaluated here strongly indicate that many of these initiatives are unsuccessful though it is not possible to say whether this position is different from efforts at diversification or economic conversion within the civilian economy. Partly in consequence of these failures there has, within the last ten years, been a remarkable growth in trade union and labour initiatives to encourage diversification and conversion, beginning with the well-known Lucas Plan. These alternative strategies have in turn helped to establish some common ground between the labour and peace movements in many Western countries, where before there had frequently been division and disharmony at grass-roots level.

The industrial approach to conversion will be discussed in three parts: in this chapter, the various studies of managerial attempts at defence industry diversification and conversion will be evaluated; in the next chapter, the more recent labour initiatives on conversion will be examined; and finally, in Chapter 12, theoretical issues posed by these developments particularly in relation to the dynamic processes of conversion, the relevance of industrial democracy and the much closer links now forged between peace researchers and the labour movement, will all be discussed.

MANAGERIAL INITIATIVES

Once more it is the USA that has provided by far the most material on the subject of managerially led defence industry diversification and conversion efforts. Nonetheless, while the contributions from the United States will constitute the main focus here, there have also been significant studies undertaken in France, Sweden and the UK. Taken together these studies, while not numerous, provide valuable insights into the detailed and complex problem of either reducing a defence company's dependence on defence work by diversification or turning a part, or the whole, of that company away from military contracts altogether.

THE STRATEGIC MANAGEMENT OF CONVERSION

The French scholar Dussauge has pointed out that a firm's defence work needs to be considered within the context of the management's overall strategic perspective.[1] A global corporation will be split into what are sometimes called 'strategic business units' that consist of activities comprising the firm's business portfolio. Some of these units will be primarily military in orientation while others will be civilian. Clearly, from a management perspective, it will be very important in any programme of conversion or diversification to understand how the defence-related activities fit into the firm's business portfolio as a whole and how they affect its overall strategy.

Dussauge identified three main consequences of defence work on a firm's business portfolio. They are the effects on technological capacities, corporate financial results and profitability, and the global risk for the firm.

Taking each of these impacts in turn, the extent to which technological knowledge derived from military programmes can be applied to civilian areas varies greatly (and, as previously discussed, is a contentious issue).[2] Dussauge argued that there are very strong synergies between military and civilian technologies in the fields of radar equipment, air control systems, airborne electronics or helicopter manufacture. On the other hand, nuclear weapons and nuclear power plants, contrary to popular notions, have very few industrial connections despite a common foundation of basic scientific research. Likewise there are few civil applications for the technologies utilised in making armoured vehicles. Dussauge's point is that the more dependent on military-generated technology the civilian business units of a firm are, the harder it will be to convert those military activities. If, instead, military technologies have no civilian applications then the conversion process will not affect civilian work within the firm directly.[3]

On the question of the financial implications of conversion, military work (particularly exports) can provide a large share of corporate profits and tend to generate a strong and positive cash flow due to government financing of the investments involved. Thus firms can often use the cash flow generated by military activities on other activities which normally absorb more funds than they generate in their early stages of development. Companies like Matra, one of the major missile and aerospace equipment manufacturers in France, have been able to use their defence activities to provide the cash for diversification into activities like automobile manufacture, public transport systems and many other areas. Similarly the complementarities between, for instance, military and civilian aircraft design and production are based as much on financial as on technological factors because long-term investments in the civil sector are dependent on the financial resources generated by their military work.[4]

Lastly, on the effect of defence work on the global risk of the firm, the different economic cycles of defence and civilian activities can be advantageous in reducing the level of risk. For example, in the early 1980s military programmes in the West helped aerospace companies compensate for the very difficult conditions in the civilian aircraft and helicopter markets. Dussauge argued that the lower level of risk in defence work is due to the procurement planning process, which is designed to ensure regular orders, and also to the commitment of most major Western countries to maintain an indigenous defence industry.[5]

It is important to emphasise that the profitability, cash generation and risk associated with military activities is not a constant but varies with time and place in relation to civilian work, sometimes to the disadvantage of the former, and also that governments can control all these factors in order to discourage military activities and encourage civilian ones. Indeed Dussauge stated that without a central governmental role in the conversion process defence firms would not, in most cases, convert because they would have much to lose and little to gain.[6] He offered a useful framework for analysing the varying strategic impact of the conversion process and what response, in terms of governmental assistance, would be needed.

Defence dependence

		Low	High
Technological synergies between the firm's military and civilian activities	Low	1	2
	High	3	4

Figure 10.1   Revaluation of the strategic impact of a firm's military activities on the conversion process

Source: Pierre Dussauge, 'The Conversion of Military Activities: A Strategic Management of the Firm Perspective' in *Peace, Defence and Economic Analysis*, edited by Christian Schmidt and Frank Blackaby (London, 1987), Figure 20.1.

The basis for this analytical framework is twofold: the level of defence dependence measured in terms of the proportion of the firm's net sales (or profits) accounted for by defence work, and the significance of the technological knowledge arising from the firm's military work for its civilian activities measured in terms of the technological synergies existing between these two activities. Figure 10.1 sets out the framework in the form of a simple matrix. While, as Dussauge admitted, it would be operationally desirable to define and quantify the threshold points between the 'low' and 'high' ratings for each dimension the matrix is quite sufficient to illustrate the main points.

Firms in zone 1 have a low level of defence dependence and their military activities are not technologically related to their civilian work. State intervention should not be necessary as the conversion process will be least complicated and have fewer long-term strategic consequences. However, for firms in zone 2, where military activities account for roughly 20–25 per cent of global activity or more, although they are not technologically related to civilian work, conversion of military activities would have an impact on the strategic position of these firms. Companies like General Electric in the USA or Thomson in France fall into this category. Government assistance in the form of contracts to develop civilian programmes would probably be necessary to compensate these firms for lost business.[7] Additionally such firms might try to expand their existing civilian businesses.

Firms in zone 3 are in a more difficult situation. Although conversion would not entail the loss of a large proportion of the company's business it would mean an end of their principal source of technology. Examples include Matra of France, cited earlier, and Rockwell in the USA. Governments would need to offer some form of civilian 'technology pump', such as the various American and European space programmes or techno- logy development schemes like Eureka.[8] Those firms in zone 4 represent the most difficult ones to convert. They include the majority of aerospace companies which are generally heavily dependent on military work and also derive many of their technologies for civilian activities from this defence work. Com- panies like Aerospatiale in France or Westland in the UK would be unlikely to survive once their military helicopter work had ended. It might not be possible, or cost-effective, to save all the firms in this position and even in less extreme cases substantial restructuring, with government assistance, would be necessary.

Dussauge's analytical framework represents an important starting-point for the discussion of defence industry diversification and conversion.[9] Although it impinges on many contentious issues such as the extent of technology transfer in major defence com- panies and the relative profitability of, and risks associated with, military and civilian work there can be no doubt that, unlike most of the studies to follow, this analysis has highlighted two major issues:

- The importance of setting defence conversion within the broader context of managerial business strategies.
- The crucial links between defence dependence and the extent of any technological synthesis, affecting military and civilian activities, in assessing the ease or difficulty in achieving conversion.

The studies that follow, on defence industry diversification and conversion, should be examined within this overall framework.

US EXPERIENCE OF DIVERSIFICATION OR CONVERSION

The US Arms Control and Disarmament Agency was foremost amongst those sponsoring such studies in the 1960s.[10] One report of special note, carried out by Gilmore and Coddington of the Denver Research Institute, analysed the diversification experi- ences of eleven defence firms, including giants like Lockheed and

Boeing, by means of detailed interviews of the executives concerned.[11] Their analysis, supplemented with other relevant information, formed the basis for a number of generalisations made in their report: on the reasons for success or failure of diversification and conversion programmes, and on what constitutes the essential elements of a diversification strategy most likely to succeed. It will not be necessary to consider different approaches to acquisition of civilian firms since this issue does not relate to the key question of whether, and if so how, *existing* defence-related resources can be transferred to civilian purposes. Hence diversification through internal changes is more important in terms of this book, though it should be admitted that often diversification through acquisition would be the quickest, or the only, way for a defence firm to rapidly reduce its military dependency.

Before examining the key question outlined above a brief word is in order regarding the reasons defence firms have, historically, attempted to diversify or even convert and why Gilmore and Coddington have concentrated their researches on diversification not conversion. The ebb and flow of interest in diversification coincides, unsurprisingly, with increases or reductions in defence expenditure and the lack of existence of, or the opportunity for entering, new commercial markets. Other factors can be important, too:

● past experiences with diversification, if unfavourable, can lead managers of defence firms to tend to avoid commercial markets;
● the likely flow of future profits must justify the new investment required, and the degree of risk involved, in diversification;
● the desire for bigger sales than seem likely from current product lines can motivate firms to diversify;
● the existing degree of diversification in a defence firm may encourage or deter new initiatives, as most firms do not like to be too dependent on a few products (though some companies consider themselves to be highly diversified within the defence field and are less concerned about their defence dependency overall);
● the resources available in a defence company based on its size, desire to capitalise on civilian spin-off opportunities, existing or excess manufacturing capacity (though this is not usually a

strong motivation to diversify given that many of these facilities are too specialised), financial, personnel and, most importantly, managerial resources, all affect the ability to diversify;

● employee attitudes to defence and civilian work can also be significant, especially as far as scientists and engineers are concerned;

● and, finally, the attitudes of major customers, especially the government, can be a constraint on efforts to diversify if they fear that it may result in a deterioration in current performance on defence contracts.[12]

Gilmore and Coddington explained the attitude of most managers in the defence industry towards conversion and diversification in the 1960s in the following terms:

> ... there are few examples of successful, rapid conversion by defense firms to commercial production in recent years. The reconversion following World War II largely involved commercially-oriented firms which had first converted to arms production and then reconverted back to their commercial product lines. The aircraft firms, lacking large and familiar commercial markets to go back to, could find no option but massive layoffs in 1945 and 1946. Employment in the Aircraft and Parts Industry averaged 1,296,600 in 1944; 788,100 in 1945; and 237,000 in 1946. That experience left [the] defense industry [in a] general [state of] pessimism about conversion and diversification, with increased awareness of the magnitude of the problem.[13]

The contrast between this view and that expressed in the economic studies of disarmament and conversion, discussed in Chapters 6 and 7, could scarcely be greater. Yet it should be remembered that the conversion envisaged in those studies did not necessarily involve maintaining existing companies and industries. The economic approach to conversion involved no commitment to sustaining current defence firms if it would be more efficient to disperse personnel and equipment to other companies in new or established civilian industries, either through the market mechanism or by direct government intervention. Hence it is important to recognise that the industrial approach to conversion is generally confined to a factory or company-based concept which does not exhaust the full range of possibilities for conversion, described in Chapter 6, nor does it necessarily provide the most socially efficient economic solution to the problem of resource utilisation.

With this reservation about the limitations of the industrial approach to conversion, and despite the differences between diversification and conversion,[14] the Gilmore and Coddington report can still be used to assist in understanding conversion problems. For the lack of success in entering new commercial markets is as much a problem for a defence company trying to diversify as for one trying to convert, the difference being one of degree. What is more the history of diversification experiences, analysed by Gilmore and Coddington, also revealed many failures and only some limited successes in entering commercial markets:

> Where diversification involved a radical change in the market being served, as in commercial diversification, the result generally was failure or limited success. Where defense firms stayed within the same customer relationship (the defense customer) there were a number of notable successes. These experiences influenced the managements of defense firms to be wary of non-defense, non-government diversification.[15]

This distinction between non-defence and non-government markets is conceptually useful. A non-defence market (e.g. housing) could still involve a government as a major customer. These *civilian, government markets* will be distinguished from *commercial markets* that are both civilian and non-government (i.e. involve many buyers). It can be argued that such public sector markets, or market segments, have somewhat greater commonality with defence as opposed to commercial markets and theoretically at least should offer greater scope for successful defence industry diversification. Hence the importance given, in the economic approach to conversion (Chapters 6 and 7), to governmental action to create these new, non-military public sector markets. Nevertheless evidence to be cited shortly will show that even these government, civilian markets are far from unproblematic for defence firms trying to diversify.

Gilmore and Coddington investigated the major obstacles to successful commercial diversification by defence firms. Contrary to the conventional wisdom at the time, they found that it was not so much a general marketing capability which defence companies lacked but an established position in the markets they wished to enter. Any lack of commercial marketing experience was likely to be only a temporary problem which could be surmounted, given sufficient time and money. The ability of defence firms to innovate, if applied to the marketing function, might enable them to move ahead of their commercial rivals.[16]

Gilmore and Coddington also found that, generally, armaments manufacturers had costs which were very high compared to normal commercial standards. However, there were exceptions amongst subcontracting specialists and smaller defence firms which were able to both carry out certain defence-related manufacturing tasks for the prime contractors in a more economical way than those contractors could themselves, and at the same time, and sometimes from the same building, compete in competitive commercial markets where control of costs was even more vital.[17]

A number of other factors posed problems for commercial diversification of defence firms. Defence industry technology is often too sophisticated for commercial customers though some companies have overcome this problem by tailoring their technology and attitudes to the needs and values of their chosen commercial markets. The requirement to separate defence from commercial engineering and production activities poses another barrier. It arises from different accounting practices, the expense of using government-owned plant and equipment for commercial purposes, and the different engineering and production operations together with contrasting personnel attitudes and pay. However, particularly amongst smaller firms, manufacturing (but not design) work could be carried out under one roof and even by the same people. Gilmore and Coddington believed that the need for complete separation of defence and commercial production activities probably only occurs after the size of commercial activity reaches a certain point. Turning to the problem of adapting defence personnel to commercial work, Gilmore and Coddington made the interesting claim, contrary to Melman and others, that such personnel had contributed successful managers and key staff to commercial diversification.[18] However, their evidence for this claim was not extensive and did appear to relate to the similarity of sales and engineering techniques between certain defence and commercial activities.

So much for the barriers to diversification. It remains to summarise the main ingredients of diversification success, according to Gilmore and Coddington's findings. The commitment of the top management to a programme of diversification is a primary requirement, but not easy to bring about given a history of past failures and evidence of a lack of interest by government. For management the major challenge is to show a capacity to innovate in the marketing field as well as in the technical arena. The defence firm must 'open windows' on the commercial world, either by employing those with commercial experience in key posts, or by associating with commercial firms already operating in a chosen market, or by various other methods including acquisition of a civilian firm. These processes save on learning time and improve the prospects of success. This emphasis on marketing necessitates close control of marketing expenses which, in turn, means more precise accounting systems and cost controls than are normally prescribed by the DoD. Such cost accounting would cover all functions, including production, in the more developed diversification programmes. Timing of a diversification programme is especially important, given the long time-lag of about five years between inception and breakeven point on an internally developed product. (In fact, Thorsson took the view that up to ten years might be required to design and develop products for civilian markets.[19]) If commercial diversification is to contribute to a firm's profit potential when defence business starts to decline, whilst being able to take advantage of the most favourable conditions of a firm's defence work, then the best time to start is /hen increased defence production is expected. However, this is a particularly inconvenient period for top management because of the demands of their defence business. Finally, two other elements of diversification success are significant: failure, paradoxically, is to be expected sometimes since not all new commercial products can be expected to succeed (in fact, many do fail); a creative environment involving many individuals and groups within a company will supplement top management's commitment and bring out the entrepreneurial initiative vital to successful commercial diversification.[20]

Gilmore and Coddington's study provides a most useful bench-mark against which to assess other research discussed in this chapter. As far as their policy proposals are concerned, they

identified many conflicting interests over the defence diversification process such that no clear, single public interest can be
stated. They argued that federal government policy must balance
diversification against other public interests in deciding what, if
anything, should be done to help defence firms prepare in good
time for major cut-backs in procurement. Gilmore and Coddington made the important observation that while (in private firms)
responsibility for diversification rests with top management
nevertheless their firms are so tied into government, as the main
defence customer, that these firms tend to follow government
wishes in their actions. Consequently government agencies
should encourage diversification if preparation for military cut-
backs is taken to be in the public interest.[21]

The other US ACDA-sponsored studies do not add much to
the above and their observations tend to be more specifically tied
to the industrial and market conditions of the 1960s. A study of
the electronics industry reached similar conclusions to the
Gilmore and Coddington report and noted that, if diversification
to the government-dominated space market is excluded, only
15–20 per cent of companies rated their diversification efforts –
by acquisition or internal development – as 'good'. (At the time,
about half of the electronics industry's sales related to defence.)
However, the electronics industry study put rather more emphasis on the apparent difficulty in reorientating personnel from
defence to civilian work. Other research suggested that the
special systems capabilities of defence firms might be applied to
public sector problems, with federal government support,
though difficulties would arise from the greater fragmentation of
government non-defence markets (which could include munici-
pal governments as well as some private customers), the lack of
the same sense of urgency, a lack of understanding by defence
firms of the problems confronted by the non-defence public
sector and an absence of innovative marketing abilities within
such firms.[22]

The barriers to diversifying into the non-defence public sector
were even more clearly illustrated a few years later by a US
Senate subcommittee investigating the possibility of employing
the resources of defence and commercial companies in meeting
public needs like housing, pollution and mass transit. Replies
from sixty-nine companies, five mayors and two labour unions
confirmed that the likelihood of a 'peace dividend' after the

Vietnam War were small unless the federal government took action on conversion.

In general, the responses indicated that private industry is not interested in initiating any major attempts at meeting critical public needs. Most industries have no plans or projects designed to apply their resources to civilian problems. Furthermore, they indicated an unwillingness to initiate such actions without a firm commitment from the Government that their efforts will quickly reap the financial rewards to which they are accustomed. Otherwise they appear eager to pursue greater defense contracts or stick to proven commercial products within the private sector.[23]

Although a few examples of successful conversion were identified – Abt Associates Inc. began as a $500 000 department in an aerospace firm and grew to become a $5 000 000 firm applying systems techniques and the social sciences to a broad range of private and public civilian problems – the Senate subcommittee '... found that the need for serious thought and action on conversion has largely been disregarded by most of the business community'.[24]

In the subcommittee's view, this necessitated a strong federal role in conversion if the end of hostilities in Vietnam were not to mean either a big rise in development and production of over-sophisticated military equipment or, alternatively, a real depression concentrated in the areas of greatest defence dependence.[25] What actually occurred was a mixture of both scenarios as the Senate subcommittee's call for action on conversion went largely unheeded.

The most recent analysis of the diversification and conversion experiences of defence firms was that carried out by DeGrasse for the US DoD's feasibility study into establishing a conversion office in the Pentagon.[26] DeGrasse followed a similar methodology to the one adopted by Gilmore and Coddington, based on case studies of selected defence contractors, backed up by other pertinent information. These case studies were mostly related to the aerospace and electronics industries and included the following: Kaman Corporation, a medium-sized subcontractor that produced helicopters;[27] Acurex Corporation, a small research and engineering firm; Boeing Vertol, which was a major producer of helicopters; and Raytheon Company, a major missile manufacturer. DeGrasse's report examined the efforts of these firms to enter civilian markets during the 1960s and 1970s, in response to reductions in defence procurement, by switching some of their defence-related resources to new civilian work.

Whilst none of the case studies were regarded as successful examples of conversion (or 'economic conversion', in American terms) Boeing Vertol was cited as a limited success as a conversion initiative, while the other three were better described as examples of diversification. However, Boeing Vertol itself re-employed only about 500 people out of the 8700 displaced during the late 1970s with the decline of helicopter production, and still had far more employees engaged on military contracts than the new mass transit car operations. Then, in 1979, Boeing Vertol decided to terminate transit car production because of design and manufacturing problems and other factors.[28] Using the definition adopted in this book Boeing Vertol's experience would also be better described as an example of diversification than conversion. From an assessment of his findings DeGrasse himself came to the somewhat disappointing conclusion that conversion is a concept still awaiting field testing.[29] This is hardly a revelation given the virtual unanimity of the many conversion studies, reviewed earlier, which stressed the role of governments and the need for advance planning if conversion programmes were to be successfully carried out.

DeGrasse discussed the factors which influence success or failure in defence contractors' efforts to adjust quickly to reductions in defence procurement through diversification or conversion. He rightly highlighted the changed economic environment in the 1970s, including greater competition and higher energy prices, which have made the risks in any adjustment effort even greater. Yet the five factors he identified as critical to success are very similar to Gilmore and Coddington's own guidelines: effective leadership by top management; adapting defence technologies to commercial use; development of a market strategy to ensure entry into the new civilian markets; acquisition of individuals or firms possessing civilian production or marketing skills; persistence and a willingness to learn from, rather than be put off by, failure. Additionally DeGrasse identified three specific problems which required special attention by defence firms attempting to diversify: unfamiliarity with the commercial market may lead to design, development, production and servicing problems (the example of Boeing Vertol's trolley cars has already been referred to); concurrency – simultaneous development and production of a product – while common enough in defence, can lead to serious problems in commercial markets through premature introduction of new products before they have been properly tested; and inaccurate assessment of government non-defence markets can led to over-optimistic market expectations, exacerbated by any federal government failure to lay down national standards.[30]

DeGrasse concluded his report by emphasising four essential requirements for successful conversion programmes:

- Federal government support in creating new, non-defence markets in areas like energy research and transportation. New product development by defence contractors will not occur quickly or successfully without such support and subsidies and this assistance needs to be carefully planned.
- It may take from five to ten years, without government support, for the process of entering civilian markets to generate a profit.
- Even with government support, defence contractors should prepare for reductions in defence expenditure in good time – preferably whilst sales to the DoD are still growing.
- Reorientation and retraining of defence-related employees, especially managers and engineers, is vital.[31]

The analysis of managerially led diversification and conversion experiences in the USA and attendant policy proposals now need to be compared, first with European studies and then with studies emanating from the economic approach to conversion.

EUROPEAN EXPERIENCE OF DIVERSIFICATION AND CONVERSION

European diversification and conversion experience has been most extensively studied by Udis who, in 1985, updated an earlier study focusing on the 1972–78 period.[32] This updating work covered the UK, France, Sweden and the FRG with supplementary information from sources in Belgium, Holland and Italy. Like the DeGrasse report, it formed part of the US DoD's feasibility study into the setting up of a conversion office.

Udis' updated report, like his earlier one, evaluated European policy instruments available to ease the adjustment to reduced expenditure on defence procurement and '... found few relevant European conversion examples or mechanisms to aid effectively the transition of military production capacity to civilian output'.[33]

Unfortunately, the updated Udis report is surprisingly unhelpful since it is mostly concerned with detailing the different industrial policies in each of the European countries under examination, policies which, as Udis readily admitted, were not designed to aid the process of transferring resources from military to civilian production. The efficacy of these policies, including regional development, financial aid, labour market programmes and subsidies for research and technology, is therefore very hard to judge, and Udis appeared to rely on impressions gleaned mostly from anonymous executives. Moreover, he offered no proposals himself as to what policies might be suitable to assist the adjustment of defence firms to civilian work.

One comparatively recent UK study merits a brief mention although it is primarily concerned with the broader question of promoting civilian spin-offs from defence electronics. The report by Sir Ieuan Maddock has, therefore, a different focus to most of the other studies considered in this chapter. Nevertheless his views on what he described as type 'A' defence companies – mostly specialised divisions of very large corporations – are relevant here. These are firms which are almost wholly dependent on producing military equipment. His researches illustrated, once again, the different environment in which such companies operate compared to commercial counterparts, and their unwillingness to apply their skills in advanced technologies to a wide range of purely civil uses. (The contrast with Dussauge's schema, on this latter point, is instructive.[34]) In fact Maddock bluntly concluded that '... the likelihood of type "A" companies making a major contribution in the civil areas (other than aerospace) is vanishingly small and even strong measures by the government are unlikely to have more than marginal effect'.[35] Instead he recommended that other, less defence dependent types of companies should be encouraged to make full use of unexploited technologies in type 'A' firms and in associated government laboratories.

Undoubtedly, though, one of the most valuable European studies is that by Frensborg and Wallensteen concerning Swedish

experiences in changing from military to civilian production.[36]
Their report concentrates on the history of two firms from the
early 1930s to the late 1960s: NOHAB, a heavy machinery
company, and Wedaverken, a light metal foundry. It charts the
experiences of these firms in moving from civilian production to
military work and back to civilian activities once more. The
authors of the report supplemented their findings with a review
of the general literature on the defence industry, and also with a
meeting between themselves and representatives of other Swedish
armaments manufacturers. What makes their study particularly
useful is the theoretical overview of the dynamics of industrial
production, as related to conversion, which takes the whole issue
far beyond a list of ingredients for successful diversification or
conversion as provided by the US studies previously discussed.

Frensborg and Wallensteen started their analysis by distinguishing defence from civilian production, in a similar way to
the comparison of defence and civilian markets in Chapter 5.
They identified three principal factors: the high quality of
defence *products*; the highly specialised *means of production* used
in the manufacture of those products; and the *nature of the
market* for military-specific equipment. The relationship between
the first two of these factors is represented in Figure 10.2.

The question of conversion arises for a company which has
highly specialised means of production but which is manufacturing products for a civilian market (square 4 in the table). This
defence firm will eventually either have to return to square 3,
producing military goods with its equipment designed for that
purpose, or dismantle some of its investments so as to turn to
square 1, if it is not to continue making high cost civilian goods
with equipment not especially designed for that task.[37] (For the
purposes of this book it will not be necessary to discuss the
question of reconversion or conversion *to* military industry which
are also within the scope of Figure 10.2.)

Thus internal factors, notably the contradiction between
product and means of production, are one source of change
within a company. Another is provided by the third factor
distinguishing military production: the nature of the market it
serves. This is the external, environmental influence which can,
as a result of reductions in defence procurement, force a company from square 3 to 4, a problematic position which cannot be
indefinitely sustained.[38]

Product	Means of production	
	Geared to civilian requirements	Geared to military requirements
Civilian products of standard type	(1) Balance between product and apparatus	(4) Problem situation
Defence materiel of specialized type	(2) Problem situation	(3) Balance between product and apparatus

Figure 10.2   Relationship between product and means of production

Source: Olof Frensborg and Peter Wallensteen, *New Wine and Old Bottles –
Product Versus Organization: Swedish Experiences in Changing from Military to
Civilian Production*, Report No. 21 (Uppsala, Sweden, May 1980), p. 21.

Frensborg and Wallensteen have now established a simple,
yet insightful, framework within which to examine the dynamic
process of fundamental industrial changes. They pointed out
that a major portion of conversion literature has dealt with
vertical shifts in Fig. 10.2, particularly from square 3 to 4,
involving diversifying the range of products but still using
existing military productive capacity. Horizontal shifts, particularly from square 4 to 1, are more significant since they involve
new investment and disposal of old machinery. Such changes are
long-term ones requiring considerable capital and, once made,
restrict a company as to what it can do thereafter. On the
principle of least effort, most companies will prefer vertical shifts
to horizontal shifts and no movement at all rather than vertical
shifts, i.e. defence companies would rather not move from square
3, but they may be forced to by external and internal influences.[39]
Consequently converting defence industries to civilian purposes has two aspects: *market extension* (a shift from square 3 to
4) which could mean a temporary use of spare military capacity
to produce civilian goods but may result in priority conflicts
between military and civilian demands; and *adaptation to civilian
production* (a shift from square 4 to 1) which means full-scale
conversion and, most likely, a significant shake up in the firm's
organisation.[40]

As the final, but extremely important, step in their analysis Frensborg and Wallensteen introduced a subjective element into what, up to now, has been a mostly objective account of the dynamics of industrial production. They referred to what is often called the 'culture' of an industry, meaning the value accorded to the particular kind of production carried on in a company by those who work there. This 'business idea', as Frensborg and Wallensteen preferred to call it, will be an important consideration in decisions on changing production:

> The selection of new products, the addition of new means of production and the development of new markets, will, we suggest, be judged by the organization with respect to its underlying 'business idea': whether this is what 'we' are here for or not ... Not only will it be difficult to find a civil product because civilian markets are different, but if there exists within the organisation a feeling that this very production is alien to the original idea, the difficulties will be greatly enhanced.[41]

This whole theoretical overview then forms the basis for an analysis of the two case studies neither of which, it must be stressed, is a success story. Nevertheless the conclusions from this analysis merit some attention before the implications of these findings for conversion and diversification initiatives are summarised.

Frensborg and Wallensteen concluded, from these case studies, that

> ... the obstacles to vigorous conversion, then is [sic] found not in the lack of products or in the lack of ideas, but in the organization itself: military production provides an easy way out compared to the hazards of civilian production.[42]

Elaborating on this point, the authors found military means of production to be labour-intensive so that finding alternative civilian manufacturing work which was able to use all the labour available in assembly and machine workshops was not easy. Moving away from work practices and levels of skill appropriate to defence production towards practices and skills relevant in civil production involves a major effort and was another obstacle to conversion. Moreover, in the firms examined, military production provided the basic work in hand so that there was insufficient commitment in looking for alternatives. Finally,

weak cost-minimising mechanisms in the design and manufacture of weapons led Frensborg and Wallensteen to the conclusion that, since there was little risk-taking or new investment
in civilian production, despite the profitable nature of the
military contracts in hand, perhaps defence work led to a loss of
the entrepreneurial spirit. So, taking all these points together:

> Civilizing military industry means infusing an organism with
> a new life. Conversion then is not simply a material change
> but also a spiritual one.[43]

The general implications drawn from this analysis contrast
with the Gilmore and Coddington findings, discussed previously,
in the greater prominence given to subjective factors, but also
complement that study in the greater weight given to conversion
rather than diversification. To that extent Frensborg and Wallensteen's general conclusions are more focused on the central
theme of this work and, as the last quote suggests, are also not
unrelated to the values of peace research and peace conversion.

The general implications of their analysis are fivefold. First,
ideas for alternative civilian products using existing means of
production and skills (i.e. diversification) are best found by
systematic searches within the company itself. It could, for
instance, be made part of a military contract. Secondly, these
searches should not be restricted to products that can be made
with existing means of production. Governments, which once
financed civilian companies to shift to military work, have a
responsibility for returning them to civilian uses (i.e. conversion). Thirdly, the former purchaser of military equipment – the
government – may need to take on the role of buyer of civilian
products if defence firms are to convert successfully. A 'civilian–
industrial complex' may be required! Fourthly, the 'business
idea' of the company needs to be redefined before there can be
any move away from military production. Management may
well have a vested interest in the 'pay-offs' from defence work
(e.g. better careers, political involvement), while for workers this
may be less so as having a job is what matters. For this reason
trade unions should be involved in the conversion process from
an early stage. Fifthly, what is valuable in military production is
the inventiveness and quality of workers and managers[44] and it
is this competence, rather than the physical assets of the firm,
which should be kept, if at all possible. Thus conversion means

not only doing away with the product, the weapon system, but also changing the type of plant and equipment used in production.[45]

A CONCLUDING NOTE

The discussion of the issues pertaining to the dynamics of industrial conversion will be taken up once more after the role of labour unions has been assessed. So far, though, it can be said that the industrial approach to conversion is a most useful and necessary adjunct to the macro-economic studies of disarmament and conversion discussed at length in Chapters 6 and 7. Moreover, those exponents of the economic approach to conversion, notably Thorsson and Melman, who have also investigated the industrial basis of conversion have reached similar conclusions to those described above. There is, though, a tendency to differ from some of the findings of Gilmore and Coddington: a more critical attitude is taken towards the top managers of defence firms, and the transfer of skills and the lack of marketing organisation and capability are regarded as more serious problems. The role of top management is by far the most significant point of difference, though, since this involves an internal political, and not simply a technical, matter. Before examining this point it is appropriate, first, to consider labour initiatives on defence industry conversion.

11 Defence Industry Diversification and Conversion (II)

LABOUR INITIATIVES

Trade unions have, from time to time since 1945, taken the initiative in propounding ways of achieving defence industry diversification, if not conversion. However, it was only with the public launching of the Lucas Aerospace Combine Shop Stewards Committee's alternative Corporate Plan in January 1976 that the potential role of the trade union movement in conversion caught the imagination of a part of the Western peace and labour movements. The UK became the launch pad for a new labour-oriented approach to conversion that was to exert a profound influence throughout Western Europe and North America in particular, and was a major factor behind the growth of international conversion activities from the mid-1970s onwards. Labour unions have both written themselves, and commissioned work from radical academics, on defence industry conversion. While the spread of these new ideas is still at an early stage, and has met with considerable hostility or indifference from some quarters of the union movement, an analysis of the significance of these developments is clearly called for.

THE LUCAS PLAN

The central elements of the Lucas Plan, as it came to be called, will therefore be discussed here.[1] At the time that this plan was made public the Combine Committee was well established, representing as it did all the staff and manual unions in Lucas Aerospace. Importantly, however, it did not form part of the official, and officially recognised, trade union machinery. The Combine's central concerns were job security and ensuring that their members could use their skills and ability in the interests of the community. Recognising that there was little enthusiasm amongst the membership for nationalisation,and fearful of recession and more redundancies in Lucas Aerospace, the Combine Committee had taken up a suggestion made by the Industry Secretary Tony Benn and drawn up an alternative plan. The basis for this plan was the idea of socially useful products, some of which might also be profitable, primarily aimed at meeting social needs. This approach challenged traditional management criteria for selecting products. Alternatives to military production were a related aspect of the Lucas Plan, as Lucas Aerospace was heavily involved in manufacturing components for military aircraft, and defence cuts were anticipated and supported by the shop stewards. Workers at every factory in the company, thirteen sites in all, were involved in the process of carrying out a skills and equipment audit and identifying socially useful product ideas which could be realised with these productive resources in Lucas Aerospace.[2] Thus the Corporate Plan presented to management in 1976 was a remarkable combination of innovative thinking and democratic involvement.

Altogether 150 product ideas emanated from the various factories and from these the executive of the Combine Committee selected five groups of proposals: medical equipment, transport vehicles and components, improved braking systems, energy products, and devices for undersea work. The Lucas Plan went further than this by proposing production processes which were ecologically sound and attempted to liberate, rather than suppress, human creativity. Changing the nature of work, not simply the products worked upon, was fundamental to the Combine's conception of industrial democracy.[3]

The response of the Lucas Aerospace top management in May 1976 was, in effect, a blunt rejection of the Plan and a restatement of the company's commitment to its traditional aerospace and defence business. It stressed that military aircraft do have social utility in that they are needed for defence purposes. The company stated that it constantly reviewed opportunities in non-aerospace fields where equivalent technologies could be applied. Only one small carrot was offered: a suggestion that local consultative machinery, comprising union representatives and local management, could review the order book and market trends so as to identify any local opportunities and difficulties.[4]

As the authors of the Combine-sponsored history of the Lucas Plan pointed out:

Many delegates had genuinely believed that management would be prepared to negotiate over it ... Terry Moran, an AUEW member from Burnley, was one of those who had high expectations: 'I was horrified when management completely rejected it. We were actually offering to work collectively with them to create wealth for the country, and they rejected the offer.' In his eyes, and those of many like him, management came out of the whole episode morally condemned.[5]

The Labour government, with its 1974 manifesto commitment to an 'irreversible shift of power towards working people', also failed to come up to expectations in providing support for the Combine initiative. Even the trade union hierarchy proved largely unresponsive and unwilling to recognise, let alone support, the Combine Committee.[6] The rights and wrongs of the differences between the Combine and these various groups and institutions will not be debated, for such a digression would be as lengthy as it is unnecessary to the main theme of this book. Suffice it is to say that the Plan was never implemented in Lucas Aerospace.

The Lucas Combine Committee clearly had a key role in the development of the Plan and its ideas are, perhaps, primarily associated with the nature of trade unionism and only secondly with disarmament and conversion. Taking the former aspect first, this also has some relevance to labour-oriented conversion initiatives since the kind of trade unionism found within any particular Western country is bound to influence the development of industrial democracy there, and hence the role it is possible for organised labour to play in the planning and implementing of conversion programmes. While the Combine was not a political party, in the sense of wanting to take power, it could not help becoming, in a broad sense, political because it was attempting to move to a new definition of trade unionism. Wainwright and Elliott explained the difficulties this caused the Combine:

... its functions as a trade-union organization directly expressing and fighting for the needs of its members has led it, out of necessity, to make proposals which go beyond the customary sphere of trade-union activity. The stewards' plan to defend their members' jobs implies changes in the priorities of government spending and purchasing. It implies a rejection of

the adequacy of the capitalist market in co-ordinating resources with needs. It seeks to release the massive resources
locked up in arms production and it requires an opening-up of
institutions of higher education and technological research for
use by trade-union and community groups. Yet at the same
time the base of the Combine Committee is a limited one: the
factory-based institutions of collective bargaining.[7]

For our purposes it is unnecessary to discuss the limits of
collective bargaining and whether, and if so to what extent, the
Lucas workers have pioneered a new kind of trade unionism.[8]
All that has to be noted at this juncture is that trade unions, even
with a degree of outside popular support and attempting to go
beyond traditional 'defensive' unionism, may not be able to force
or persuade management to negotiate over the strategic aspects
of company business. If this is the case, then is the Lucas
experience generalisable and, in particular, what significance
can it have for the peace movement and industrial conversion
initiatives?

The first part of the question is easily answered. The Lucas
management may have rejected the plan – and all that concerns
us here is that they did reject it – but the international response
from trade union and disarmament groups was tremendous.
However, as will be elaborated upon shortly, whether in Lucas
Aerospace itself or in other companies in the UK or abroad, the
extent to which ensuing labour diversification or conversion
proposals, based on socially useful products, were accepted by
management proved very limited, even when some of the
products were commercially viable (as was the case at Lucas
Aerospace). Neither traditional trade unionism, nor attempts at
a new unionism, were to succeed in breaking down the barrier
to successful implementation.

Despite the lack of success in implementing diversification or
conversion plans Lucas-type initiatives were largely welcomed
by peace and disarmament groups because they provided a way
out of the dilemma posed by advocating cuts in military spending which threatened defence workers with unemployment. As
Wainwright and Elliott succinctly put it:

> ... [The Lucas shop stewards] reversed the whole way
> seeing the relationship between disarmament and unemploy-
> ment. The Lucas Plan implied that instead of the problem

alternative employment being seen as a residual problem to be cleared up after the other decisions about disarmament had been taken, the possibility of liberating the skills and energies of defence workers for socially useful production became part of the positive case for disarmament.[9]

This possibility, albeit largely unrealised so far, was perhaps the single most important factor in bringing a part of the peace and labour movements together. It also influenced the economic studies on disarmament and conversion, discussed previously, in emphasising factory-based conversion opportunities and this positive case for disarmament.

Summarising the central elements of the Lucas Plan, the main objectives were job security and control of the labour process in the interests of society. Socially useful products and an improved work environment were integral to achieving these objectives which, in turn, involved seeking alternatives to military production. The Combine Committee did not, however, anticipate that aerospace would cease to be a major part of Lucas Aerospace's activities.[10] Thus its strategy of trying to negotiate the introduction of alternative products to compensate for declining defence sales was essentially one of diversification rather than conversion. It raises a number of important theoretical issues regarding the dynamics of industrial change, industrial democracy and the relationship between the peace movement and labour unions which need to be examined. Before doing this a few more details are required on labour diversification and conversion initiatives since the Lucas Plan.

OTHER EUROPEAN AND US LABOUR INITIATIVES

One of the most thorough reviews of trade union-inspired diversification and conversion plans was commissioned by the Central Organisation of Finnish Trade Unions and carried out by Lindroos, in cooperation with the Tampere Peace Research Institute.[11] More recently, a study by the European Trade Union Institute, *Disarmament and the Conversion of Arms Industries to Civil Production: A Review of Possibilities and Experiences in Western Europe* (1983), brings the history of some of these initiatives more up to date. Other international trade union organisations, which have taken up this issue in the last few years, include the International Metalworkers' Federation and the International Confederation of Free Trade Unions, while the UN specialised agency, the International Labour Organisation, has also instituted research studies.[12] These developments reflect the increasing interest in conversion expressed by various national trade unions and federal bodies.

In Western Europe, the Metalworkers' Union in the FRG created a special discussion group on armament technology and employment to examine various matters related to conversion.[13] This union, I. G. Metall, also set up working parties in different arms companies, mostly in Northern Germany. The main objective has been to safeguard jobs through the development of alternative products. Although sometimes successful in persuading or forcing management to the negotiating table, as at Krupp Mak Maschinenbau GmbH in Kiel, the unions have rarely, if at all, succeeded in getting any of these alternative products adopted.[14] While, as Suzanne Gordon has argued, the German system of co-determination may provide a more favourable starting point for discussions on alternative product options with management,[15] so far it cannot be said that German unions have been any more successful than their UK counterparts in securing effective implementation of diversification plans.

Elsewhere in Western Europe, the metalworkers' unions have also led the way in diversification and conversion proposals in recent years. In Italy the FLM (Italian Metalworkers' Federation) has made diversification one of its demands through collective bargaining at plant level in various arms firms.[16] While, again, there are no successful examples of conversion, the factory council at Oto Melara did manage to force the management to divide production equally between military and agricultural vehicles at its new Brindisi plant,[17] although this does not appear to have involved adoption of any alternative products. According to the European Trade Union Institute, formal agreements on diversification into the civilian sector were reached with the managements of four large arms companies but were not enforced except at Agusta, which started production of an ambulance-helicopter. The international economic recession and the Italian government's massive increases in military expenditure were factors behind the weakening of company diversification plans.[18]

Likewise in Sweden the metalworkers' union there has pressed for diversification in some of the major defence companies. In 1979 a public committee of enquiry comprising representatives of managements and unions throughout Sweden was established to consider defence industry diversification. It proposed government purchasing of new civilian technologies, similar to procurement of military technologies, as a means to assist the diversification process.[19] While the Lucas Plan has been an inspiration to some trade unions in Sweden, as in the FRG and Italy, examples of successful negotiation of new, alternative products are hard to come by though the Swedish unions do appear to have had some influence on management. One major successful conversion experience, cited by Gordon, involved the closure of the state-owned Oresundsvarvet shipyard in Landskrona in 1981, and its replacement by more than forty new enterprises in the town utilising the buildings at the shipyard and the workers' skills.[20] However, this was not a factory-based conversion; rather it had more in common with the approach taken by the US Office of Economic Adjustment in helping communities adjust to base closures and military contract cancellations.[21]

Most trade union initiatives on defence industry diversification and conversion have occurred in the UK, the FRG, Italy and Sweden. Unsurprisingly, given the analysis of the role of arms exports in France provided in Chapter 5, the trade unions there have exhibited little interest in conversion. Politically, too, the support of both left-wing political parties for President Mitterrand's rearmament and pro-nuclear policies has helped to ensure that no strong peace movement, and few active conversion groups, emerge.[22]

Turning to the USA, proposals for conversion were made by Walter Reuther, President of the United Automobile Workers' Union, as long ago as 1943 but the government did not take them seriously.[23] More recently the International Association of Machinists and Aerospace Workers has commissioned a study on the employment effects of the arms industries, where many of its members are employed.[24] The union has strongly supported conversion progammes, for which it has demanded government support, and it appears from a recent book published by this union, *Let's Rebuild America* (1984), that this position emanates from concern about economic decline and unemployment in the

United States, with hardly any noticeable influence from European Lucas-type initiatives.

Nevertheless the Lucas Plan has had an impact in America, as evidenced by the United Automobile Workers' campaign to re-employ some of the thousands of workers who had lost their jobs from McDonnell Douglas Corporation's Long Beach plant in Southern California.

The resulting McDonnell Douglas Project involved the setting up of a labour–management committee to look at alternative product ideas. This initiative was particularly noteworthy because it began in a plant where the dominant commercial production (in an otherwise overwhelmingly militarised company) had proved rather unsuccessful over the years, and where the pressures to increase military dependency were mounting.[25]

CONCLUSION

As far as a comparison between US and West European experiences are concerned, it may be said that on both continents trade union diversification and conversion initiatives have increased markedly in recent years but without overcoming the many obstacles to implementation. However, in terms of the number of grass-roots campaigns, the US unions have so far organised fewer than the European, and particularly the UK, unions. A full analysis of these diverse campaigns appears premature and unnecessary here, and would anyway involve consideration of factors that have not been discussed so far, for example the differences between American and European trade unions.[26] It is sufficient that, on the positive side, the potential role of labour unions in conversion progammes has been demonstrated, while, on the negative side, the unions alone, or even with community backing, have been shown to be largely unable to win sufficient political support to require the managers of defence firms to negotiate seriously with them about alternative product or production plans.

This seems an appropriate point at which to turn to the theoretical issues posed by the industrial approach to conversion.

12 Defence Industry Diversification and Conversion (III)

THE DYNAMICS OF CONVERSION

Despite the aura of radicalism surrounding the Lucas Plan it was in fact a diversification, not a conversion, programme. The modest nature of its objectives become clearer by comparing the plan with the general implications of Frensborg and Wallensteen's analysis of conversion. One of their most important observations was that the main obstacle to conversion lay not in a lack of ideas or products but in the organisation itself. Indeed almost all the many alternative product proposals came from within Lucas Aerospace itself but, quite deliberately, they were largely restricted to products which could be made with existing skills and equipment. While the Labour government was not willing directly to assist Lucas Aerospace in moving out of military production, nor to become a major buyer of civilian products from this or any other defence company, some of the alternative products proposed by the Combine appeared profitable even by commercial criteria. Moreover, the Lucas shop stewards, even with a diversification not a conversion strategy, found themselves up against the 'business idea' of the company which management was unwilling to change. And although the Combine Committee stressed retention of the skills and ingenuity of the workforce, rather than new investment in plant and machinery, that did not appear to make their proposals any more acceptable. So, in terms of making industrial change happen, the Lucas workers were no closer to making progress through what was essentially a diversification initiative than if they had proposed a wholesale conversion programme. When to this consideration is added the preliminary results from other labour led initiatives in the UK and abroad, many of them far less political, less ambitious and more moderate in presentation than the Lucas Plan, it is hard to escape from one of two conclusions. Either there is some basic technical fault in all the labour alternative product proposals so far, or the opposition to these plans has some political content to it which is of general relevance to the way in which industry is governed.

It would be hard to exaggerate the significance of these issues, complex as they undoubtedly are. For whilst it may be readily admitted, from the evidence presented earlier in this book, that there are serious structural obstacles to defence industry diversification and conversion, arising from different production and marketing characteristics compared to civilian industries, in so far as such industrial change can occur it depends on the full commitment of those involved, especially top management. If the objections of management to labour union proposals are genuine – that is technical – that is one thing, but if they are political then that is quite another.

This discussion will focus on the internal political questions relevant to the individual defence company since the external political issues, notably the role of government in supporting conversion, have already been dealt with in some detail. Nevertheless it will be recalled that the major Western states control directly varying parts of their respective defence industries, so they can have a greater say in the internal running of these firms compared to those in the private sector. Accepting this point, it should still be noted that, in the normal course of events, Western governments have generally preferred to 'pass the buck' on conversion to management, rather than get involved themselves, thus reinforcing the strategic position which the top managers of defence companies have in order to implement, or not to implement, diversification and conversion plans – where these are possible even without government support.

Yet, as the record of experience to date illustrates, top management have not been very successful in commercial diversification, particularly through internal developments, and even less so in conversion. The end result has been that many defence-oriented managers lack the interest and competence to diversify the companies they control. Conversely, some labour unions have the interest, the ideas and an avowed, but untested, competence in implementing alternative plans to diversify those same firms, which they do not control. Time and again diversification and thus, ultimately, the prospects for conversion are placed on the horns of a dilemma: management lacks the interest but has the power; labour has the interest but lacks the power.

There are exceptions, of course, in that management is not always a stumbling block and, no doubt, labour unions sometimes are. However, the evidence accumulated so far is quite sufficient to require further examination on whether, and how, this log-jam can be removed. This raises the broader issue of industrial democracy.

Before turning to this topic, it is necessary to take on board the question of technical objections to labour unions' alternative plans, raised earlier on. These objections can only be answered on a case-by-case basis since they are specific to particular companies at certain times. To that extent no definitive rebuttal can be given though the burden of proof in sustaining such objections ought to lie with management where labour unions have taken the trouble to present a detailed and reasoned case for diversification. Specific technical criticisms of workers' plans have frequently been lacking because managements, as in the case of Lucas Aerospace, have preferred to rest their case on more general and abstract objections. Moreover it seems implausible that only technical issues are behind the fact that some defence companies are only too pleased to take up the alternative product ideas of their employees – through suggestion box schemes, for instance – yet, somehow, hardly ever find such ideas acceptable if channelled through the unions and made an object of discussion and negotiation. Consequently it should be stated here that there is no prima facie case for assuming that some basic technical fault inheres to any, let alone all, labour proposals for diversification.

INDUSTRIAL DEMOCRACY

Now if progress can only be made in securing for labour a share in decision-making concerning defence industry diversification and conversion when the structure of power and authority in defence firms is altered, it is clear that such changes are dependent on more general advances in industrial democracy. The defence industry can claim no special case for exclusive rights in this respect. If there is a strong case for participation in management decision-making within defence firms, it need be no less strong within textile or automobile firms as well. Thus no major changes in the authority structure of the defence industry can be expected until wider political support for industrial democracy, and consequent legislative changes, are achieved.

Whilst this is not the place for a major exposition on the subject of industrial democracy, some general comments are necessary in order to set the prospects for increased worker participation in defence companies within their proper context. The significance of attaining greater participation within defence firms can then be highlighted, before assessing what can realistically be achieved in the economic and political climate of the West at the advent of the 1990s.

At the risk of some over-simplification it may be said that, historically, there have been waves of interest in participation and new institutional growth in Britain and some other market economies.[1] These waves tend to correspond with periods of crisis when there is a labour shortage and output has to be kept high by employers and the state but wages are constrained (to contain inflation, in particular). In this situation labour's bargaining power increases and, in the presence of restrictions on wage increases combined with continuous pressure for higher output and improved efficiency, participation becomes an outlet for easing the strains between management and workers. Nevertheless neither of these groups nor government itself always pursue similar goals and institutional reaction varies between different countries.

However, once the crisis moves to slump the unions lose much of their bargaining power, whilst management becomes more willing to adopt a confrontational posture. As the economy moves out of the slump the pressures for wage constraints are reduced, and trade unions once again become more interested in wage demands which employers and governments become less reluctant to concede. Although interest in participation then tends to fall away some aspects of the institutional growth associated with the earlier crisis remain to be revitalised on the crest of the next wave. Thus Brannen's view, based on an extensive review of research into participation, is that over time workforce expectations grow and the limits of managerial authority are increasingly challenged.[2]

Yet, as Brannen rightly cautioned, the pressure for participation should not be exaggerated even during waves of interest. What is more, from the mid-1960s up to the late 1970s such pressures as existed were focused at the lower, socio-technical levels of the enterprise; little demand existed for a measure of control at the political level. Most workforces in the primary sectors of the labour force, amongst whom the majority of studies have been carried out, are highly unionised and offer the greatest potential for participation. However, most of these workforces '... expressed no wish to challenge management's right to manage, but simply wished to influence the operation of that right; collective bargaining was seen as the most effective way of exerting that influence.'[3]

Likewise most trade unions and their officials have been generally opposed to participation either at the political or socio-technical levels of the individual firm. Whilst, as Brannen pointed out, opportunity creates potential as historically the desire for participation has increased with greater workforce experience of it,[4] the foregoing observations correspond with the difficulties encountered by the Lucas shop stewards in attempting to extend collective bargaining to the political level of the firm.

Management, too, has been very hostile to participation at the political level, although where it has been forced upon them attitudes tend to become more positive. Involvement by employees at the socio-technical level is seen as the appropriate focus by management although, unlike employees who aspire to partial or full participation, management defines this as meaning consultation at most, or simply improved communication. Studies have strikingly emphasised the homogeneity of management attitudes and '... their deep commitment to existing organisational structures and managerial prerogatives'.[5] Brannen concluded that management does not generally initiate change:

> Participation is considered by management only when there are threats to managerial authority, and paradoxically in order to maintain it.[6]

With the onset of deep recession and high unemployment accompanied by rapid technological change, the most recent wave of interest in participation had come to an end by the close of the 1970s. Labour market power had swung back to management with a consequent reassertion of their prerogatives. Many participative structures are a constraint on management flexibility and are not required as incentives to work. Hence the

Western market economies have returned to the non-participative period in the economic cycle.[7]

While, as Brannen stressed, this is an over-simplification since the evolution of industrial democracy over many decades cannot just be switched off, there can be no doubt that the prospects during the 1980s were not good. However, as unemployment declined and economic growth rates improved in the West during the latter part of the decade, future prospects for industrial democracy were beginning to improve slightly at the outset of the 1990s. The role of labour in defence industry diversification and conversion has to be evaluated in this context.

Yet, before assessing the implications of this rather negative outlook for advances in participatory frameworks within defence firms, it is necessary to draw attention to the great importance that an enlarged workplace democracy throughout industry has been given by one conversion advocate in particular: Seymour Melman. One of his most recent books, *Profits Without Production* (1983), contains the strongest condemnation of US (and in passing, UK) industrial management and the most detailed case for worker participation to derive from any proponent of conversion. Given the high profile Melman has had in this book a brief word on his thoughts on these subjects would seem in order so as to complete the picture. It should also be recalled that his support for worker involvement in management decision-making goes back to at least the early 1960s.

Melman's theoretical framework has already been fully discussed.[8] The aforementioned work emphasises the decline of production competence in the USA due to profit-taking derived from expanded, private, non-productive or foreign investments and the capability of state managers to extend their decision-making powers over an increased military economy. This combination of short-term, money-making strategies of private management, together with the greater power of state managers, have stripped the economic system of its productive capital and led to the slowest productivity growth in the world, as well as unemployment and inflation.[9]

A movement of management back towards production rather than money-making strategies, since profit is based finally on production, cannot be expected to be initiated by management itself. Their social status, self-image and particular skills are bound up in their current method of operating. Whilst in the past the 'manager's right to manage' was usually not questioned but rather reinforced by unions Melman believed that this will change:

> As one union after another, across the country and in many industries, faces the prospect of permanent unemployment traceable to the technical/economic inability of management to organize work, or the preference of management to make money with no production, the trade unions are compelled to broaden their view. They can no longer leave production decision-making to management on the assumption that management will surely do the job in its own self-interest.[10]

Melman argued that the spread of workplace democracy is essential to restoring industrial productivity while worker control over financial resources, together with a greater say in production matters, is necessary for increased, productive investment. He believed that these and other developments, necessary to achieve the goal of useful work for all, will be the consequence of a breakdown in the social contract between management and the rest of society:

> Management has been expected to organize work, and in exchange has been permitted to control production and to take a large share of the profits and power. But managerialism, oriented with primacy to profits/power, has developed a trained incapacity to organize work. The traditional basis for legitimacy of managerial power is being destroyed by the controlled deterioration of the US production system and the parallel efforts of management to sustain its money-making in the presence of a growing workless population. Once the social contract breakdown is displayed for all to see, there will come a national demand for alternative ways to organize work and rebuild the American economy [including] ... enlarged workplace democracy ... production-oriented management, more decentralized decision-making and a substantially smaller military economy.[11]

The special significance of Melman's analysis, highly condensed as it is here, lies in the linkage between conversion, on the one hand, and increased participation throughout industry, on the other hand. Moreover, the case for increased workplace democracy was made by going back to basic principles, in

Melman's terms the tacit social contract. While it is quite possible to argue from a different basis, for instance by questioning managerial legitimacy in terms of ownership,[12] the crucial point is to place conversion within the wider context of advances in workplace democracy, assuming that one wishes to encourage labour unions to play a constructive role in conversion planning. These advances will only occur, as Melman pointed out, in response to society-wide pressures which go beyond individual union initiatives to extend collective bargaining, as the Lucas Combine attempted to do, and instead create the political and legislative conditions for fundamental changes in the structure of power and authority in industry.

In the immediate future, though, the prospects for industrial democracy are obviously not very propitious either in the USA or the UK. A less confrontational approach by the unions might be expedient, though in the face of aggressive managements, determined to recover and then consolidate their own control over decision-making within defence companies, there can be little confidence that even this will bear much fruit. Why, after all, should managements concede voluntarily, and at a time when they are bargaining from strength, what they would not accept even under pressure, when their bargaining power was weaker? For theory and practice have suggested that managements will not willingly surrender power at the political level of the enterprise and that such participation as they will countenance will be, as far as they can make it, on their own terms.

AN ASSESSMENT OF THE CONVERSION PROCESS

These thoughts lead to some final conclusions on the likely nature of defence industry diversification and conversion in the USA and UK in the next few years. (The position in the other major Western countries may vary from this, though perhaps not too much.) Those initiatives which occur are almost certain to continue to be managerially led, with minimal labour union involvement, unless and until the state intervenes either to extend industrial democracy more generally throughout industry, or to provide assistance to defence firms to diversify or convert as part of the government's overall industrial policy. Assistance could also be made available because of a change in defence policy in the direction of unilateral or multilateral disarmament. Since the propensity of even labour or socialist Western governments to intervene in the economy is usually limited, and a successful conversion programme affecting major parts of the defence industry might cost a great deal of money initially in terms of creating new public sector markets, it appears that the prospects for the factory-based concept are probably limited in scope, though rather better for diversification than conversion. However, the economic adjustment process of transferring resources from closed military bases or defence firms to new companies and industries offers more potential in the immediate future. This would follow an already tried and tested approach by the Office of Economic Adjustment in the USA.

It should be emphasised that these sober, if not sombre, conclusions reflect prevailing political, economic and industrial realities. Individual defence enterprises may be capable of converting, but not without a great deal of assistance of the type described at length in Chapter 10.

THE LABOUR MOVEMENT AND PEACE RESEARCH

One last theoretical issue remains to be examined. The closer links between the labour and peace movements have, in large measure, come about as a result of the impact of the Lucas Plan and other similar initiatives. Intellectual expression of this linkage can be found in United Nations', some government-sponsored, and many peace research monographs or articles on disarmament and conversion. It is the influence on peace research of labour movement ideas on conversion which will form the focus of attention here, though it should not be forgotten that the unions have, in turn, derived most of their views on the harmful economic and social consequences of the arms race from the findings of peace research and radical academics. Nor should it be overlooked that many parts of the national union movements remain largely untouched or unmoved by these ideas. The purpose of this short review is to understand the ways in which peace research has incorporated the potential role of labour into its writings on conversion.

As early as 1977 the Richardson Institute for Conflict and

Peace Research in the UK was highlighting the significance of the Lucas workers' Corporate Plan and related initiatives. D. Smith incorporated the notion of effective participation in the planning process by workers and their communities as one of five basic features of a conversion programme.[13] A year later Albrecht, writing in the *Bulletin of Peace Proposals*, analysed the Lucas experience and concluded:

> ... the Lucas campaign has demonstrated the action-potential of [the] organised labour movement for peaceful conversion of military industries, to a greater extent and with far more vigour than most analysts of the conversion problem have tended to assume. Labour is not just an object of conversion strategies: it can also attain a crucial subjective role.[14]

Albrecht's other observations included the following: that Lucas-type initiatives appeared transferable to other countries (as, indeed, they were to be); that conversion strategies ought to be based upon consideration of technological trends so as to encourage the development of those technologies which will maintain employment; that decision-making in a converted factory would be more decentralised down to shop-floor level; that the strength of the Combine Committee was that the plan was prepared well in advance of a crisis, and it did not attempt to go it alone but simply to widen the scope of collective bargaining.[15] Only on the latter point would it be necessary to question Albrecht's judgement since the Combine really had no option except to try to persuade management to negotiate, and when that failed they had to fall back on traditional union methods to defend members' jobs and terms and conditions of service.

Another German peace researcher, Christian Wellmann, discussed the problems of a factory-based concept of conversion in a densely worded article in *Current Research on Peace and Violence*.[16] He centred his analysis around the attempts to close the VFW-Fokker plant in Speyer and claimed, with some justification, that while peace researchers and peace movement activists had often come to the somewhat hasty conclusion that the question of conversion was all but settled, in fact many unresolved difficulties remained, as his case study demonstrated. The lack of political motivation for conversion was, in Wellmann's view, often lacking precisely because these difficulties

existed, especially affecting the production workers and office
staff in defence firms, and their resolution would assist in getting
the idea of conversion accepted and developed by employees and
their unions. He criticised the emphasis on macro-economic
reasoning in peace research studies on disarmament and conversion which obscure the problems faced by workers at the factory
level. Wellmann theorised that, contrary to the conventional
viewpoint, one cannot first create the political conditions for
conversion and then carry out the practical tasks involved;
rather an iterative process is involved in which each component
influences and pushes forward the other.[17]

Perhaps the most ambitious synthesis of ideas, linking labour
to the concept of peace conversion itself, was that by Marek
Thee of the International Peace Research Institute in Oslo. His
contribution in the *International Labour Review*, which is almost
impossible to summarise because it encapsulates virtually every
dimension of conversion ever discussed, is best captured by this
inspiring and visionary passage:

> Conversion is not a purely technical issue with solutions that lie
> exclusively in econometrics and organisational measures. Far
> more decisive is the socio-political context: human versus
> military needs; socially useful production versus barren waste;
> science and technology for human development versus their
> misuse for destructive purposes; and participatory and demo-
> cratic working conditions versus hierarchical and authoritarian
> production structures. Like disarmament, and as its corollary,
> conversion is an existential and spiritual historical necessity for
> the advancement of the human race. It is the way of the
> future...[18]

This quotation implicitly identifies labour as an agent in the
process of gaining democratic control over the driving forces
behind the arms race. Its positive emphasis contrasts rather
starkly with the conclusions arrived at, earlier in this chapter,
concerning the likely role of labour in conversion within the next
few years. While Thee's perspective is a much longer term one it
can certainly be argued that not only he, but some other peace
researchers, have tended to be over-optimistic about the potential of unions in converting defence industries. Nevertheless such
a positive outlook has been instrumental in forging closer ties

between some parts of the labour and peace movements than has probably ever been achieved before.

That concludes not only this chapter but also the assessment of the last of the three main approaches to conversion. It only remains to consider the various efforts over the last thirty years or so to support, or greatly expand the scope of, defence industry diversification and conversion programmes. This will complete the analysis of the history of post-war conversion studies and experiences. Then a theoretical framework for conversion in the major Western industrialised countries can be outlined.

13 Historical Legacy of Conversion Initiatives

The activist aspect of the history of conversion in the post-war period dates mostly from the Lucas Plan onwards, with the rare exception of managerial initiatives in individual defence firms. So most of the foregoing has dealt with the theoretical and empirical studies of the economics of defence spending and disarmament, the structure of Western defence industries and the possibilities for conversion. Nevertheless the practical efforts outside of industry, modest though they were, to stimulate interest in conversion or create an environment in which defence companies, workers and their communities could more easily switch to civilian work should not be overlooked. Such efforts, begun in the pre-Lucas period, helped to lay the groundwork for the subsequent nexus between some peace and labour organisations and the emergence of various organisations to support and promote defence conversion. This earlier work was mainly conducted by two different groups: academic researchers who from time to time organised conferences in the USA and Western Europe,[1] and legislators in the USA who have tried unsuccessfully for over twenty-five years to persuade Congress to pass legislation on defence industry conversion. Additionally the US government, through the Office of Economic Adjustment (OEA), has actively supported community-based conversion while remaining indifferent, or hostile, to the factory-based concept. Much more recently, the UN itself has very tentatively begun to take practical steps to support conversion activities whilst a growing network of grass-roots organisations has given new impetus to efforts at conversion planning.

LEGISLATION

On the legislative front in the USA there has been a great deal of activity, beginning in October 1963 when Senator McGovern and fourteen others introduced a bill to provide for a National Economic Conversion Commission. Since then a formidable

189

body of specific legislation has been put to both Houses of Congress on the subjects of defence industry conversion or the reduction of military expenditure. In one year alone, 1971, some thirty separate conversion-related bills were before Congress. Whilst more details of this legislation have been given elsewhere,[2] it needs to be noted that despite almost complete lack of success these efforts have had an important impact on the conversion policy debate abroad, for instance in the UK.[3] For this reason a brief summary of one of the two conversion-related bills currently before Congress will be given shortly.

The only successful pieces of national legislation concerned the setting up of the OEA in the Department of Defense in the 1960s, at a time when the US government itself was interested in the economic effects of disarmament. It was mainly concerned with assisting communities affected by military base closures and contract cancellations and was, therefore, only indirectly linked to the question of defence industry conversion. Nevertheless the historical development of the OEA and its achievements will also need to be outlined as it provides one of the few practical examples of successful conversion so far.

At no time has any American administration, Democratic or Republican, shown the slightest support for industrial conversion planning. On the contrary, they have consistently opposed all legislation aimed at assisting such planning.[4] One of the rare occasions on which even partial conversion-related legislation had any real chance of becoming law was in 1978–79 when McKinney and Dodd (a Republican and a Democrat, respectively) attached their conversion proposals as amendments to the renewal of the Economic Development Act. While the House of Representatives passed the renewal legislation the Senate was split and eventually allowed the whole bill to fail rather than accept the McKinney/Dodd amendments.[5] The only successes, as far as conversion legislation is concerned, have been at state or local level, e.g. the Connecticut state legislature passed 'The Defense Readjustment Act of 1980' which applied a series of existing state-wide economic development instruments to the problem of defence-dependent firms. Even so the provisions of this act would not, according to one expert, be able to cope with a major alteration in the mix of defence procurement within Connecticut.[6]

Of the two conversion-related bills before Congress, Represen-

tative Ted Weiss' 'Defense Economic Adjustment Act'[7] is the
most comprehensive and follows most closely the kind of proposals put forward every year since 1963. However, the original
version of his bill was that placed before Congress by Senator
McGovern and one other on 2 November 1977.[8] The Weiss bill,
which reflects to some extent the influence of American unions
interested in conversion, has four main parts:

- A national Defense Economic Adjustment Council to encourage concrete plans for national non-defence projects, coordinate information on such projects with communities and
  facilities faced with cut-backs in military programmes, develop a 'Conversion Guidelines Handbook' for displaced
  defence workers and set up criteria for deciding when a
  community is eligible for federal assistance.
- Alternative use committees, comprised of management and
  workers in equal numbers, to be set up at every military base
  or industrial facility with 100 employees or more to develop
  alternative plans for civilian production within two years.
- A one year advance notification of military base closures or
  major defence contract cancellations.
- Financial and retraining assistance for affected workers supported by an Economic Adjustment Fund based on a 1.25 per
  cent surcharge on all Pentagon prime contracts.[9]

A more modest version of this bill is that presented by
Representative Nicholas Mavroules, the 'Economic Conversion
Act'. Although this piece of legislation had more support in the
House of Representatives neither appeared to have any prospect
of becoming law at the time of writing. This question – whether
national legislation on conversion can ever be passed into law –
is more important here than the precise details of the bills.

As noted previously, it is only when conversion is linked to
broader issues, like defence or economic policy, that it is able to
achieve greater prominence and the prospects for its successful
adoption within the political programme of a government are
heightened.[10] It is surely no coincidence that the one notable
occasion in American Congressional experience of conversion-
related bills when such legislation came closest to being enacted
was at the time of the McKinney/Dodd amendments of 1978–
79. There must be grave doubt as to whether federal legislation
on defence industry conversion is ever likely to be successful on

its own – a point made by Gordon Adams in a critique of conversion in 1986, which will be assessed in the last section of this chapter.

MILITARY BASE CONVERSION

A rather more encouraging picture is presented by the history of US military base conversion over the last twenty years or so. By all accounts this base conversion programme has been, on balance, successful. The OEA was set up in March 1961, by the then Secretary of State for Defense McNamara, to alleviate the damaging economic effects of a large number of planned military base closures. It had only a small staff and no funding but the comparatively buoyant state of the economy in the 1960s helped to facilitate efforts to create new civilian jobs to replace those lost through base closures. Then, in March 1970, President Nixon created the Economic Adjustment Committee (EAC) within the OEA to coordinate assistance from twenty federal departments and agencies to affected communities. In April 1973 the size of the OEA staff was increased and between that time and October 1977 over $420 million in federal funds was appropriated for the EAC to finance its activities in the affected communities.[11]

OEA/EAC assistance to communities adjusting to defence cut-backs is aimed at stimulating the local economy through finding alternative uses of the former military base, economic diversification and cutting red tape in obtaining assistance from federal and other agencies. The process involves all levels of government, from central to local, as well as the business community in the area affected.[12] According to the OEA itself, 94 military base economic adjustment projects between 1961 and 1981, involving the loss of 87 703 former DoD or contractor jobs, resulted in the creation of 123 777 civilian jobs of which 109 262 were new jobs and 14 515 were jobs relocated from the communities to improved facilities on the bases. In many cases the loss of military personnel may have significantly affected the local economy in terms of reduced spending power, but not in direct employment loss.[13] Uniformed personnel and their families were sent from the community, with guarantees of employment, when a base was closed down. A CBO report noted that since 1969 70 per cent of DoD civilian workers laid off when military installations were closed had been placed in jobs at other installations.[14] Thus the creation of jobs at redundant military sites, as a result of economic adjustment projects, is by no means limited to protecting existing defence jobs.

While the severe economic conditions, particularly in the early 1980s, will have made community-based conversion more difficult to achieve, there is no doubt that this concept now represents a tried and tested approach.[15]

UNITED NATIONS' ACTIVITIES

Turning from governmental to inter-governmental initiatives, it has been revealed earlier in this book that the UN has contributed many studies and one of the main models of conversion. However, it was only in 1987 that this organisation held its first conference on the relationship between disarmament and development. It is within this relationship that much of the UN's conversion work has been undertaken. The conference was held at the UN Headquarters in New York between 24 August and 11 September and it was attended by 150 states, 183 non-governmental organisations and various specialised agencies and inter-governmental bodies. A significant absentee was the USA, apparently on the grounds that it saw no interrelationship between disarmament and development.[16]

The Final Document, adopted by consensus, set out many of the principles discussed in the 1981 UN report[17] and made recommendations on an action programme. However, the proposals on future action were not strong and, as far as conversion was concerned, states only committed themselves to 'consider' various activities like undertaking studies and planning which had all been proposed before. The UN itself was asked to facilitate an international exchange of views and experience in the field of conversion.[18]

Nevertheless the conference represented a step forward, albeit a small one, in terms of translating ideas into practical, policy proposals. A further impetus to UN activities in this area was provided by the Soviet leader Mikhail Gorbachev in his address to the UN General Assembly on 7 December 1988. He publicly stated his confidence that conversion is a realistic idea and committed the USSR to drawing up, and making public, an internal plan of conversion within the overall framework of Soviet economic reforms. Additionally, during the course of 1989, the USSR would, as an experiment, draw up conversion plans for two or three defence plants and, also, make public their experience in providing employment for specialists from military industry and in using defence-related equipment, buildings and structures in civilian production.[19] Previously almost all Soviet comment on conversion had related to Western capitalist countries or the relationship between disarmament and development. Mr Gorbachev's statement to the UN was, therefore, an important and remarkable departure. If the USSR fulfils its commitments to conversion, and planned cuts in the military budget will provide an added incentive to do so, then this could conceivably provide a spur to action in the West as well.

AN EVOLVING FRAMEWORK OF SUPPORT ORGANISATIONS

The growth of support groups for trade union-inspired conversion planning in the West, as well as more general educational work on defence industry conversion, has been most apparent in the USA, the UK, the FRG and in Scandinavian countries. Since a detailed analysis of the development of conversion organisation ought to be related to what has happened in the peace and trade union movements as well as to practical involvement by sympathetic regional or local government authorities the assessment here can only be of a very preliminary nature.

However, Woodhouse's overview of conversion activities in the USA, in the context of the Nuclear Weapons Freeze Campaign during the early 1980s and the previous hiatus in the American peace movement, illustrates a number of ways in which they differ from European experience.[20] In particular, the earlier reference to the post-Lucas period betrays a Western European perspective, which should not obscure the fact that most US conversion work emerged out of specifically American conditions and some of it pre-dated the publication of the Lucas Plan. Defence conversion was being discussed by the American Society of Friends during the early 1970s whilst one of the oldest and most effective of the conversion groups, the Center for

Economic Conversion (formerly the Mid-Peninsular Conversion Project), was founded in 1975. Although trade union organisation in the USA is weaker, the multitude of local peace groups formed to research, educate and organise around the conversion issue puts the USA far ahead of Western Europe in this respect. No doubt this situation is partly due to greater freedom of information in the USA, particularly concerning the defence industry, which allows these groups to do more useful work for the unions and provide more material for general public education.[21] Nevertheless even in other Western countries there are now many individuals and groups involved in conversion planning, as a weighty compendium produced by Bomann-Larsen bears witness.[22]

Perhaps the clearest sign of the greater presence and activity of grass-roots organisations and the increased awareness of the need for closer international links was the International Economic Conversion Conference in 1984, arguably the first time that shop stewards, peace activists and academics from Western Europe and North America had met to exchange information and support conversion activities. One of the outcomes of this conference was the setting up of the Economic Conversion Clearinghouse by the Center for Economic Conversion to assist the interchange of information and resources amongst groups at local, national and international levels and promote the coordination of conversion planning.[23]

Various efforts have been made to analyse the impact of this pressure group, or nascent movement, for conversion.[24] One of the most optimistic accounts of Western European experience so far, that by Gordon, highlighted several features of note: conversion is seen not just as a solution to the problem of unemployment resulting from disarmament, but as a positive, job-creation strategy forming a vital part of any industrial policy designed to reverse the decline in manufacturing industry; through conversion planning the role of unions is altered from that of protecting narrow sectional interests to being defenders of the rights of all citizens to rewarding work; also as conversion planning moves into the factory and workers become involved in product and investment decisions that serve the community and maintain employment, producers and consumers will develop a common interest; European conversion campaigns, following English and German regional examples, can be linked to alternative economic development strategies to ensure a healthy work and community environment; and, finally, these conversion pro-grammes can be built without national plans or legislation.[25] While Gordon did refer to the tremendous problems which exist in overcoming management resistance and winning workers' support it must be said that, in the context of what has been written in the preceding chapter, her analysis is more a state-ment of hope than an indication of current realities. It is an inspiring positive vision of the future much along the lines of Thee (cited at the end of the last chapter).

The assessment made by Ball, based on both US and Western European experience, was much more salutary. Looking to the future she stated:

> The various conversion-related activities described in this section are but the beginning of serious campaigns to promote the transfer of resources from the military to the civil sector. Attempts to inaugurate alternative use planning have for the most part failed to capture the support they need from governments, management, unions and individual workers.[26]

Conversion groups are, however, significant in various ways: educating governments and the public concerning the need for, and the means of achieving, conversion; demonstrating that workers can find alternatives to military equipment; and con-vincing workers that they should participate in matters which have historically been the prerogative of management. Yet Ball still added another cautionary note:

> Despite the clear growth of interest at the grass-roots level in defence-industry conversion since the mid-1970s, it is still the case that only a relatively few individuals are actively involved in working for conversion. Most workers and most members of communities in which defence industries are located continue to see military expenditure as a means of guaranteeing eco-nomic prosperity and jobs. Most union officials are similarly not motivated to work for conversion. It also remains true that workers are primarily concerned with maintaining their jobs – particularly in the uncertain economic climate of the 1980s.[27]

Ball pointed out the importance of support from organised labour, at all levels, but recognised that many union officials have seen the advocacy of conversion plans by members of local branches or combine committees, as in the Lucas case, as a threat to their position in the union hierarchy. Sometimes the rank-and-file have also been indifferent or even opposed to conversion planning when such proposals have not been adequately explained.[28]

Ball also acknowledged that the attitude of central governments is vital since it will be very hard to make progress in promoting conversion whilst governments continue to purchase weapons in the quantities in which they have done.

By far the harshest judgement on conversion activities has come from Adams, whose attack was particularly surprising because he has himself supported, and been involved in, such work in the USA for many years. In an article published in February 1986 he provocatively claimed:

> Economic conversion has come to a dead end ... nearly 25 years of analysis, organizing and legislative effort aimed at local conversion and national legislation – a campaign often supported by this writer – have borne little fruit. A close examination of this failure would suggest that the context for such work must be enlarged to include genuine concern with federal spending priorities and with the direction of U.S. economic and industrial development and change. Unless this change in view takes place, conversion advocates will cause successive generations of activists and legislators to beat their heads against an impossible, utopian wall.[29]

(Adams was, of course, using the term economic conversion in the American way, broadly speaking equivalent to the term defence conversion in this work.)

His article produced an outraged response from, amongst others, Dumas and Gordon and some consideration of the issues at stake is required here since the whole *raison d'être* of the nascent conversion movement was being questioned.

It is important to recognise at the start that the argument was not really about Adams's proposal to take economic issues seriously both at a national and at local level. Dumas and Gordon themselves 'partly' agreed with the spirit of his recommendation at the local level,[30] and changing national economic priorities has been a central objective of major conversion advocates like Melman for years. In similar vein to the US DoD report discussed previously, Adams identified conversion solely with factory-based change, and implicitly differentiated this from economic adjustment (or community-based conversion) involving the dispersion of resources from defence firms or military bases to other civilian firms or new industries in their respective localities. His main point was that this conversion approach had not worked in the past and was not likely to work in the future. The debate was, therefore, essentially about the appropriate organising strategy and, in terms of this book, the type of conversion to be pursued – whether a factory-based or a local economic development model – rather than about the ultimate objectives, namely national security and economic health.

That (factory-based) conversion initiatives have generally been unsuccessful was not seriously disputed, though Dumas and Gordon made the point that conversion has not been a major priority for any large group of activists during its over-twenty year history.[31] Moreover, given the ambitious objectives of conversion advocates, it is unsurprising that conversion has not worked so far. However, for Adams more modest initial goals were important since success is the litmus test for politics.[32]

Whatever criticisms can be made of Adams's attack on conversion, especially in terms of style or weak analysis, he did make two points which ought not to be ignored in assessing the future of conversion organisations: activists could burn themselves out quite quickly if the limited potential of factory-orientated conversion in some cases is not recognised, particularly in the absence of wider changes in defence policy as well as in economic and industrial policy; and, also, the broader questions of national security and economic and industrial priorities, together with regional and local economic planning, provide a vital framework for conversion, in the full sense of that term (i.e. not limited to individual enterprises). In a word, what is true for conversion planning is true for the growth of grass-roots conversion organisations: their scope for autonomous activity is limited. Their future is inextricably linked to the success or failure of the labour and peace movements of which they form a part.

14 Conversion: A Theoretical Framework

This extensive review of the processes of armament and disarmament since 1945 and of the economic, the defence policy and the industrial approaches to conversion in the major Western industrialised countries had two main objectives. First, an evaluation of the dynamics of the arms race and the prospects for disarmament would set the main Western countries with indigenous defence industries in their international context. Second, a thorough grasp of the structure of Western defence industries and of the economics of disarmament and conversion makes possible an initial assessment of the scope for conversion in any advanced Western democracy. The first objective has already been achieved. It is the aim of this chapter to meet the second objective by providing a theoretical framework from which a preliminary view can be formed on the prospects for conversion. The need for such a model arises from the fact that earlier works, notably that of Melman and the 1981 UN report, tended to concentrate on what was required for a conversion programme to be successfully implemented and so, from this positive perspective, almost inadvertently overemphasised the degree of autonomy involved in conversion planning. The model presented here not only illustrates the very real external constraints on conversion, that is the very limited autonomy such activities have, but shows how the prospects for successful conversion progammes can alter in the light of both changing external factors and the nature of the policies proposed to, or adopted by, governments on conversion itself. Although the theoretical framework provided does not cover the subject of peace conversion as defined in this book, the relationship between defence conversion and peace conversion will be summarised later.

PURPOSES OF CONVERSION

Before outlining a conversion model a brief reminder of the purposes of conversion is in order. The long-term perspective is one of disarmament. Within this context preparations for the transfer of resources from military to civilian production are required both to meet that eventuality and to help reduce opposition to disarmament and foster a climate of international confidence. Conversion can also be seen as part of an altered perception of international security, one embracing economic and social as well as military factors. Finally conversion planning can foster, and be integrated with, wider economic changes both nationally and globally. The shorter-term perspective for conversion is based on changes in national defence policy and procurement planning resulting from strategic, technological or budgetary factors and affecting the profitability or employment prospects of a portion of the defence industry. Thus as Thorsson concluded:

> Irrespective of when disarmament were to start, it is vital that preparations are initiated immediately for the conversion of the defence industry.[1]

She herself gave several further reasons for this: the long lead time of up to ten years involved in designing and developing competitive products for civilian markets; the consequent need for early planning of the conversion process in order that defence firms can maintain employment and profitability when defence orders decline; and, in particular, to avoid either the forced dismissal of defence workers should an expected contract not be awarded, or the undesirable possibility that considerations about the maintenance of employment might unduly influence procurement decisions.[2]

THE PROSPECTS FOR CONVERSION

Turning from the purposes of conversion to its dynamic aspects, that is what can help or hinder in making it happen, the major factors affecting defence industry diversification or conversion in the six Western countries with indigenous defence industries[3] are shown in italics in the left-hand columns of Tables 14.1 and 14.2. The former table provides the overall context, identifying as it does the environmental, structural and political conditions which can either improve or reduce the prospects for successful conversion programmes. The latter table (which should never be

Table 14.1   Defence industry diversification and conversion: the context

Prospects for success	
Improved by	*Reduced by*

(a) Environmental conditions (Western/national perspective)

● Boom *economic conditions* – low unemployment	● Recession – high unemployment
● *Political commitment* to greater state intervention in private enterprise economy Government willingness to increase non-defence public expenditure	● Political commitment to reduce state intervention in private enterprise economy Government curbs on public expenditure, except defence
● Strategic threats reduced – relaxation of *international tensions* – arms control/ disarmament agreements signed	● Increased strategic threats – heightened international tensions – few or no arms control agreements
● Lower absolute levels of military expenditure Increased government/public recognition of harmful economic and social consequences of *arms race* Government willingness to give greater emphasis to non-military factors affecting security	● Higher absolute levels of military expenditure Little recognition by, or influence on, governments/public of harmful economic and social consequences of arms race Government emphasis on armaments-based security and deterrence
● Global *development prospects* rise – establishment of new international economic order	● Global development neglected – maintenance of current north– south divide

(b) Structural conditions (Western/national defence industries or industry sector perspective)

● Temporary *historical involvement* by commercial firms in defence work	● Permanent defence industry of highly specialised contractors
● Reduced *size and extent* of domestic defence industry	● Indigenous defence industry maintained or scope enlarged
● Weakened *political influence* of military–industrial complex/ state management of defence industry	● Strengthened political influence of military–industrial complex/ state management of defence industry
● State *ownership* of defence firms and industrial sectors	● Private ownership of defence firms and industrial sectors
● Lower regional and industrial *concentration* of defence industry	● Higher regional and industrial concentration of defence industry

Table 14.1   (*contd*)

	Prospects for success
Improved by	*Reduced by*

(b) Structural conditions (*contd*)

● Many producers in defence industry sector (i.e. competitive *markets*)	● Few or no rivals in defence industry sector (i.e. monopolistic or oligopolistic markets)
● Less reliance on/potential for *defence exports*	● Greater reliance on/potential for defence exports
● Increasing reliance on *arms imports* by government	● High/increasing level of domestic defence procurement
● Higher level of government and industry support for civilian *R&D*	● Higher level of government and industry support for military R&D
● Less *international equipment collaboration*	● More international equipment collaboration (unless international conversion planning is feasible)
● Less commercial/state *secrecy* involving the defence industry	● More or continuing commercial/ state secrecy involving the defence industry

(c) Political conditions (national/regional perspective)

(i) State policies

● *Foreign policy: détente* – agreed link between disarmament and development (in practice)	● Aggressive/militaristic posture – no link made between disarmament and development (in practice)
● *Defence policy:* unilateral/ multilateral nuclear disarmament or nuclear freeze vigorously pursued Major changes in force structure and procurement requirements	● Increased military strength and/or limited arms control measures

Reinforcement of existing force structure and accompanying weapons platforms/systems |
| Conversion closely linked to a disarmament strategy | Disarmament pursued without regard to conversion planning |
| ● Maintaining aggregate demand while reducing military expenditure Low integration of defence industry into *national economic strategy* | ● No compensation for reduction in military expenditure – strict curbs on government spending High integration of defence industry into national economic strategy |

Table 14.1 *(contd)*

| Prospects for success | |
| *Improved by* | *Reduced by* |

(c) Political conditions *(contd)*

(i) State policies *(contd)*

- Strong *regional economic policies* to deal with regions in economic difficulty from whatever cause
  Closer links between conversion and economic planning for regions
- Creation of, or extension of existing, public sector, non-defence markets
  Strong *industrial policies* to deal with industrial sectors in difficulty from whatever cause
  Closer links between conversion and industrial policy
- Government role in, and *policy for,* defence industry diversification and *conversion*
  Recognition by government, employers and unions of need for advance planning
  Decentralised approach to conversion planning
  Legislative and financial support for conversion integrated with other government policies

- Weak (or no) economic policies to deal with regions in economic difficulty from whatever cause
  Few or no links between conversion and regional economic planning
- Reduced public expenditure, especially of non-defence programmes
  Weak (or no) industrial policies to deal with industrial sectors in difficulty from whatever cause
  Few or no links between conversion and industrial policy
- No government role in, or policy for, defence industry diversification and conversion
  No recognition by government, employers and unions of need for advance planning
  Centralised approach to conversion planning
  No, or separate, legislative and financial support proposed for conversion

(ii) Public pressure/social movements

- Strong *public support* for lower defence budgets
  Strong support for disarmament/arms control
- Strong *labour movement* support for economic planning/industrial democracy and conversion

- Strong *peace movement* support for disarmament/freeze proposals and conversion
- Popular grass-roots *organisations to support* conversion

- Strong public support for high/higher defence budgets
  Weak support for disarmament/arms control
- Opposition of union hierarchy and/or rank-and-file to economic planning/industrial democracy and conversion
- Weak/no peace movement – disinterest in conversion
- Few/no grass-roots organisations to support conversion

Sources: See previous review of literature.

Table 14.2 Defence industry diversification and conversion: the industrial firm

	Prospects for success	
Improved by	*Reduced by*

(d) Internal conditions (defence company perspective)

(i) Relevant to diversification[1] and conversion

Improved by	Reduced by
● Low *dependency* on domestic defence contracts Low level of dependency on defence exports	● High dependency on domestic defence contracts High level of dependency on defence exports
● Compatibility between defence and civilian *technologies* – concentration on high technology	● Defence technologies not easily adapted to civilian work
● Previous *experience* of successes in diversification Proven managerial competence	● Past failures in diversification Demonstrable incompetence of management
● Future *profits* likely to justify new investment Low *risk* in diversification	● Future profits unlikely to justify new investment High risk involved in diversification
● Low degree of *existing diversification*– alternative products available	● High degree of existing diversification – few more alternative products available
● Opportunities for entering new civilian (especially public sector) *markets* available Desire for greater sales than is possible from defence work Innovative ability in commercial markets	● Few/no opportunities for entering new civilian (especially public sector) markets Any requirement for increased sales can be met from defence work Little innovative ability/marketing expertise in commercial markets
● Availability of *resources* (managerial, technical, capital) for diversification	● Existing resources (managerial, technical, capital) heavily tied to defence work
● Longer *time span* (5–10 years) for diversification Beginning diversification when defence sales increase	● Little time (2–5 years) available for diversification Beginning diversification when defence sales decline
● Little government-owned *plant and equipment* More adaptable plant and equipment	● Most plant and equipment being government-owned Highly specialised plant and equipment

Table 14.2   (*contd*)

Prospects for success	
Improved by	*Reduced by*

(d) Internal conditions (*contd*)

(i) Relevant to diversification[1] and conversion (*contd*)

● Similar engineering *production operations* in defence and civilian fields	● Very different engineering production operations in defence and civilian fields
Ability to carry out defence and civilian production simultaneously or even using same facilities (ensure tight control of costs)	High degree of separation required between defence and civilian facilities
● Adaptability to commercial *cost controls*/accounting procedures	● Little experience with commercial cost controls/accounting procedures
● Acquisition of *personnel* or firms with civil production or marketing skills	● Lack of individuals or firms with civilian production or marketing skills and unwillingness to recruit the same
Labour-intensive production requirements of civilian alternatives	More capital-intensive or less labour-intensive requirements of civilian alternatives
● Similar *pay and conditions* of service to that in chosen civilian industries	● Higher pay/better conditions of service in defence work
● Establishment of *retraining/* reorientation programmes	● Lack of retraining/reorientation programmes
● Company *culture*: innovative/ entrepreneurial atmosphere	● Company culture unfavourable to civilian work
Commitment of top management	No commitment from top management
Positive employee attitudes (especially of scientists and engineers)	Negative employee attitudes (especially of scientists and engineers)
Positive customer attitudes (especially of government)	Negative customer attitudes (especially of government)
Willingness to accept some product failures	Unwillingness to countenance any product failures
● Avoidance of *pitfalls* in defence industry practice, e.g. over-designing, concurrency, poor cost controls, over-optimistic market expectations	● Lack of awareness of the need to avoid defence industry malpractices

Table 14.2 *(contd)*

	Prospects for success
Improved by	*Reduced by*

(d) Internal conditions (*contd*)

(ii) Relevant to conversion in particular

● Searches for *alternative products* not limited to those made with existing means of production	● Searches for alternative products limited to products which can be made with existing means of production
● Military activities not the principal *source of technology* for civilian work	● Civilian activities heavily reliant on military-generated technology
● *Business idea* (purpose of organisation) redefined – compatability of conversion with corporate strategies	● Conservative attitude to redefining the business idea (purpose of organisation) – conversion regarded as incompatible with corporate strategies
● Commitment to major new *investment*	● Unwillingness to countenance any major new investment
● *Involvement of trade unions* (as management may be more interested in defence industry 'pay offs')	● Involvement of trade unions prevented or not sought (seen as interference with managerial prerogatives)

[1] Prospects for success/failure are particularly relevant to diversification through internal development rather than acquisition.

Sources: See previous review of literature.

divorced from the former) is designed with the individual defence firm in mind, that is one producing military-specific equipment. Together the two charts, which represent a synthesis of all that has been learnt from the three main approaches to defence conversion, enable an analysis to be undertaken of the prospects for conversion at any level: the major Western countries as a whole, individual Western states,[4] specific defence industries or industry sectors, defence dependent regions, or individual defence firms. The conditions and possibilities itemised in the charts represent a schematic summary of a large part of all that has been learnt from the foregoing review of the literature, although it cannot do justice to the wealth of material covered nor prove a substitute for a more detailed analysis of the country, industry or firm involved. This latter point must be stressed: a framework has been established for the analysis of any of a range of conversion problems but in no sense can this be a substitute for detailed study. Rather the framework offers a comprehensive and logical basis upon which to conduct further study. In the conclusion to this book an initial assessment will be given of the major Western defence industries and their prospects for conversion to civilian production in the 1990s.

The limitations of the model are obvious. It applies only to the post-1945 period and is directly relevant to just a few Western market economies with powerful defence industries of their own. Like all models it is based on generalisations which simplify the immense complexity of real-world institutions and processes, and it leaves out some of the issues dear to the hearts of peace researchers but not of immediate practical relevance. (The usefulness of maintaining a distinction between defence conversion and peace conversion will be referred to shortly.) Moreover, the model is qualitative not quantitative and provides no indication of the weighting to be attached to each factor listed. Some factors will be more relevant at one time or for one place and less at or for another.

Yet this theoretical framework does illustrate a number of points: that whilst conversion planning may sometimes have some limited autonomy it is more often highly dependent on factors beyond the control of individual firms, although diversification possibilities are certainly greater and there is more scope for independent action; that the prospects for conversion are constantly changing though some factors (e.g. the general economic climate) may remain the same for years; that conversion cannot thrive as a separate entity since the prospects for a viable conversion policy increase as it is integrated into the government's overall policy framework and the interests of wider social movements.

As far as the type of conversion is involved Table 14.2 clearly refers to the possibilities for the factory-based variety. However, Table 14.1 can also be considered with respect to economic adjustment or community-based conversion, that is where resources from defence firms or military bases are dispersed into new or existing firms and industries to revitalise the local or regional economy. Different factors and conditions listed may favour one type of conversion more than another (e.g. government aversion to direct intervention in the economy may still have a less adverse effect on the possibilities for economic adjustment, compared to factory-based conversion), or may have similar consequences for both types. Moreover, it should be recalled that factory-based conversion may be managerially led or initiated by the union movement, though the prospects for success with union-initiated conversion plans are severely constrained by the lack of much advance in industrial democracy at the present time. These points need to be borne in mind in using the framework provided in Table 14.1 since in current circumstances in the UK, for example, it would appear that, while future possibilities are limited, either economic adjustment or, to a lesser degree, managerially led factory-based diversification (with the possibility of some worker involvement) offer the most likely way forward.

THE DEFENCE SECTOR: A SPECIAL CASE?

Yet the question was posed earlier in Chapter 7 as to whether structural adjustment programmes under conditions of low growth and high unemployment would be no more than palliatives? The answer given was that, under such conditions, they surely would be but that it might still be justifiable although highly controversial in political terms. Thorsson, while admitting that the restructuring of the Swedish defence industry attendant upon disarmament involved a much less dramatic process over a much longer time-scale than other sectors of the Swedish economy had experienced, still argued that the defence sector should receive special attention. She identified three main factors. First, it was vital from a political perspective that disarmament should not lead to unemployment since, if this seemed likely, the promotion of peace and reductions in military expenditure would be hampered. Second, incentives for the transfer of resources from the defence industry to civilian production were vital in order to develop the country's technological and industrial base and maintain employment. Third, the Swedish defence industry's main customer is the government on whose behalf human and technical resources devoted to weapons development and production have been constructed. Society has a greater responsibility for the future of those who work in the defence industry than for other industrial employees not so dependent on the government.[5] Clearly these points are relevant in all Western countries with major defence industries.

While the case for treating the defence sector as a special case is a strong one in the context of disarmament where society as a whole benefits, and it seems unjust to make defence employees pay all the costs of adjustment, special case pleading in other circumstances is more contentious. The whole of society does not necessarily benefit from changes in technology or procurement planning, or at least the benefit is less obvious than in the case of disarmament. Nevertheless the points about ensuring technology transfer and recognising a defence firm's dependency on the government clearly do still have some force. It would be less contentious to provide assistance to the defence industry for conversion if this was tied as closely as possible to the government's overall industrial and regional policies (see Table 14.1). Some special aid might then be provided in relation to the particular problems of turning a defence firm from military to civilian activities.

With this reservation about the justification for the government giving special treatment to assist defence industry conversion, it can be re-emphasised that virtually every major study ever undertaken on the economics of disarmament (as examined exhaustively in Chapters 6 and 7) has confirmed that conversion is economically and technically feasible. This does not mean, though, that the factory-based type of conversion would always, or even often, be possible or socially efficient. Only an examination of the precise circumstances involved could determine that.

PEACE CONVERSION

Lastly, there is the role of peace conversion to consider. In the first place it links defence conversion to peace research themes like the causes of the arms race and the factors which contribute to wars – topics usually neglected in conversion literature. Following from this, peace conversion emphasises the importance of setting defence conversion in a wider context of disarmament and social transformation. Writers like Oberg and Kaldor have focused attention on the social structures behind the armaments build-up and on how to bring about fundamental social change rather than simply modify the consequences of reliance on purely military notions of security (as defence conversion tends to do). An alternative security concept, involving full human and social development, is required for a true disarmament strategy and this should be tied to alternative social structures if a more peaceful society is to be established.[6]

As was pointed out at a previous stage, the criticisms of traditional notions of conversion do appear to have been implicitly recognised, at least by some writers who have linked conversion more firmly to a detailed disarmament strategy.[7] Also peace conversion has helped to reveal the causes of the difficulties in implementing conversion programmes. Yet a conceptual distinction between the two seems appropriate because of the (as yet) apparently completely impractical nature of the proposals to which peace conversion gives rise and also the historical division in the literature, reviewed in this book, between the mainstream of 'reformist' writing on the subject and the limited but much more 'radical' contributions of a few academics. Although the accent in this work is on defence rather than peace conversion, it is still important not to lose sight of the latter.

15 Conclusion

The time has come for the conversion of military industries to be placed on the national political agenda of each Western country with a major domestic defence industry. The principal reason for this contention is that conversion is an integral part of the process of disarmament, which gained new momentum in the mid-1980s, and without it there is a risk that fears over job losses in defence firms may be exploited by politicians opposed to disarmament to help frustrate that objective. As this book has illustrated, numerous studies over the last thirty years have demonstrated, beyond all serious doubt, the feasibility of defence conversion, with the exception of the one category discussed below. Moreover, various in-depth reports have shown that disarmament need not cause unemployment; rather it could be the opportunity for boosting the civilian economy through new investment, particularly in civil R&D.

Before summarising the key policy requirements, a preliminary assessment of the prospects for conversion in the West is needed. At the end of the 1980s the most positive sign is the progress on disarmament attendant upon the earlier thaw in East–West relations. The Treaty on intermediate-range nuclear forces signed in December 1987 has helped pave the way for possible further agreements on cuts in the strategic nuclear forces of the USA and USSR, conventional force reductions in Europe and a ban on the production, possession and use of chemical weapons. Any such agreements would obviously primarily affect the United States, amongst Western countries. Both the UK and France, the former under a Conservative administration the latter with a Socialist government, have made clear their strong opposition to cuts in their own nuclear arsenals even if the superpowers reduce their strategic nuclear weapons by 50 per cent. Thus only an agreement on reductions in conventional forces and weaponry would be likely to have any significant impact on West European powers. In the case of Sweden, its neutral status would preclude any direct link to a NATO/WTO agreement on conventional forces but a significant reduction might be expected to lead, in due course, to Swedish arms cuts, too.

Despite these hopeful, if precarious, signs of progress the general climate for conversion of military industries is by no means entirely propitious. Most Western economies are expected to slow and unemployment increase again in the early stages of the 1990s. Although the pace of growth in military expenditure eased in the latter part of the 1980s there is little indication of any willingness on the part of NATO to reduce spending substantially or to respond to the USSR's planned 14.2 per cent cut in military expenditure over the next two years to 1991.[1] Moreover, there is, so far, scant attention paid by most Western governments to the evidence concerning the harmful economic and social consequences of high levels of military spending (except, perhaps, over defence R&D) and none whatsoever to the notion of broadening the concept of security to include non-military factors. And this is despite the valiant efforts of the UN to persuade all governments to take these matters seriously. Further factors which militate against the prospects for conversion include the dominance of ideologies which seek to reduce state intervention in the private enterprise economy and place strong curbs on non-defence public expenditure, and the poor prospects for global development, as Third World countries struggle to cope with the international debt crisis.

Turning from the environmental to the structural conditions for conversion there are similarities, as well as some significant differences, in the opportunities and problems faced by different Western defence industries. All the Western countries discussed in this book – the USA, UK, France, FRG, Italy and Sweden – have permanent defence industries with highly specialised contractors and also powerful lobbies to sustain or even increase levels of military expenditure (whether or not these lobbies are described as military–industrial complexes). Their defence industries tend to be concentrated both regionally and industrially which can militate against conversion efforts, especially in areas which are otherwise depressed economically and socially.

However, there are pressures favouring diversification and conversion, not least being the soaring cost of military equipment and, in particular, combat aircraft and naval vessels. The expense associated with the advanced electronics, and the cost of assimilating these technologies into the weapons platforms themselves, have forced Western governments to renew their efforts to reduce waste and inefficiency in defence procurement by encouraging greater competition and international collaboration. Although Sweden has faced greater difficulties in following this path because of its desire not to compromise its neutral status by favouring West or East, the other Western defence industries have had, to varying extents, to confront these pressures for improved productivity and industrial restructuring, notably in electronics. As a result job losses have occurred on a significant scale: in the UK, according to the government's own figures, a total of 145 000 jobs have been lost between 1978–79 and 1986–87 despite a 28 per cent increase in the defence budget, a 3.4 per cent increase in the share of the budget spent on equipment and a greatly improved record of arms exports during this period.[2] While no government shows any sign of completely abandoning a commitment to an indigenous defence industry and throwing all equipment tenders open to international competition, the moves towards a greater integration of European defence industries seem likely to continue in the 1990s.

To some extent, though, the resulting scope for diversification and conversion may be undermined by an increased commitment to arms exports by major contractors. Where this is at least partially successful, as in the USA and France and now also the UK, arms exports become a substitute for diversification or conversion. Unless tighter controls on military transfers can be achieved, or emerging defence industries in developing countries supplant a significant part of the developed countries' global market share of the arms trade, this will remain a serious obstacle to conversion efforts in the future. Further barriers include the privatisation of many defence firms which reduces the capacity of governments to support conversion directly; the growth of international collaboration in procuring military equipment which necessitates a similar internationalisation of conversion planning; and continued excessive secrecy involving the activities of military firms in Western Europe, although there has been some improvement recently particularly in the UK. The widely varying contributions of government and industry to civil R&D, as between different major Western countries,[3] is also likely to influence significantly the prospects for conversion: a country like the FRG, whose government spends proportionately more on civil R&D than the USA, UK or France, being in a better position overall to exploit opportunities which arise.

Thus the potential for diversification and conversion of Western defence industries is clearly present, even at this high level of
generalisation. The key ingredient, if this potential is to be
realised and the undoubted impediments to progress overcome,
is the adoption of appropriate policies by government. There is
little reason to dissent from Brzoska's judgement, over a decade
ago, that conversion in the FRG would be easier to accomplish
but less necessary than in France, the UK and Italy where it is
particularly desirable (for long-term economic reasons) yet more
difficult to achieve (because of greater short-term economic
problems).[4] Sweden would probably belong in the former category while the USA in the latter, on the basis of the Thorsson
and Melman studies, respectively, discussed in Chapters 6 and 7
above.

Since what is anticipated, and hoped for, is a modest level of
disarmament and less inefficient and wasteful defence industries
rather than an immediate leap to general and complete disarmament, the corollory ought to be modest and practical schemes of
diversification and conversion. The wider vision and long-term
goal of general and complete disarmament should not be abandoned but it might be best for us to learn to walk before we run.
Those employed in defence industries are unlikely to be impressed, and are more likely to be frightened, by vast experi-
ments in disarmament and conversion, taken mainly at their risk
and expense, even if such were a practical proposition.

On this assumpton, there are three main requirements in
formulating a policy on conversion, at the national and international levels, for the 1990s:

● *To develop a conversion strategy within the context of a disarmament-oriented defence policy.* Historically it is all too obvious
   that neither NATO nor WTO have geared their respective
   strategic, political and military positions to the objective of
   substantially reducing their nuclear and conventional force
   levels and associated weaponry. Progress on disarmament,
   and therefore conversion, will be increasingly dependent on
   the major powers giving practical effect to the broader
   concept of security – one which includes economic and social
   factors, as well as military – and also to the development of
   revised defence policies which move the two main power blocs
   away from confrontational postures to more defensive positions.

The evidence concerning the harmful economic and social consequences of the arms race should then be used to buttress the case for substantially reducing military expenditures.

This will be seen to be more realistic than it might sound if it is remembered that the post-Second World War period is unique in terms of the level of 'peacetime' forces and overkill capacity of the Great Powers. Once the strategic threat is perceived by both sides to have lessened progressive steps to reduce force levels and armaments ought to be possible – though the process is fraught with dangers.

● *To emphasise community-based conversion and defence company diversification rather than factory-based conversion.* The evidence presented in this book has illustrated that economic adjustment, as community-based conversion is sometimes called, is a tried and tested approach in the USA to dealing with military base closures and contract cancellations. It is also compatible with most market-oriented economic policies. There is, additionally, considerable scope for learning from past mistakes in defence industry diversification but here there is still a major educational task to be undertaken to persuade governments that they have an important facilitating role. The more this can be encouraged (as discussed in Chapters 10 and 12 above) the more likely firms are to diversify successfully out of even difficult situations. The potential for union involvement in what will generally be managerially led diversification is very important, too, as many constructive initiatives have suggested.

However, the most ambitious type of conversion – the factory-based variety – should represent a longer-term goal rather than an immediate one. Under existing defence managements the likelihood of success is next to zero.

● *To establish a track record of successful diversification and conversion programmes which, like successful disarmament agreements, will build confidence for bigger initiatives in the future.* Progress in the field of conversion has been held back by too much theorising on too small a base of experience. There are some fields of human activity where very radical ideas blaze the way for enormous social and economic changes. Yet defence conversion is too dependent on other factors to allow for this autonomy. A record of achievement on the more modest, experimental scale suggested by disarmament prospects in the 1990s (as seen at the end of the previous decade) is far more likely to pave the way for ambitious programmes of conversion than excessive idealism. The political obstacles to conversion, identified at the end of Chapter 5, are formidable in all the major Western countries, especially France and the UK, but a more gradual approach may begin to undermine this resistance to change.

These three requirements ought to be common to all the Western states considered in this book. The detailed conversion policies would need to take account of the specific conditions pertaining to each country, as outlined in Tables 14.1 and 14.2. Likewise it is impossible to generalise on how advocates of conversion might seek to ensure the adoption of these policies in their respective countries.

It is hoped, though, that this book will have provided everyone who is interested in these matters with useful insights into the value and feasibility of turning at least some of our 'swords into plowshares'. Governments, who by their demands, created and sustained the manufacturers of armaments in the first place have a clear responsibility to assist in returning them to commonality with their civilian counterparts. The turnaround required to achieve this will involve more than trusting to the 'invisible hand' because market forces did not make the military firm what it is: a different kind of animal to the civilian firm. If the one is to eventually lie down with the other – as the lion with the lamb – the commitment of governments and peoples to peace will need to be active and enduring.

Notes and References

INTRODUCTION

1. Hakan Wiberg, 'JPR 1964–1980: What Have We Learnt about Peace?', *Journal of Peace Research*, 18, no. 2 (1981), pp. 112–13.
2. Ibid., pp. 118–21.
3. Ibid., pp. 119 and 122.
4. Ibid., p. 142.

CHAPTER 1

1. Isaiah 2: 4; and also, similarly, Micah 4: 3. However, Joel 3: 9–10 might serve, perhaps, as a reminder that the conversion process is reversible:

   ... Prepare war, wake up the mighty men, let all the men of war draw near; let them come up: Beat your plowshares into swords, and your pruninghooks into spears: let the weak say, I am strong.

2. Leon Trotsky, *History of the Russian Revolution* (London, 1967), p. 929.
3. Since most conversion literature has been written in, or translated into, English this should not be a significant drawback.
4. This framework was applied by the writer to the United Kingdom defence industry. See P. M. Southwood, 'Arms Conversion and the United Kingdom Defence Industry' (unpublished PhD dissertation, University of Bradford, 1987).
5. Kenneth E. Boulding, 'The Domestic Implications of Arms Control', Arms Control Issue of *Daedalus* (Fall 1960), p. 848.
6. Seymour Melman, *Problems of Conversion from Military to Civilian Economy: An Agenda of Topics, Questions and Hypotheses*, Paper for a Symposium on Conversion from Military to Civilian Economy held in Moscow, 14–16 June 1984, p. 1.
7. *Defense Industry Diversification: An Analysis with 12 Case Studies*, A Report Prepared by John S. Gilmore and Dean C. Coddington for the US Arms Control and Disarmament Agency (Washington DC, 1966), p. 2.
8. Ibid., p. 3.
9. *Democratic Socialism and the Cost of Defence: The Report and Papers of the Labour Party Defence Study Group*, edited by Mary Kaldor, Dan Smith and Steve Vines (London, 1979), p. 94.
10. Ulrich Albrecht, 'New Concepts for Conversion Strategies in Western Europe: Analysing the Lucas Experience', *Bulletin of Peace Proposals*, 9, no. 4 (1978), p. 349.
11. *The Defense Economy: Conversion of Industries and Occupations to Civilian Needs*, edited by Seymour Melman, (Conversion of Industry from a Military to Civilian Economy, 6 vols) (New York, 1970), p. 7.
12. Ibid.
13. Albrecht, op. cit., p. 349.

14. Jan Oberg, 'Is the Conversion Idea to be Converted? Some Sceptical Comments from a Non-Convert', in *Militarization and Arms Production*, edited by Helena Tuomi and Raimo Väyrynen (Beckenham, England, 1983), pp. 294–5.
15. Ibid., p. 295.
16. Tom Woodhouse, *A Peaceful Economy? Defence Conversion and the Arms Industry in the USA: A Survey of Recent Trends*, Peace Research Reports no. 7 (Bradford, March 1985), p. 13.
17. *International Economic Conversion Conference: Transforming the Economy for Jobs, Peace and Justice*, Proceedings of a Conference held on 22–24 June 1984 (Boston, undated), p. 1.
18. Economist Intelligence Unit (EIU), *The Economic Effects of Disarmament* (London, 1963), pp. 115–16.
19. Judith Reppy, 'The United States', in *The Structure of the Defense Industry: An International Survey*, edited by Nicole Ball and Milton Leitenberg (Beckenham, England, 1983), pp. 21–2.
20. EIU, op. cit., p. 117. The total expenditure of 111 per cent of net national expenditure during 1944 was made possible by the rundown of fixed assets and by borrowing from abroad.
21. Anon., 'Planning for Victory', *Labour Research*, 74, no. 5 (May 1985), p. 119.
22. Ibid., p. 119.
23. EIU, op. cit., pp. 120–1.
24. Ibid., p. 121.
25. Anon., op. cit., p. 119.
26. A. J. Brown, *The Economic Consequences of Disarmament*, Annual Memorial Lecture, December 1964 (London, undated), p. 16.
27. *Economic and Social Consequences of Disarmament: Replies of Governments and Communications from International Organizations*, Report of the Secretary-General Transmitting the Study of his Consultative Group (New York, 1962), pp. 209–10.
28. Reppy, op. cit., pp. 22–3.
29. Ibid.
30. *Economic and Social Consequences of Disarmament: Replies of Governments and Communications from International Organizations*, op. cit., p. 211.
31. Juliet Saltman, 'The Economic Consequences of Disarmament', *Peace Research Review*, 4, no. 5 (April 1972), pp. 1–84.
32. Ulrich Albrecht, 'Researching Conversion: A Review of the State of the Art', in *Experiences in Disarmament: On Conversion of Military Industry and Closing of Military Bases*, edited by Peter Wallensteen, Report no. 19 (Uppsala, Sweden, June 1978), pp. 11–43.
33. Nicole Ball, *Converting Military Facilities: Shared Responsibilities and the Need for Planning* (Stockholm, 31 July 1985).

CHAPTER 2

1. *Economic and Social Consequences of the Arms Race and of Military Expenditures*, A/37/386 (New York, 1983), pp. 7, 9–11. This report is

referred to in the text as the 1982 UN report (dating being by year of submission to the UN Secretary-General, which in the case of this and other reports is not the same as the publication date). A further UN report on the arms race was published towards the end of 1989, too late for the material to be included here. See *Study on the Economic and Social Consequences of the Arms Race and Military Expenditures*, A/43/368 (New York, 1989).

2. *The Relationship Between Disarmament and Development*, A/36/356 (New York, 1982), pp. 54–5. This report is referred to in the text as the 1981 UN report.
3. *Economic and Social Consequences of the Arms Race* (1983), op. cit., pp. 40–4.
4. *Economic and Social Consequences of the Arms Race and of Military Expenditures: Report of the Secretary-General*, A/8469/Rev. 1 (New York, 1972), p. 7. This report is referred to in the text as the 1971 UN report.
5. Ibid., pp. 3–4.
6. *Economic and Social Consequences of the Arms Race and of Military Expenditures: Updated Report of the Secretary-General*, A/32/88/Rev. 1 (New York, 1978), p. 8. This report is referred to in the text as the 1977 UN report.
7. Ibid., p. 9.
8. Ibid., pp. 9–10.
9. Ibid., pp. 10–11.
10. Ibid., pp. 12–13.
11. Ibid., p. 14.
12. *Economic and Social Consequences of the Arms Race* (1983), op. cit., p. 3.
13. See Stockholm International Peace Research Institute, *SIPRI Yearbook 1988: World Armaments and Disarmament* (Oxford, 1988), pp. 375–485, for full details of the INF Treaty.
14. *Economic and Social Consequences of the Arms Race* (1978), op. cit., pp. 17–18.
15. Ibid., p. 18.
16. This is discussed in more detail in Chapter 5.
17. *Economic and Social Consequences of the Arms Race* (1978), op. cit., p. 18, which is based on Mary Kaldor, *European Defence Industries: National and International Implications*, ISIO Monographs, 1st Series, no. 8 (Brighton, England, 1972), pp. 7–14.
18. *Economic and Social Consequences of the Arms Race* (1978), op. cit., p. 19.
19. Ibid., p. 20.
20. For a discussion of Soviet military expenditure and conversion issues see Milton Leitenberg, 'The Counterpart of Defense Industry Conversion in the United States: The USSR Economy, Defense Industry, and Military Expenditure', *Journal of Peace Research*, 16, no. 3 (1979), pp. 263–77; Seymour Melman, *Barriers to Conversion from Military to Civilian Industry: In Market, Planned and Developing Economies*, Prepared for the United Nations Centre for Disarmament, Ad Hoc Group of Governmental Experts on the Relationship Between Disarmament and Development (New York, April 1980); and Lloyd J. Dumas, 'Disarmament and Economy in Advanced Industrialized Countries: The US and the USSR', *Bulletin of Peace Proposals*, 12, no. 1 (1981), pp. 1–10. President

Gorbachev's statement on conversion, which was made to the United Nations in December 1988, is discussed in Chapter 13.

21. Several countries with smaller defence industries, such as Norway, have also produced a limited number of works on conversion. These are not, however, discussed in this book.

CHAPTER 3

1. Some Marxists like R. Smith, whose work is discussed later in this chapter, also agree that military spending can harm the economy.

2. *Economic and Social Consequences of the Arms Race* (1972), op. cit., pp. 19–20.

3. *Economic and Social Consequences of the Arms Race* (1978), op. cit., p. 40.

4. Ibid., pp. 40–1.

5. Ibid., p. 41.

6. Ibid., pp. 49–50.

7. Ibid., pp. 41–2.

8. *The Relationship Between Disarmament and Development*, op. cit., pp. 181–9.

9. *Economic and Social Consequences of Disarmament: Report of the Secretary-General Transmitting the Study of his Consultative Group*, E/3593/Rev. 1 (New York, 1962), p. 18, which is referred to in the text as the 1962 UN report; *Disarmament and the Economy*, edited by Emile Benoit and Kenneth E. Boulding (New York, 1963), pp. 272–4.

10. *Economic and Social Consequences of the Arms Race* (1978), op. cit., pp. 43–4.

11. Ibid., pp. 45–6, citing the US Department of Labor, *Projections of the Post-Vietnam Economy* (Washington DC, 1972).

12. *Economic and Social Consequences of the Arms Race* (1978), op. cit., pp. 46–7.

13. *Economic and Social Consequences of the Arms Race* (1972), op. cit., p. 27.

14. *Economic and Social Consequences of the Arms Race* (1978), op. cit., pp. 48–50.

15. For a discussion of the role of the French defence industry in the national economy see Chapter 5. It is also possible that the FRG may be entering this category. See Michael Lucas, 'West Germany: Can Arms Save the Export Giant', *ADIU Report*, 7, no. 4 (July–August 1985), pp. 1–2, 4–5.

16. Goran Lindgren, 'Review Essay: Armaments and Economic Performance in Industrialized Market Economies', *Journal of Peace Research*, 21, no. 4 (1984), pp. 375–87. Other recent reviews of the literature are: Steve Chan, 'The Impact of Defense Spending on Economic Performance: A Survey of Evidence and Problems', *Orbis*, 29, no. 2 (Summer 1985), pp. 403–34; Hugh G. Mosley, *The Arms Race: Economic and Social Consequences* (Lexington, USA, 1985); and G. Adams and D. A. Gold, 'The Economics of Military Spending: Is the Military Dollar Really Different', in *Peace, Defence and Economic Analysis*, edited by Christian Schmidt and Frank Blackaby (London, 1987), pp. 266–300.

17. Chan, op. cit., p. 433.

18. Lindgren, op. cit., p. 375.

19. Ibid., p. 376.
20. Ron Huisken, 'Armaments and Development', in *Militarization and Arms Production*, op. cit., p. 10.
21. Frank Blackaby, 'Introduction: The Military Sector and the Economy', in *The Structure of the Defense Industry*, op. cit., p. 10.
22. Ibid., pp. 10–11.
23. Ibid., p. 11.
24. Ibid., pp. 7–8; Mosley, op. cit., p. 113. However, for a contrary view see Seymour Melman, 'Inflation and Unemployment as Products of War Economy: The Trade Union Stake in Economic Conversion and Industrial Reconstruction', *Bulletin of Peace Proposals*, 9, no. 4 (1979), pp. 359–74.
25. Robert DeGrasse with Paul Murphy and William Ragen, *The Costs and Consequences of Reagan's Military Buildup*, A Report to the International Association of Machinists and Aerospace Workers, AFL-CIO and the Coalition for a New Foreign and Military Policy from the Council on Economic Priorities (New York, 1982), pp. 3–6; Gordon Adams and David Gould, 'Recasting the Military Spending Debate', *Bulletin of the Atomic Scientists* (October 1986), p. 28. See also the US Congressional Budget Office, *Defense Spending and the Economy* (Washington DC, February 1983), p. xvi, which also concluded that the proposed rapid defence build-up need not rekindle inflation in the near term.
26. Harvey Starr *et al.*, 'The Relationship Between Defense Spending and Inflation', *Journal of Conflict Resolution*, 28, no. 1 (March 1984), pp. 103–22.
27. Ibid., p. 105.
28. Lindgren, op. cit., p. 376.
29. Ibid., citing Bruce Russett, 'Who Pays for Defense?', *American Political Science Review*, 63 (1969), pp. 412–26 and also *What Price Vigilance?* (New Haven, USA, 1970); Emile Benoit, *Defense and Economic Growth in Developing Countries* (Lexington, USA, 1973); Jacques Fontanel, *Formalized Studies and Econometric Analyses of the Relationship between Military Expenditure and Economic Development*, Paper Prepared for the UN Group of Governmental Experts on the Relationship Between Disarmament and Development (1980); K. A. Rasler and W. R. Thompson, *Longitudinal Change in Defense Burdens, Capital Formation and Economic Growth*, Paper Delivered at the Annual Meeting of the International Studies Association, Atlanta, Georgia (1984); and Adne Cappelen, Nils Petter Gleditsch and Olav Bjerkholt, 'Military Spending and Economic Growth in the OECD Countries', *Journal of Peace Research*, 21, no. 4 (1984).
30. Lindgren, op. cit., p. 376, citing Eric Chester, 'Military Spending and Capitalist Stability', *Cambridge Journal of Economics*, 2, no. 3, (1978) pp. 293–8.
31. Lindgren, op. cit., pp. 379–80, also citing Benoit, op. cit.; Fontanel, op. cit.; Ron P. Smith and George Georgiou, 'Assessing the Effect of Military Expenditure on OECD Economies: A Survey', *Arms Control*, 14, no. 1 (May 1983), pp. 3–15; and Cappelen, op. cit.
32. R. P. Smith, 'Military Expenditure and Capitalism', *Cambridge Journal of Economics*, 1 (1977), p. 70.

33. Lindgren, op. cit., p. 380; and, for the UN view, see note 4 above.
34. Lindgren, op. cit., p. 380 citing Clark Nardinelli and Gary B. Ackerman, 'Defense Expenditures and the Survival of American Capitalism', *Armed Forces and Society*, 3, no. 1 (November 1976), pp. 13–16; Riccardo Faini, Patricia Annez and Lance Taylor, *Defense Spending, Economic Structure and Growth: Evidence Among Countries and Over Time*, Report to the UN Group of Governmental Experts on the Relationship Between Disarmament and Development (1980); and Robert W. DeGrasse, *Military Expansion Economic Decline: The Impact of Military Spending on US Economic Performance* (New York, 1983).
35. Lindgren, op. cit., p. 380, citing Chester, op. cit.
36. Lindgren, op. cit., p. 380. For similar conclusions on the relationship between military expenditure and growth see Mosley, op. cit., p. 63, and Chan, op. cit., p. 405.
37. Lindgren, op. cit., p. 380.
38. Ibid., p. 381.
39. Albrecht (June 1978), op. cit., pp. 23–5; Reijo Lindroos, *Disarmament and Employment: A Study on the Employment Aspects of Military Spending and on the Possibilities to Convert Arms Production to Civilian Production* (Helsinki, 1980), pp. 116–17; and DeGrasse (1983), op. cit., pp. 12–13. Most studies on this subject have been conducted in the USA.
40. *Defense Spending and the Economy*, op. cit., p. xiii.
41. See Albrecht (June 1978), op. cit., pp. 25–26; Ball, op. cit., pp. 30–1; and *Defense Spending and the Economy*, op. cit., p. 43 (note 4). An updated version of the Anderson report (under the same title) was published in 1982.
42. DeGrasse (1983), op. cit., pp. 182, 216–17.
43. Lindgren, op. cit., p. 381, and Huisken, op. cit., pp. 6–8.
44. Mary Kaldor, Margaret Sharp and William Walker, 'Industrial Competitiveness and Britain's Defence', *Lloyds Bank Review*, no. 162 (October 1986), p. 46.
45. Council for Science and Society, *UK Military R&D* (Oxford, 1986), p. 58; David Greenwood, *The SDI and Europe*, Aberdeen Studies in Defence Economics No. 26 (Aberdeen, Autumn 1985), p. 27.

CHAPTER 4

1. Melman (1974), op. cit., p. 261.
2. Seymour Melman, *Our Depleted Society* (New York, 1965), p. viii, and also 'The Arms Race: An Economic Alternative', *END Papers*, Sixteen (Summer, 1987), p. 33. For a detailed study on the harmful effects of high military expenditure on the UK economy see Malcolm Chalmers, *Paying for Defence: Military Spending and British Decline* (London, 1985).
3. Seymour Melman, *The Peace Race* (London, 1962).
4. Melman (1965), op. cit.
5. Seymour Melman, *Pentagon Capitalism: The Political Economy of War* (New York, 1970).
6. One of Melman's more recent books is *Profits without Production* (New York, 1983), aspects of which are discussed in Chapter 12.

7. Melman (1974), op. cit., p. 16.
8. Ibid., p. 17.
9. Ibid., pp. 33–4.
10. This is a contentious point. Arms exports have economic value and even domestic military procurement can lead to valuable commercial spin-offs (see Chapter 3, note 14, above). However, these comments may be regarded as a qualification rather than an abnegation of Melman's contention.
11. Melman (1974), op. cit., pp. 62–73.
12. Ibid., p. 97.
13. Ibid., p. 106. (Emphasis in the original.)
14. Ibid., p. 107.
15. Ibid., p. 146.
16. Paul A. Baran and Paul M. Sweezy, *Monopoly Capital: An Essay on the American Economic and Social Order* (Harmondsworth, 1977), p. 87.
17. Ibid., p. 23, and a note which explains how their concept of 'surplus' differs from Marx's 'surplus value'.
18. Ibid., p. 150.
19. Ibid., pp. 150–1.
20. Ibid., pp. 155–6.
21. Ibid., pp. 190, 205–8, 211–14.
22. See Melman (1974), op. cit., pp. 261, 274–9.
23. For a critique of other Marxist writers on this subject see also Gavin Kennedy, *Defense Economics* (London, 1983), pp. 67–9 on Mandel and pp. 182–6 on Kidron.
24. R. Smith (1977), op. cit., p. 68.
25. Ibid.
26. Ibid., p. 69.
27. Ibid., pp. 74–6.
28. Lindgren, op. cit., pp. 382–3.
29. Albrecht (June 1978), op. cit., p. 12.
30. This is all the more surprising given the obvious difficulties in conducting UN studies. See Ulrich Albrecht, 'The Aborted United Nations Study on the Military Use of Research and Development: An Editorial Essay', *Bulletin of Peace Proposals*, 19, no. 3 (1988), pp. 245–59.
31. Blackaby, op. cit., p. 19.
32. A more sceptical view was expressed by Adams *et al.* (1987), op. cit., pp. 272–7.
33. See Chapter 2, note 19, above.
34. See Adams *et al.* (October 1986 and 1987), op. cit.; *Defense Spending and the Economy*, op. cit.

CHAPTER 5

1. The term 'defence industry' is used here to describe those industrial resources which provide goods and services to domestic or foreign armed forces.

2. For a more detailed and up-to-date study of the UK defence industry see P. M. Southwood, op. cit., Chapters 4 and 5, and Trevor Taylor and Keith Hayward, *The UK Defence Industrial Base: Development and Future Policy Options*, A Royal United Services Institute Study (London, 1989).

3. *The Structure of the Defense Industry*, op. cit., p. 3.

4. These countries include all the Western powers listed by the UN as being amongst the top six global military spenders (discussed in Chapter 2). Italy is added to this group on the grounds of its being a major Western European power and because of its close links with the UK and FRG in various collaborative weapons projects. Sweden, although much smaller than the others in terms of the level of military expenditure, is also added because of the value of its contributions to the literature on conversion. Japan, on the other hand, although undoubtedly a major industrialised country in the Western bloc, is excluded because, at least until very recently, it spent no more than 1 per cent of its GNP on defence.

5. For further information on source material see Manne Wangborg, 'The Use of Resources for Military Purposes: A Bibliographical Starting Point', *Bulletin of Peace Proposals*, 10, no. 3 (1979), pp. 319–31.

6. Judith Reppy, 'The United States', in *The Structure of the Defense Industry*, op. cit., pp. 23–5. This section of the chapter relies principally on this authority, partly to aid comparison with Western European counterparts. For a much fuller treatment of the subject see Jacques S. Gansler, *The Defense Industry* (Cambridge, USA, 1982). Another concise study is that by Tom Woodhouse, op. cit.

7. This point is discussed again in more depth when the literature on the military–industrial complex is examined in Chapter 8.

8. Reppy, op. cit., pp. 25–6.

9. Ibid., pp. 26–7. Compare also with Melman's assessment of the nature of defence markets in the previous chapter.

10. Reppy, op. cit., p. 27.

11. Ibid., p. 28.

12. Ibid.

13. Ibid., pp. 28 and 30.

14. Ibid., p. 31.

15. Ibid., pp. 30–3.

16. Ibid., p. 33.

17. Ibid., pp. 31, 34–5.

18. Ibid., pp. 35–6.

19. Ibid., pp. 36–7.

20. Ibid., pp. 37–8.

21. Ibid., pp. 42–4.

22. Michael Brzoska, 'The Federal Republic of Germany', in *The Structure of the Defense Industry*, op. cit., p. 111.

23. Ibid., pp. 111–16.

24. Sergio A. Rossi, 'Italy', in *The Structure of the Defense Industry*, op. cit., pp. 216–17.

25. Edward A. Kolodziej, 'France', in *The Structure of the Defense Industry*, op. cit., pp. 82–3.

26. SIPRI, *World Armaments and Disarmament: SIPRI Yearbook 1985* (London, 1985), pp. 288 and 291.

27. See, for example, Council for Science and Society, op. cit.; *Civil Research and Development*, House of Lords Select Committee on Science and Technology, HL 20–I to III (London, 26 November 1986); and Trades Union Congress, *The Future Business: Britain's Research and Development Crisis* (London, May 1985). The Conservative government's response is to be found in *Civil Research and Development*, Cmnd 185 (London, July 1987).

28. Kolodziej, op. cit., p. 101; Brzoska, op. cit., p. 121; and Rossi, op. cit., pp. 250–1.

29. *Statement on the Defence Estimates 1989*, Cmnd 675–II (London, 1989), Table 2.9, p. 14; Brzoska, op. cit., p. 117.

30. *UK Defence 1986: Volume I Industry Trends*, compiled by Grieveson Grant & Co. (London, February 1986), p. 3; Brzoska, op. cit., p. 128; Rossi, op. cit., p. 221; and Inga Thorsson, *In Pursuit of Disarmament: Conversion from Military to Civil Production in Sweden*, 2 vols. (Stockholm, 1984–85), IA, p. 90.

31. Brzoska, op. cit., pp. 130–1.

32. Kolodziej, op. cit., pp. 83–5; and Rossi, op. cit., pp. 225–9.

33. Brzoska, op. cit., p. 129.

34. France appears to be an exception in that, although aerospace and electronics are the two most defence-dependent sectors, the third one cited is that of 'Mechanics, Automobiles and Armour' which was 17 per cent dependent on domestic and foreign arms contracts in 1979. Shipbuilding was not mentioned though it is probably not far behind. Kolodziej, op. cit., pp. 98–100.

35. Ibid., p. 107; Southwood, op. cit., Chapter 5, Figure 5.1 and also Appendix 3 for regional location maps; Brzoska, op. cit., pp. 123–4; Rossi, op. cit., pp. 239–42; and Per Holmstrom and Ulf Olsson, 'Sweden', in *The Structure of the Defense Industry*, op. cit., pp. 165–6.

36. Jacques Aben and Ron Smith, 'Defence and Employment in the UK and France: A Comparative Study of the Existing Results', in *Peace, Defence and Economic Analysis*, op. cit., pp. 390–1.

37. Kolodziej, op. cit., pp. 91–3.

38. SIPRI (1988), op. cit., Table 7.2, pp. 178–9.

39. Brzoska, op. cit., pp. 131–2; Holmstrom *et al.*, op. cit., p. 170; and Rossi, op. cit., pp. 243–9.

40. Ibid., p. 220; Holmstrom *et al.*, op. cit., pp. 147–8; Brzoska, op. cit., p. 118; and *Statement on the Defence Estimates 1985*, Cmnd 9430–I (London, 1985), p. 33.

41. Reppy, op. cit., p. 47.

42. Kolodziej, op. cit., p. 108.

43. Brzoska, op. cit., p. 136.

44. Rossi, op. cit., p. 255.

45. Holmstrom *et al.*, op. cit., p. 150.

CHAPTER 6

1. See Chapter 1, notes 31–3, above.
2. See Judith Roswell, *Arms Control, Disarmament and Economic Planning: A List of Sources*, Political Issues Series Vol. 2, No. 3 (Los Angeles, 1973); United Nations Educational, Scientific and Cultural Organisation, *Review of Research Trends and an Annotated Bibliography: Social and Economic Consequences of the Arms Race and of Disarmament* (Paris, 1978); C. Wong, *Economic Consequences of Armament and Disarmament* (Los Angeles, 1981); and *Bibliography on Economic Adjustment/Conversion*, Reprinted from the Report to the Congress on Economic Adjustment/Conversion (Washington DC, February 1986).
3. Thorsson, op. cit., p. 221.
4. See, for instance, Norwegian Ministry of Foreign Affairs, Department of Policy Planning and Research and the Norwegian Committee for Arms Control and Disarmament, *The Sandefjord Report on Disarmament and Development* (Norway, 1980); Independent Commission on International Development Issues, *North–South: A Programme for Survival* (London, 1981); *Disarmament and World Development*, edited by M. Graham, R. Jolly and C. Smith, second edition (Oxford, 1986); and Jacques Royer, *The Long-Term Employment Impact of Disarmament Policies*, Disarmament and Employment Programme, Working Paper No. 3 (Geneva, February 1986).
5. *Economic and Social Consequences of Disarmament: Report of the Secretary-General*, op. cit., p. 1.
6. Ibid., pp. 7–8.
7. Ibid., p. 16.
8. Ibid., p. 28.
9. Ibid.
10. Ibid., p. 31.
11. Ibid., p. 52.
12. *Economic and Social Consequences of the Arms Race* (1972), op. cit., p. 25; *Economic and Social Consequences of the Arms Race* (1978), op. cit., p. 53; *Economic and Social Consequences of the Arms Race* (1983), op. cit., p. 43.
13. *Economic and Social Consequences of the Arms Race* (1978), op. cit., pp. 52–4.
14. *Disarmament and Development: Report of the Group of Experts on the Economic and Social Consequences of Disarmament*, ST/ECA/174 (New York, 1972), p. 1. This report is referred to in the text as the 1972 UN report.
15. Ibid., pp. 3–7, 14 and Annex II.
16. Ibid., pp. 15–16 and Annex III.
17. *The Relationship Between Disarmament and Development*, op. cit., p. 7.
18. Ibid., pp. 11–14.
19. Ibid., p. 14.
20. Ibid., p. 15.
21. Ibid., pp. 35–6.
22. See Chapter 1, section on 'The Meaning of Conversion and Related Terms'.

23. *The Relationship Between Disarmament and Development*, op. cit., pp. 101–3.
24. Ibid., p. 118.
25. Ibid., pp. 118–19.
26. Ibid., p. 124.
27. Ibid., pp. 124–6.
28. Ibid., pp. 167–8.
29. Ibid., p. 168. So far only the Swedish government has followed up this proposal. See Thorsson, op. cit., discussed in the next subsection.
30. See Chapter 3, note 8, above.
31. Ball, op. cit., p. 14.
32. Milton Leitenberg, 'Efforts at Reducing Military Expenditure in the United States, 1960–1978' in *Militarization and Arms Production*, op. cit., pp. 109–12.
33. *The Economic Impact of Reductions in Defense Spending: Summary of Research Prepared for the United States Arms Control and Disarmament Agency* (Washington DC, 1972), p. 4.
34. Ibid.
35. Ibid., pp. 3–5.
36. *The Economic Consequences of Reduced Military Spending*, edited by Bernard Udis (Lexington, USA, 1973), p. 3.
37. Amitai Etzioni, 'Societal Turnability: A Theoretical Treatment', in ibid., pp. 337–80.
38. *Economic Conversion: What Should Be the Government's Role – A Special Study* (Washington DC, 1980).
39. Ibid., p. 21.
40. Ibid., pp. 21–2.
41. Ibid., pp. 22–3.
42. Ibid., p. 23.
43. Ibid., pp. 25–6.
44. Ibid., p. 27.
45. *Economic Adjustment/Conversion*, Report Prepared by the President's Economic Adjustment Committee and the Office of Economic Adjustment (Washington DC, July 1985), p. i.
46. Ibid., p. ii. See Chapter 10, note 45, where Frensborg and Wallensteen argue that new investment is essential for successful conversion, as opposed to diversification.
47. The Office of Economic Adjustment is one of the conversion initiatives discussed in Chapter 13.
48. *Economic Adjustment/Conversion*, op. cit., pp. 10–12.
49. Thorsson, op. cit., pp. 45–6, 221–3, 233–6. Her emphasis was on conventional force reductions because the size of nuclear weapon forces, maintained in Europe, does not directly influence Swedish defence planning (p. 28).
50. Ibid., pp. 271–2.
51. Ibid., p. 272.
52. Ibid., p. 296.
53. Ibid., pp. 178–9, 296–8.

54. Ibid., p. 297.
55. Ibid., p. 302.
56. Thorsson, op. cit., IB, pp. 46–50.
57. Ibid., p. 52.
58. Ibid., pp. 50–2.
59. Ball, op. cit., p. 14.

CHAPTER 7

1. See, for instance, Udis, op. cit., pp. 1–3, and Emile Benoit, 'The Economic Impact of Disarmament in the United States', in *Disarmament: Its Politics and Economics*, edited by Seymour Melman (Boston, 1962), p. 135.
2. Melman (1962), op. cit., pp. 82–3.
3. Boulding, op. cit., p. 858.
4. Saltman, op. cit., pp. 18–19.
5. See, in particular, Wassily Leontief and Marvin Hoffenberg, 'The Economic Effects of Disarmament', *Scientific American* (April 1961), pp. 47–55. Leontief has been a pioneer in economic modelling of defence expenditures using input-output tables.
6. Saltman, op. cit., p. 81.
7. For a discussion of their views see Chapter 4, section on 'A Marxist Critique'.
8. EIU, op. cit., pp. 126–8. It regarded a shorter time-scale of two years for the transition period as being preferable since that would reduce the likelihood of wrong decisions being made as a result of uncertainty, increase the psychological impact of disarmament and the readiness of people to accept the changes involved and, finally, keep to a minimum the wasteful use of resources.
9. *Disarmament and the Economy*, op. cit.
10. Ibid., p. ix.
11. Emile Benoit, 'Economic Adjustments to Disarmament', in ibid., p. 286. This view is clearly in conflict with that expressed in the 1962 UN report which gave equal weight to maintaining aggregate demand and dealing with structural problems. See Chapter 6, note 7, above.
12. Benoit (1963), op. cit., p. 286.
13. Ibid., pp. 286–7.
14. See Chapter 4, section on 'Melman's Studies'.
15. Melman (1965), op. cit., pp. 214, 242–4.
16. Melman (1974), op. cit., p. 188.
17. Ibid., pp. 188–9.
18. Ibid., pp. 184–203.
19. Ibid., pp. 208–23.
20. Ibid., p. 225.
21. Ibid., p. 226.
22. Ibid., pp. 227–8.
23. Ibid., pp. 228–9.

24. Seymour Melman, *From Military to Civilian Economy: Issues and Options*, Occasional Papers Series No. 8 (Los Angeles, 1981), pp. 34–5.

25. *The Freeze Economy: A Short Primer for Partisans on How A Bilateral Nuclear Weapons Freeze Could Help Revitalize the Ailing American Economy*, edited by Dave McFadden and Jim Wake (Mountain View, USA, 1983); William D. Hartung, *The Economic Consequences of a Nuclear Freeze* (New York, 1984).

26. See Randall Forsberg, 'The Freeze and Beyond: Confining the Military to Defense as a Route to Disarmament', *World Policy*, 1, no. 2 (Winter 1984), pp. 285–318. Her ideas are discussed in Chapter 9.

27. See DeGrasse *et al.* (1982), op. cit.

28. Hartung, op. cit., pp. 1–13, 23–4, 27, 43–9.

29. Ibid., pp. 88–91, 99–100, 110–12.

30. See Chapter 6, section on 'Government-Sponsored Reports: the USA'.

31. Hartung, op. cit., pp. 99–100, 113–14.

32. See note 8 above.

33. See Chapter 11.

34. See also *Democratic Socialism and the Cost of Defence*, op. cit.

35. Bill Niven, 'An Approach to Defence Industry Conversion', *END Papers*, Five (Spring 1983).

36. Herbert Wulf, 'The Economic Importance of the Arms Industry in the Federal Republic of Germany and the Feasibility of Converting It to Civilian Production', *Peace and the Sciences*, no. 2 (1979), p. 37.

37. Michael Brzoska, 'Economic Problems of Arms Production in Western Europe: Diagnoses and Alternatives', in *Militarization and Arms Production*, op. cit., pp. 84–6.

38. For a discussion of these issues see Trevor Taylor, *European Defence Cooperation* (London, 1984), pp. 17–18, who comes down on the side of those who are in favour of allowing the EC to expand its interest into the realm of defence.

39. The European Parliament has been active in considering defence procurement and high technology industries. Ibid., pp. 60–1. See, for instance, *Report Drawn Up on Behalf of the Political Affairs Committee on European Armaments Cooperation (Klepsch Report)*, European Parliament Working Documents 1978–79, Doc. 83/78 (Brussels, 8 May 1978); *Report Drawn Up on Behalf of the Political Affairs Committee on Arms Procurement Within a Common Industrial Policy and Arms Sales (Fergusson Report)*, European Parliament Working Documents 1983–1984, Doc. 1-455/83 (Brussels, 27 June 1983).

40. Melman (1974), op. cit., p. 191, which outlines four ways of viewing economic needs but does not explicitly refer to the underdeveloped countries.

41. However, it may take considerably longer (up to eight years or so) for new civilian products, developed within defence firms, to reach financial viability. This will be discussed in the industrial approach to conversion in Chapter 10.

42. In the UK the opposition Labour Party adopted a policy on arms conversion at its 1986 annual conference. See also Labour Party, *Meet the Challenge Make the Change: A New Agenda for Britain*, Final Report

of Labour's Policy Review for the 1990s (London, 1989), p. 88, where the most recent policy on conversion is outlined.

CHAPTER 8

1. Roswell, op. cit., p. vi.
2. Albrecht (June 1978), op. cit., p. 29.
3. See Chapter 1, section on 'The Meaning of Conversion and Related Terms'.
4. For the most famous part of Dwight D. Eisenhower's last official address to the American people, delivered by television and radio on 17 January 1961, see *Defense and Disarmament: The Economics of Transition*, edited by Roger E. Bolton (New Jersey, USA, 1966), pp. 173–5.
5. *Testing the Theory of the Military–Industrial Complex*, edited by S. Rosen (Lexington, USA, 1973), p. 1.
6. See, for instance, V. R. Berghahn, *Militarism: The History of an International Debate, 1861–1979* (Leamington Spa, England, 1981).
7. The summary is taken from *Testing the Theory of the Military–Industrial Complex*, op. cit., pp. 2–3; see also Berghahn, op. cit., pp. 88–9.
8. A UNESCO review identified two major interpretations in the analysis of the military–industrial complex (MIC): an *elitist* interpretation, whereby the MIC is a fairly tightly coordinated 'power elite' fully capable of shaping the course of the arms race according to its own interests; and a *pluralist* interpretation, in which the MIC is a loosely coordinated group of actors with some common interests and who consequently work for the same type of policies, but whose components also form a countervailing power to each other. UNESCO, op. cit., p. 8.
9. Woodhouse, op. cit., pp. 2–5, enlarges on this.
10. J. Slater and T. Nardin, 'The Concept of a Military–Industrial Complex', in *Testing the Theory of the Military–Industrial Complex*, op. cit., p. 27.
11. Ibid., pp. 27–59.
12. *Testing the Theory of the Military–Industrial Complex*, op. cit., p. 25.
13. UNESCO, op. cit., p. 8.
14. *Testing the Theory of the Military–Industrial Complex*, op. cit., p. 5; and Slater *et al.*, op. cit., pp. 35–6. A parallel appears to exist between the debates on the military–industrial complex and those on the economic and social consequences of the arms race. In both cases it is doubtful how compelling the respective arguments are to those who are not already convinced that the external threat is being exaggerated or military spending is too high. On the latter see the conclusion to Chapter 4.
15. Melman (1970), op. cit.
16. Melman (1974), op. cit. His work was discussed in detail in Chapters 4 and 7.
17. S. Lieberson, 'An Empirical Study of Military–Industrial Linkages', in *Testing the Theory of the Military–Industrial Complex*, op. cit., pp. 61–83.
18. J. R. Kurth, 'Aerospace Production Lines and American Defense

Spending', in ibid., pp. 135–56. See also Mary Kaldor, 'The Weapons Succession Process', *World Politics*, 38, no. 4 (July 1986), pp. 577–95.

19. Albrecht (June 1978), op. cit., p. 31.
20. M. Reich, 'Military Spending and the US Economy', in *Testing the Theory of the Military–Industrial Complex*, op. cit., p. 85.
21. Ibid., pp. 86–9. But see also R. J. Art, 'Why We Overspend and Underaccomplish: Weapons Procurement and Military–Industrial Complex', in *Testing the Theory of the Military–Industrial Complex*, op. cit., pp. 247–66, for a contrary view to that of Reich. More recent discussions on the question of how profitable military contracts are, compared to civilian work, can be found in Thorsson, op. cit., 1A, pp. 145–55, and II, pp. 227–30 (relating to Sweden); and Gansler, op. cit., pp. 85–9 (relating to the USA).
22. Reich, op. cit., pp. 95–8.
23. Ibid., p. 99.
24. See Chapter 5, Table 5.1.
25. Richard B. DuBoff, 'Converting Military Spending to Social Welfare: The Real Obstacles', *Quarterly Review of Economics and Business*, 12 (Spring 1972), pp. 19.
26. In this respect Melman followed in the tradition of Radicals in the pre-1914 Liberal Party in Britain and of J. A. Hobson's critique of nineteenth-century British imperialism. The industrial capitalist system, they believed, could be reformed, indeed had to be, in order to save it from collapse. Berghahn, op. cit., p. 99.
27. See Chapter 6, section on 'United Nations Reports'.
28. Independent Commission on Disarmament and Security Issues, *Common Security: A Programme for Disarmament* (London, 1982), p. 139. (Emphasis in the original.)
29. See also Seymour Melman, 'Limits of Military Power: Economic and Other', *International Security*, 11, no. 1 (Summer 1986), pp. 72–87.
30. Kaldor (1982), op. cit., p. 3.
31. Ibid., pp. 4–5.
32. Ibid., pp. 3–5.
33. Ibid., pp. 7–8.
34. Ibid., pp. 8–9.
35. Ibid., pp. 229–30.
36. Ibid., p. 226.
37. Ibid., p. 230. (Emphasis in the original.)
38. Oberg, op. cit., pp. 289–92.
39. Ibid., p. 294.
40. Ibid., p. 295.
41. The 1981 UN report *did* place heavy emphasis on an alternative security concept and on democratic participation in conversion activities. See Chapter 6, section on 'United Nations' Reports'.
42. Jan Oberg, 'Disarmament, Conversion and Transformation: Some Elements of a Strategy Towards Constructive Defence and Peaceful Development', *Bulletin of Peace Proposals*, 10, no. 3 (1979), p. 309.
43. Ibid., pp. 309–10.
44. Ibid., p. 311, citing Galtung.

45. Ibid., pp. 311–12.
46. Ibid., p. 312, citing G. Sharp, *The Politics of Nonviolent Action. Part Three: The Dynamics of Nonviolent Action* (Massachusetts, 1973), pp. 802–3.
47. Oberg (1979), op. cit., pp. 312–13.
48. Indeed the term 'peace conversion' has been used pejoratively against those peace activists whose approach to defence workers is very counter-productive. See Gene Carroll, 'How to Get Labour Involved', in *Economic Conversion: Revitalizing America's Economy*, edited by Suzanne Gordon and Dave McFadden (Cambridge, USA, 1984), pp. 227–9, for examples which illustrate how excessive idealism is not only impractical in itself but militates against the prospects for conversion planning.
49. Melman has not really gone beyond stressing the importance of economic security and prosperity. See note 29 above.
50. Kaldor (1972), op. cit., pp. 27–28.
51. Oberg (1983), op. cit., p. 295. It might well be argued that the US DoD's Office of Economic Adjustment (to be discussed in Chapter 13) represents just such a co-option of conversion by the establishment in a way that clearly does not threaten the underlying structures behind the arms race.

CHAPTER 9

1. Boston Study Group (1982), op. cit., pp. 3–11, 298–309.
2. Forsberg, op. cit., pp. 285–318.
3. See Woodhouse, op. cit., pp. 45–8.
4. Michael Clarke, *The Alternative Defence Debate: Non-Nuclear Defence Policies for Europe*, ADIU Occasional Paper No. 3 (Brighton, England, August 1985), p. 1.
5. Ibid., pp. 2–6.
6. As outlined in Kaldor (1982), op. cit., discussed in the previous chapter, and *Democratic Socialism and the Cost of Defence*, op. cit. The latter publication was categorised under the economic approach to conversion because it was premised on a major reduction in the share of GDP devoted to military expenditure, to bring it into line with the UK's main European allies. In so far as an alternative defence policy was developed it was within that economic framework.
7. Clarke, op. cit., p. 7.
8. More recently an updated version has been published: Alternative Defence Commission, *Without the Bomb: Non-Nuclear Defence Policies for Britain* (London, 1985).
9. Alternative Defence Commission, *Threat or Opportunity: The Economic Consequences of Non-Nuclear Defence*, Peace Research Reports No. 6 (Bradford, September 1984).

CHAPTER 10

1. Pierre Dussauge, 'The Conversion of Military Activities: A Strategic Management of the Firm Perspective', in *Peace, Defence and Economic Analysis*, op. cit., pp. 424–37.

2. See Chapter 3, sections on 'United Nations' Reports' and 'Peace Research (and Other) Studies' which relate contradictory views on civilian spin-offs from military activities; see also David Weston and Philip Gummett, 'The Economic Impact of Military R&D: Hypotheses, Evidence and Verification', *Defense Analysis*, 3, no. 1 (1987), pp. 69–73 in particular. An apparently contrary view to that of Dussauge is expressed by Maddock later in this chapter – see note 34 below.

3. Dussauge, op. cit., pp. 425–6.

4. Ibid., pp. 427–9.

5. Ibid., pp. 429–30.

6. Ibid., p. 431.

7. Ibid., pp. 434–5.

8. Ibid., pp. 435–6. The French-inspired Eureka programme has been portrayed as a European alternative to the US Strategic Defense Initiative involving the development of high technologies for civilian purposes. However, the distinction is not so clear-cut: see A. Tucker, 'Who Really Needs Eureka?', *Guardian*, 1 August 1985.

9. For another useful discussion of the relationship between defence and civilian technologies see Thorsson, op. cit., IA, pp. 131–6.

10. See Betty Goetz Lall, 'Arms Reduction Impact', *Bulletin of Atomic Scientists* (September 1966), pp. 41–4, for a summary of some of these industrial studies. Also, for a fuller summary, see *The Economic Impact of Reductions in Defense Spending*, op. cit., pp. 7–11.

11. *Defense Industry Diversification*, op. cit.

12. Ibid., pp. 7–24.

13. Ibid., p. 3.

14. These terms were defined in Chapter 1.

15. *Defense Industry Diversification*, op. cit., pp. 9–10. In this book, though, diversification always refers to a move out of defence into civilian work.

16. Ibid., pp. 54–5.

17. Ibid., p. 55.

18. Ibid., pp. 56–8.

19. Thorsson, op. cit., IA, p. 301.

20. *Defense Industry Diversification*, op. cit., pp. vii–ix, 59–66.

21. Ibid., pp. viii–ix.

22. *The Economic Impact of Reductions in Defense Spending*, op. cit., pp. 7–11.

23. *National Economic Conversion Commission: Responses to Subcommittee Questionnaire*, Report submitted by the Subcommittee on Executive Reorganization and Government Research to the Committee on Government Operations, United States Senate on S. 1285, A Bill to Establish a National Economic Conversion Commission and Other Purposes (Washington DC, 1970), pp. 1–2.

24. Ibid., p. 2.

25. Ibid., pp. 3–4.

26. *Economic Conversion and Diversification for Defense Industry*, Reprinted from the Report to Congress on Economic Adjustment/Conversion (Washington DC, February 1986).

27. See also W. H. Gregory, 'Kaman Plucking Profits from Guitars', *Aviation Week and Space Technology* (5 August 1974), pp. 51–7.

28.   *Economic Conversion and Diversification for Defense Industry*, op. cit., pp. 18–24, 36–7.
29.   Ibid., p. 37. The DoD did, though, make full political use of DeGrasse's report, especially that his '... search failed to identify any products in our economy today developed and marketed through the conversion approach', in order to reject this approach and the proposed office of conversion.
30.   Ibid., pp. 38–40.
31.   Ibid., pp. 40–1.
32.   Bernard Udis, *From Guns to Butter: Technology Organisations and Reduced Military Spending in Western Europe* (Cambridge, USA, 1978); *Economic Adjustment/Conversion: Appendices*, Report Prepared by the President's Economic Adjustment Committee and the Office of Economic Adjustment (Washington DC, July 1985), L1–81.
33.   *Economic Adjustment/Conversion*, op. cit., pp. 31 and 36.
34.   Dussauge seems to believe that in certain industries, including substantial parts of the defence electronics and missile industries, technology transfer to civilian activities is considerable, not only potentially but in practice. Maddock apparently takes a diametrically opposed view as regards the UK.
35.   Sir Ieuan Maddock, *Civil Exploitation of Defence Technology*, Report to the Electronics Economic Development Committee of the National Economic Development Committee (London, February 1983), p. 10.
36.   Olof Frensborg and Peter Wallensteen, *New Wine and Old Bottles – Product Versus Organisation: Swedish Experiences in Changing from Military to Civilian Production*, Report No. 21 (Uppsala, Sweden, May 1980). The research was undertaken in connection with the 1981 UN report although the UN is not responsible for its content.
37.   Ibid., pp. 20–2.
38.   Ibid., pp. 23–5.
39.   Ibid., pp. 24–5.
40.   Ibid., p. 26.
41.   Ibid., p. 27.
42.   Ibid., p. 47.
43.   Ibid., pp. 43–7. This point was also discussed when defining the term conversion in Chapter 1.
44.   A different view on managerial competence, or the lack of it, in turning from defence to civilian work is expressed in Chapter 12 on theoretical issues arising from management and labour conversion initiatives.
45.   Frensborg *et al.*, op. cit., pp. 48–51.

CHAPTER 11

1.   The account here is based on Hilary Wainwright and Dave Elliott, *The Lucas Plan: A New Trade Unionism in the Making?* (London, 1982). I understand that Mike Cooley, the former chairman of the Combine Committee, has a microfiche of the original complete Corporate Plan which was never published in full. A later report, published under the

auspices of the Confederation of Shipbuilding and Engineering Unions, incorporated many ideas from the original Plan and became the main source of reference. See Lucas Aerospace Confederation Trade Union Committee, *Lucas Aerospace: Turning Industrial Decline into Expansion – A Trade Union Initiative*, Interim Report of the Lucas Aerospace Trade Union Committee of the Confederation of Shipbuilding and Engineering Unions (February 1979). For a short summary of the Lucas story see Lucas Aerospace Combine Shop Stewards Committee, *Diary of Betrayal* (London, undated).
2. Wainwright *et al.*, op. cit., pp. 7–10 and 99.
3. Ibid., p. 10.
4. Ibid., pp. 114–15.
5. Ibid., p. 11.
6. Ibid., pp. 11, 13 and 179. See also Lucas Aerospace Combine Shop Stewards Committee, op. cit.
7. Wainwright *et al.*, op. cit., p. 14.
8. See ibid., pp. 231–65.
9. Ibid., p. 156.
10. Ibid., p. 111.
11. Lindroos, op. cit.
12. Ibid., p. 149; International Metalworkers' Federation Central Committee, *Metalworkers Unions and the Armament Industry: An Enquiry of the Impact of Armament Production on Employment* (Geneva, 18–19 October 1979); International Labour Office, *Disarmament and Employment Research Programme: Progress Report (1984–86)*, WEP 2–41 (Geneva, 1986).
13. International Metalworkers' Federation Central Committee, op. cit., p. 16.
14. European Trade Union Institute, op. cit., pp. 77–80; Suzanne Gordon, 'Economic Conversion Activity in Western Europe', in *Economic Conversion*, op. cit., pp. 118–21. See also Peter Wilke and Herbert Wulf, 'Conversion of the Arms Industry', *END Papers*, Seventeen (Winter/ Spring 1988), pp. 20–37.
15. Gordon, op. cit., pp. 118–19.
16. European Trade Union Institute, op. cit., p. 83.
17. Gordon, op. cit., p. 124.
18. European Trade Union Institute, op. cit., pp. 83–4.
19. Ibid., pp. 86–8.
20. Gordon, op. cit., p. 112.
21. To be discussed in Chapter 13.
22. Gordon, op. cit., p. 111.
23. Lindroos, op. cit., pp. 147–8. See also Derek Shearer, *Swords into Ploughshares: A Program for Conversion*, Working Papers for a New Society, Reprint (Summer 1973).
24. See Marion Anderson, *The Impact of Military Spending on the Machinists Union* (Lancing, USA, January 1979).
25. Joel S. Yudken, 'Conversion in the Aerospace Industry: The McDonnell Douglas Project', in *Economic Conversion*, op. cit., pp. 130–43.
26. See Christopher S. Allen, 'Trade Unions and Paths Towards Economic

Conversion: European and American Contrasts', in *Economic Conversion*, op. cit., pp. 204–18.

CHAPTER 12

1. The analysis provided here is based on Peter Brannen, *Authority and Participation in Industry* (London, 1983), p. 148.
2. Ibid., pp. 148–9.
3. Ibid., p. 149.
4. Ibid., pp. 149–51.
5. Ibid., pp. 96 and 151.
6. Ibid., p. 96.
7. Ibid., p. 152.
8. See relevant sections in Chapters 4 and 7.
9. Melman (1983), op. cit., p. xiv.
10. Ibid., pp. 275–7.
11. Ibid., pp. 279, 290–1.
12. See, for instance, Peter F. Drucker, *Managing in Turbulent Times* (London, 1981), pp. 186–8.
13. Dan Smith, 'Principles of a Conversion Programme', in *Alternative Work for Military Industries: Military Spending and Arms Cuts – Economic and Industrial Implication*, edited by Dan Smith (London, 1977), pp. 28–35.
14. Albrecht (1978), op. cit., pp. 356–7.
15. Ibid., p. 357.
16. Christian Wellmann, 'Problems with the Creation of Factory Orientated Concepts of Conversion: A Selection – Using as an Example the Conflict on the Attempts to Close Down the VFW-Fokker Plant at the Town of Speyer', *Current Research on Peace and Violence*, 3, no. 2 (1980), pp. 99–117.
17. Ibid., pp. 99–100, 116–17.
18. Marek Thee, 'Swords into Ploughshares: The Quest for Peace and Human Development', *International Labour Review*, 122, no. 5 (September–October 1983), pp. 544–5.

CHAPTER 13

1. See bibliography for reports on various conversion-related conferences.
2. Leitenberg, op. cit., pp. 118–24.
3. Niven, op. cit., pp. 34–45.
4. Leitenberg, op. cit., p. 127.
5. Lloyd J. Dumas, 'Making Peace Possible: The Legislative Approach to Economic Conversion', in *Economic Conversion*, op. cit., pp. 80–1.
6. Hartung, op. cit., pp. 95–6.
7. The most recent version of this Bill for which I have the full text is HR 813, introduced into the United States House of Representatives on 28 January 1987.

8. Leitenberg, op. cit., p. 124.
9. Hartung, op. cit., pp. 91–3. It is worth mentioning that there has been some criticism of the short time-scale of assistance envisaged (two years) which might be far too short for factory-based conversion. See *Economic Adjustment/Conversion*, op. cit., p. 80; *Economic Adjustment/Conversion: Appendices*, op. cit., N-26.
10. See conclusion to Chapter 7.
11. Ball, op. cit., pp. 72–4.
12. Ibid., p. 74.
13. *Summary of Completed Military Base Economic Adjustment Projects, 1961–81: 20 Years of Civilian Reuse*, Survey Compiled by President's Economic Adjustment Committee and the Office of Economic Adjustment (Washington DC, November 1981).
14. *Economic Conversion: What Should Be the Government's Role*, op. cit., p. 39.
15. See bibliography for fuller details of titles relating to base conversion experiences.
16. Saadet Deger, 'The United Nations International Conference on the Relationship Between Disarmament and Development', in SIPRI (1988), op. cit., pp. 517–23.
17. See Chapter 6, section on 'United Nations' Reports'.
18. *Final Document*, International Conference on the Relationship Between Disarmament and Development, New York, 24 August – 11 September 1987 (New York, 1987), pp. 7–10.
19. *Press Release*, Mikhail Gorbachev – United Nations Address – Full Text (London, 8 December 1988), p. 21.
20. Woodhouse, op. cit., pp. 54–9.
21. See, for instance, Randy Schutt, *The Military in your Backyard: How to Determine the Impact of Military Spending in your Community* (Mountain View, USA, May 1984).
22. Jacob Bomann-Larsen, *A Preliminary List of International Contacts on 'Alternative Production' (i.e. Conversion to Peaceful and Socially Useful Production)* (Boston, USA, February 1980).
23. Ball, op. cit., p. 68.
24. See Lloyd J. Dumas, 'The Political Economy of Reversing the Arms Race', in *The Political Economy of Arms Reduction: Reversing Economic Decay*, edited by Lloyd J. Dumas (Boulder, USA, 1982), pp. 145–62, which concentrated on the US position; Gordon, op. cit., pp. 108–29, which looked at Western European experiences; and Ball, op. cit., pp. 56–72 which examined both the US and European conversion organisations and initiatives.
25. Gordon, op. cit., pp. 126–9.
26. Ball, op. cit., p. 68.
27. Ibid., p. 69.
28. Ibid., p. 70.
29. Gordon Adams, 'Economic Conversion Misses the Point', *Bulletin of Atomic Scientists* (February 1986), p. 24.
30. Lloyd J. Dumas and Suzanne Gordon, 'Economic Conversion: An Exchange', *Bulletin of Atomic Scientists*, 42, no. 6 (June–July 1986), p. 48.

31. Ibid., p. 45, though these authors do take Adams to task over certain factual errors about conversion 'failures'.
32. Gordon Adams, 'A Rejoinder', *Bulletin of Atomic Scientists*, 42, no. 6 (June–July 1986), p. 51.

CHAPTER 14

1. Thorsson, op. cit., IA, p. 301.
2. Ibid.
3. The USA, UK, FRG, France, Italy and Sweden.
4. Although not specifically designed for small states in Europe the model might still constitute a reasonable starting point.
5. Thorsson, op. cit., pp. 298–9.
6. See also Tom Woodhouse, 'To Live our Lives so as To Take Away the Occasion for War: Some Observations on the Peaceful Economy', in *Articles of Peace: Celebrating Fifty Years of Peace News*, edited by Gail Chester and Andrew Rigby (Bridport, England, 1986), pp. 70–89. Another aspect of peace conversion, not considered in this book, might be an alternative perspective on economic development, based on a critique of conventional notions of economic growth. To the extent that defence conversion is linked to these traditional ideas it may be hamstrung, particularly in the current historical period.
7. See Hartung, op. cit., discussed in Chapter 7.

CHAPTER 15

1. *International Herald Tribune*, 25–26 March 1989, p. 1.
2. *Statement on the Defence Estimates 1989*, op. cit., Table 2.2, p. 9, and Table 6.8, p. 61, which includes direct and indirect industrial employment dependent on equipment and non-equipment defence expenditure, and exports; *The Government's Expenditure Plans 1987–88 to 1989–90*, Cmnd 56–II (London, January 1987), Chart 2.26, p. 35; and *Statement on the Defence Estimates 1984*, Cmnd 9227–II (London, 1984), Table 2.1, p. 8.
3. *Defence R&D: A National Resource*, Advisory Council on Science and Technology Report (London, 1989), Table 3.2, p. 14.
4. Brzoska, op. cit., pp. 84–6.

Bibliography

The literature relating to conversion is now very considerable. This bibliography includes direct citations in the references section and further works judged relevant to the theme of conversion. In particular, there are several studies of conversion potential in the UK and USA which, for reasons of space, could not be discussed in the text. Consequently, although this bibliography is by no means a full one, it is intended to provide the interested reader with a comprehensive overview of the subject area.

Adams, Gordon, 'Economic Conversion Misses the Point', *Bulletin of Atomic Scientists* (February 1986), pp. 24–8

Adams, Gordon, 'A Rejoinder', *Bulletin of Atomic Scientists*, 42, no. 6 (June–July 1986), pp. 50–1

Adams, Gordon, and David Gould, 'Recasting the Military Spending Debate', *Bulletin of Atomic Scientists* (October 1986), pp. 26–32

Albrecht, Ulrich, 'New Concepts for Conversion Strategies in Western Europe: Analysing the Lucas Experience', *Bulletin of Peace Proposals*, 9, no. 4 (1978), pp. 348–58

Albrecht, Ulrich, 'The Aborted United Nations Study on the Military Use of Research and Development: An Editorial Essay', *Bulletin of Peace Proposals*, 19, no. 3 (1988), pp. 245–59

Alternative Defence Commission, *Defence Without the Bomb* (Taylor & Francis, London, 1983)

Alternative Defence Commission, *Threat or Opportunity: The Economic Consequences of Non-Nuclear Defence*, Peace Research Reports No. 6 (University of Bradford, Bradford, September 1984)

Alternative Defence Commission, *Without the Bomb: Non-Nuclear Defence Policies for Britain* (Paladin Books, London, 1985)

Alternative Employment Study Group, *Polaris and Trident: The Myths and Realities of Employment* (AESG, Dumbarton, Scotland, April 1985)

Alternative Employment Study Group, *Future Imperfect: Trident and the Clyde* (AESG, Dumbarton, Scotland, 1988)

Anderson, Marion, *The Impact of Military Spending on the Machinists Union* (International Association of Machinists, Washington DC, January 1979)

Anderson, Marion, *The Empty Pork Barrel: Unemployment and the Pentagon Budget* (Employment Research Associates, Lansing, USA, 1982)

Angus, Rae, *The Organisation of Defence Procurement and Production in the United Kingdom*, Aberdeen Studies in Defence Economics No. 13 (Centre for Defence Studies, Aberdeen, December 1979)

Anon., 'Planning for Victory', *Labour Research*, 74, no. 5 (May 1985), pp. 118–19

Association of Scientific, Technical and Managerial Staffs, *The Leading Edge* (ASTMS, London, undated)

Ball, Nicole, *Converting Military Facilities: Shared Responsibilities and the Need for Planning* (Swedish Institute for International Affairs, Stockholm, 31 July 1985)

240 *Bibliography*

Ball, Nicole, *Disarmament and Industries*, Report for L'Annuaire Ares (Swedish Institute for International Affairs, Stockholm, 24 September 1985)

Ball, Nicole, and Milton Leitenberg, eds, *The Structure of the Defense Industry: An International Survey* (Croom Helm, Beckenham, England, 1983)

Baran, Paul A., and Paul M. Sweezy, *Monopoly Capital: An Essay on the American Economic and Social Order* (Penguin, Harmondsworth, 1977)

Barrow Alternative Employment Committee, *Oceans of Work: The Case for Non-Military Research, Development and Production at VSEL, Barrow* (BAEC, Barrow-in-Furness, England, August 1987)

Baylis, John, ed., *Alternative Approaches to British Defence Policy* (Macmillan, London, 1983)

Bellany, Ian, *British Defence Expenditure and Its Impact on Jobs and Energy Use: An Input-Output Analysis*, Bailrigg Paper on International Security No. 8 (Centre for the Study of Arms Control and International Security, University of Lancaster, Lancaster, 1985)

Benoit, Emile, ed., *Disarmament and World Economic Interdependence* (Columbia University Press, New York, 1967)

Benoit, Emile, and Kenneth E. Boulding, eds, *Disarmament and the Economy* (Harper & Row, New York, 1963)

Berghahn, V. R., *Militarism: The History of an International Debate, 1861–1979* (Berg, Leamington Spa, England, 1981)

A Better Future for Defence Jobs: Job Security, Military Spending and Alternative Production, An Interim Report of a Conference for Trade Unionists Working in the Defence Industries held at University of Bradford on 7–8 April 1984 (Conference Steering Committee, Trade Union Campaign for Nuclear Disarmament, London, June 1984)

Beynon, Huw, and Hilary Wainwright, *The Workers' Report on Vickers* (Pluto Press, London, 1979)

Bibliography on Economic Adjustment/Conversion, Reprinted from the Report to the Congress on Economic Adjustment/Conversion (DoD, Washington DC, February 1986)

Bolton, Roger E., ed., *Defense and Disarmament: The Economics of Transition* (Prentice-Hall, New Jersey, USA, 1966)

Bomann-Larsen, Jacob, *A Preliminary List of International Contacts on Alternative Production (i.e. Conversion to Peaceful and Socially Useful Production)* (Boston, USA, February 1980)

Boston Study Group, The, *Winding Down: The Price of Defense* (W. H. Freeman & Co., San Francisco, 1982)

Boulding, Kenneth E., 'The Domestic Implications of Arms Control', Arms Control Issue of *Daedalus* (Fall 1960), pp. 846–59

Boulding, Kenneth E., ed., *Peace and the War Industry* (Aldine, USA, 1970)

Brannen, Peter, *Authority and Participation in Industry* (Batsford, London, 1983)

Breheny, Michael J., ed., *Defence Expenditure and Regional Development* (Mansell, London, 1988)

Brown, A. J., *The Economic Consequences of Disarmament*, Annual Memorial Lecture (The David Davies Memorial Institute of International Studies, London, December 1964)

Burns, Richard Dean, *Arms Control and Disarmament: A Bibliography* (American Bibliographical Center – Clio Press, California, USA, 1977)

Carlton, David, and Carlo Schaerf, eds, *Arms Control and Technological Innovation* (Croom Helm, London, 1977)

Centre for Alternative Industrial and Technological Systems, *Arms Conversion* (CAITS, London, July 1981)

Chalmers, Malcolm, *Paying for Defence: Military Spending and British Decline* (Pluto Press, London, 1985)

Chan, Steve, 'The Impact of Defense Spending on Economic Performance: A Survey of Evidence and Problems', *Orbis*, 29, no. 2 (Summer 1985), pp. 403–34

Chester, Gail, and Andrew Rigby, eds, *Articles of Peace: Celebrating Fifty Years of Peace News* (Prism Press, Bridport, England, 1986)

Civil and Public Services Association, *The Employment Effects of Nuclear Disarmament*, Research Paper (CPSA, London, January 1983)

Civil Research and Development, House of Lords Select Committee on Science and Technology, HL 20-I to II (HMSO, London, 26 November 1986)

Civil Research and Development, Cmnd 185 (HMSO, London, July 1987)

Clarke, Michael, *The Alternative Defence Debate: Non-Nuclear Defence Policies for Europe*, ADIU Occasional Paper No. 3 (Armament and Disarmament Information Unit, University of Sussex, Brighton, England, August 1985)

Cooper, Sir Frank, *Pre-conditions for the Emergence of a European Common Market in Armaments*, Centre for European Policy Studies Papers No. 18 (Brussels, 1985)

Council for Science and Society, *UK Military R&D* (Oxford University Press, Oxford, 1986)

Counter Information Studies, *The Arms Industry*, Anti-Report No. 31 (CIS, London, Spring 1982)

Defence R&D: A National Resource, Advisory Council on Science and Technology Report (HMSO, London, 1989)

Defence Technology Enterprises Limited, *Defence Research for Industry* (DTE, Milton Keynes, undated)

Defense Industry Diversification: An Analysis with 12 Case Studies, A Report Prepared by John S. Gilmore and Dean C. Coddington for the US Arms Control and Disarmament Agency (ACDA, Washington DC, 1966)

Defense Spending and the Economy (CBO, Washington DC, February 1983)

DeGrasse, Robert, *Military Expansion: Economic Decline* (M. E. Sharpe, New York, 1983)

DeGrasse, Robert, with Paul Murphy and William Ragen, *The Costs and Consequences of Reagan's Military Buildup* (Council on Economic Priorities, New York, 1982)

Disarmament and Development: Report of the Group of Experts on the Economic and Social Consequences of Disarmament, ST/ECA/174 (UN, New York, 1972)

Drucker, Peter F., *Managing in Turbulent Times* (Pan Books, London, 1981)

DuBoff, Richard B., 'Converting Military Spending to Social Welfare: The Real Obstacles', *Quarterly Review of Economics and Business*, 12 (Spring 1972), pp. 7–22

Dumas, Lloyd J., 'Economic Conversion, Productive Efficiency and Social Welfare', *Journal of Sociology and Social Welfare*, 4, nos 3 and 4 (January–March 1977), pp. 567–96

Dumas, Lloyd J., 'Disarmament and Economy in Advanced Industrialized

Countries: the US and USSR', *Bulletin of Peace Proposals*, 12, no. 1 (1981), pp. 1–10.

Dumas, Lloyd J., ed., *The Political Economy of Arms Reduction: Reversing Economic Decay* (Westview Press, Boulder, USA, 1982)

Dumas, Lloyd J., *The Overburdened Economy: Uncovering the Causes of the Chronic Unemployment, Inflation, and National Decline* (University of California Press, Berkeley, USA, 1986)

Dumas, Lloyd J., and Suzanne Gordon, 'Economic Conversion: An Exchange', *Bulletin of Atomic Scientists*, 42, no. 6 (June–July 1986), pp. 45–8

Duncombe, Richard, *GEC-Marconi: What Future in Defence?* An Independent Report Compiled for Trade Unionists at GEC-Marconi (CAITS and ASTMS, London, December 1985)

Dunne, J.P., and R.P. Smith, *The Economic Consequences of Reduced UK Military Expenditure*, Birkbeck College Discussion Paper No. 144 (University of London, London, November 1983)

Economic Adjustment/Conversion, Report Prepared by the President's Economic Adjustment Committee and the Office of Economic Adjustment (DoD, Washington DC, July 1985)

Economic and Social Consequences of Disarmament: Report of the Secretary-General Transmitting the Study of his Consultative Group, E/3593/Rev. 1 (UN, New York, 1962)

Economic and Social Consequences of Disarmament: Replies of Governments and Communications from International Organizations, Report of Secretary-General Transmitting the Study of his Consultative Group (UN, New York, 1962)

Economic and Social Consequences of the Arms Race and of Military Expenditures: Report of the Secretary-General, A/8469/Rev. 1 (UN, New York, 1972)

Economic and Social Consequences of the Arms Race and of Military Expenditures: Updated Report of the Secretary-General, A/32/88/Rev. 1 (UN, New York, 1978)

Economic and Social Consequences of the Arms Race and Military Expenditures, A/37/386 (UN, New York, 1983)

Economic Conversion and Diversification for Defense Industry, Reprinted from the Report to Congress on Economic Adjustment/Conversion (DoD, Washington DC, February 1986)

Economic Conversion: What Should Be the Government's Role – A Special Study (CBO, Washington DC, 1980)

The Economic Impact of Reductions in Defense Spending: Summary of Research Prepared for the United States Arms Control and Disarmament Agency (ACDA, Washington DC, 1972)

Economist Intelligence Unit, *The Economic Effects of Disarmament* (EIU, London, 1963)

Elliott, Dave, *Defence Industry Conversion: A Review of the Options* (Network for Alternative Technology and Technology Assessment, Milton Keynes, England, February 1985)

Employment Research Associates, *The Price of the Pentagon: The Industrial and Commercial Impact of the 1981 Military Budget* (Employment Research Associates, Michigan, USA, 1982)

European Trade Union Institute, *Disarmament and the Conversion of Arms*

Industries to Civil Production: A Review of Possibilities and Experiences in Western Europe (ETUI, Brussels, October 1983)

Final Document, International Conference on the Relationship Between Disarmament and Development, New York, 24 August – 11 September 1987 (UN, New York, 1987)

Forsberg, Randall, 'The Freeze and Beyond: Confining the Military to Defense as a Route to Disarmament', *World Policy*, 1, no. 2 (Winter 1984), pp. 285–318

Freedman, Lawrence, *Arms Production in the United Kingdom: Problems and Prospects* (Royal Institute of International Affairs, London, 1978)

Frensborg, Olof, and Peter Wallensteen, *New Wine and Old Bottles – Product Versus Organisation: Swedish Experiences in Changing from Military to Civilian Production*, Report No. 21 (Uppsala University, Uppsala, Sweden, May 1980)

Gansler, Jacques S., *The Defense Industry* (MIT Press, Cambridge, USA, 1982)

Gilchrist, Alison, *A Better Future for Defence Jobs*, Report of a Conference held on 20 October 1984 (Bristol, November 1984)

Gordon, Suzanne, and Dave McFadden, *Economic Conversion: Revitalizing America's Economy* (Ballinger, Cambridge, USA, 1984)

The Government's Expenditure Plans 1987–88 to 1989–90, Cmnd 56-I and II (HMSO, London, January 1987)

Graham, M., R. Jolly and C. Smith, eds, *Disarmament and World Development*, second edition (Pergamon Press, Oxford, 1986)

Greater London Council, Industry and Employment Branch, *London Industrial Strategy: Arms Conversion* (GLC, London, 1985)

Greater London Trade Union Resource Unit, *Lost Jobs – Wasted Skills: The Impact of Defence Procurement on the Electronics Sector in London* (GLTURU, London, undated)

Greenwood, David, *The Employment Consequences of Reduced Defence Spending*, Aberdeen Studies in Defence Economics No. 8 (University of Aberdeen, Scotland, May 1976)

Greenwood, David, *The SDI and Europe*, Aberdeen Studies in Defence Economics No. 26 (Centre for Defence Studies, Aberdeen, Scotland, Autumn 1985)

Greenwood, David, and John Short, *Military Installations and Local Economies – A Case Study: The Moray Air Stations*, Aberdeen Studies in Defence Economics No. 4 (University of Aberdeen, Aberdeen, Scotland, December 1973)

Gregory, W. H., 'Kaman Plucking Profits from Guitars', *Aviation Week and Space Technology* (5 August 1974), pp. 51–7

Grieveson Grant, *UK Defence 1986*, 2 vols (London, February 1986)

Gummett, Philip, and Michael Gibbons, 'Redeployment and Diversification at Harwell', *Omega*, 6, no. 1 (1978), pp. 65–9

HR4805, A Bill Introduced into the House of Representatives, 98th US Congress, 2nd Session on 8 February 1984 by Mr Mavroules, and others

HR813, A Bill Introduced into the House of Representatives, 100th US Congress, 1st Session on 28 January 1987 by Mr Weiss, and others

Harbor, Bernard, *British Aerospace: A Kingston Perspective* (London, August 1986)

Hartley, Keith, *NATO Arms Co-operation: A Study in Economics and Politics* (George Allen & Unwin, London, 1983)

Hartung, William D., *The Economic Consequences of a Nuclear Freeze* (Council on Economic Priorities, New York, 1984)

Heriot-Watt University, Defence Finance Unit, *The Defence Business in the United Kingdom: Part 2 The Defence Suppliers*, Defence Finance Report No. 3 (Heriot-Watt University, Edinburgh, April 1985)

Holy Bible (Authorized Version)

IECC, *International Economic Conversion Conference: Transforming the Economy for Jobs, Peace and Justice*, Proceedings of a Conference held in Boston College on 22–24 June 1984 (IECC, Boston, USA, undated)

Independent Commission on Disarmament and Security Issues, *Common Security: A Programme for Disarmament* (Pan Books, London, 1982)

Independent Commission on International Development Issues, *North–South: A Progamme for Survival* (Pan Books, London, 1981)

Institute of Public and Civil Servants, *Switching Over: Nuclear Arms, Defence Spending and Jobs* (IPCS, London, undated)

International Association of Machinists and Aerospace Workers, *Let's Rebuild America* (IAM, Washington DC, 1984)

International Institute for Peace, *The Economic Necessity of Disarmament: Report on the Economic Conference of the International Institute for Peace* (International Institute for Peace, Vienna, undated)

International Labour Office, *Disarmament and Employment Research Programme: Progress Report, 1984–86* (ILO, Geneva, 1986)

International Metalworkers' Federation, Central Committee, *Metalworkers Unions and the Armament Industry: An Enquiry of the Impact of Armament Production on Employment* (IMF, Geneva, 18–19 October 1979)

Kaldor, Mary, *European Defence Industries: National and International Implications*, ISIO Monograph, 1st Series, No. 8 (Institute for the Study of International Organisation, University of Sussex, Brighton, England, 1972)

Kaldor, Mary, *The Baroque Arsenal* (Andre Deutsch, London, 1982)

Kaldor, Mary, 'The Weapons Succession Process', *World Politics*, 38, no. 4 (July 1986), pp. 577–95

Kaldor, Mary, Margaret Sharp and William Walker, 'Industrial Competitiveness and Britain's Defence', *Lloyds Bank Review*, no. 162 (October 1986), pp. 31–49

Kaldor, Mary, Dan Smith and Steve Vines, eds, *Democratic Socialism and the Cost of Defence: The Report and Papers of the Labour Party Defence Study Group* (Croom Helm, London, 1979)

Kennedy, Gavin, *Defense Economics* (Gerald Duckworth & Co., London, 1983)

Kenny, Brian, 'The Defence Industry Environment and Its Impact on the Military–Industrial Firm' (unpublished PhD dissertation, University of Salford, Salford, England, 1982)

Labour Party, *Meet the Challenge Make the Change: A New Agenda for Britain*, Final Report of Labour's Policy Review for the 1990s (Labour Party, London, 1989)

Labour Party Defence Study Group, *Sense About Defence* (Quartet Books, London, 1977)

Labour Party Defence Study Group, *Defence Industry Conversion and Economic Planning*, Unpublished draft statement (London, March 1983)

Labour Party National Executive Committee, *Defence and Security for Britain* (Labour Party, London, 1984)

Labour Party National Executive Committee, *Defence Conversion and Costs*, Statement by the NEC to the 85th Annual Conference (Labour Party, London, 1986)

Labour Party South Western Region, *Non-Nuclear Defence and Jobs in the South West* (Labour Party South Western Region, Bristol, 1984–85)

Lall, Betty Goetz, 'Arms Reduction Impact', *Bulletin of Atomic Scientists* (September 1966), pp. 41–4

Leitenberg, Milton, 'The Counterpart of Defense Industry Conversion in the United States: The USSR Economy, Defense Industry, and Military Expenditure', *Journal of Peace Research*, 16, no. 3 (1979), pp. 263–77

Leontief, Wassily, and Marvin Hoffenberg, 'The Economic Effects of Disarmament', *Scientific American* (April 1961), pp. 47–55

Levitt, M. S., *The Economics of Defence Spending*, Discussion Paper No. 92 (National Institute of Economic and Social Research, London, May 1985)

Lindgren, Goran, 'Review Essay: Armaments and Economic Performance in Industrialised Market Economies', *Journal of Peace Research*, 21, no. 4 (1984), pp. 375–87

Lindroos, Reijo, *Disarmament and Employment: A Study on the Employment Aspects of Military Spending and on the Possibilities to Convert Arms Production to Civilian Production* (Central Organisation of Finnish Trade Unions, Helsinki, 1980)

Lovering, John, 'Regional Intervention, Defence Industries, and the Structuring of Space in Britain: the Case of Bristol and South Wales', *Environment and Planning D: Society and Space*, 3 (1985), pp. 85–107

Lovering, John, *The Restructuring of the Defence Industries and the Role of the State*, Working Paper No. 59 (University of Bristol, February 1986)

Lucas, Michael, 'West Germany: Can Arms Save the Export Giant', *ADIU Report*, 7, no. 4 (July–August 1985), pp. 1–5

Lucas Aerospace Combine Shop Stewards Committee, *Diary of Betrayal* (CAITS, London, undated)

Lucas Aerospace Confederation Trade Union Committee, *Lucas Aerospace: Turning Industrial Decline into Expansion – A Trade Union Initiative*, Interim Report of the Lucas Aerospace Trade Union Committee of the Confederation of Shipbuilding and Engineering Unions (February 1979)

McFadden, Dave, and Jim Wake, eds, *The Freeze Economy: A Short Primer for Partisans on How a Bilateral Nuclear Weapons Freeze Could Help Revitalize the Ailing American Economy* (Centre for Economic Conversion, Mountain View, USA, 1983)

Maddock, Sir Ieuan, *Civil Exploitation of Defence Technology*, Report to the Electronics Economic Development Committee of the National Economic Development Committee (National Economic Development Organisation, London, 1983)

Melman, Seymour, *The Peace Race* (Victor Gollancz, London, 1962)

Melman, Seymour, ed., *Disarmament: Its Politics and Economics* (American Academy of Arts and Sciences, Boston, USA, 1962)

Melman, Seymour, *Our Depleted Society* (Dell, New York, 1965)

Melman, Seymour, *Pentagon Capitalism: The Political Economy of War* (McGraw-Hill, New York, 1970)

Melman, Seymour, ed., *Conversion of Industry from a Military to Civilian Economy* (Praeger, New York, 1970). This series comprises:

  Berkowitz, Marvin, *The Conversion of Military-Oriented Research and Development to Civilian Uses* (Praeger, New York, 1970)

  Christodoulou, Aris P., *Conversion of Nuclear Facilities from Military to Civilian Uses* (Praeger, New York, 1970)

  Lynch, John E., *Local Economic Development after Military Base Closures* (Praeger, New York, 1970)

  Mack-Forlist, Daniel M., and Arthur Newman, *The Conversion of Shipbuilding from Military to Civilian Markets* (Praeger, New York, 1970)

  Melman, Seymour, ed., *The Defense Economy: Conversion of Industries and Occupations to Civilian Needs* (Praeger, New York, 1970)

  Ullmann, John E., ed., *Potential Civilian Markets for the Military-Electronics Industry: Strategies for Conversion* (Praeger, New York, 1970)

Melman, Seymour, ed., *The War Economy of the United States: Readings on Military Industry and Economy* (St Martin's Press, New York, 1971)

Melman, Seymour, 'Ten Propositions on the War Economy', *American Economic Review*, 62, no. 2 (May 1972), pp. 312–18

Melman, Seymour, *The Permanent War Economy: American Capitalism in Decline* (Simon & Schuster, New York, 1974)

Melman, Seymour, 'Inflation and Unemployment as Products of War Economy: The Trade Union Stake in Economic Conversion and Industrial Reconstruction', *Bulletin of Peace Proposals*, 9, no. 4 (1979), pp. 359–74

Melman, Seymour, *From Military to Civilian Economy: Issues and Options*, Occasional Paper Series No. 8 (Center for the Study of Armament and Disarmament, Los Angeles, 1981)

Melman, Seymour, *Profits Without Production* (Alfred Knopf, New York, 1983)

Melman, Seymour, *Barriers to Conversion from Military to Civilian Industry: In Market, Planned and Developing Economies*, Paper Prepared for the UN Centre for Disarmament April 1980 (UN, New York, 1984)

Melman, Seymour, *Problems of Conversion from Military to Civilian Economy: An Agenda of Topics, Questions and Hypotheses*, Paper for a Symposium on Conversion from Military to Civilian Economy held in Moscow, 14–16 June 1984

Melman, Seymour, 'Limits of Military Power: Economic and Other', *International Security*, 11, no. 1 (Summer 1986), pp. 72–87

Melman, Seymour, 'The Arms Race: An Economic Alternative', *END Papers*, Sixteen (Summer 1987), pp. 16–36

Mills, C. Wright, *The Power Elite* (Oxford University Press, New York, 1986)

Mosley, Hugh G., *The Arms Race: Economic and Social Consequences* (D.C. Heath & Co., Lexington, USA, 1985)

Mottur, Ellis, *Conversion of Scientific and Technical Resources: Economic Challenge – Social Opportunity*, Monograph No. 8 (The George Washington University, Washington DC, March 1971)

Myrdal, Alva, *The Game of Disarmament: How the United States and Russia Run the Arms Race* (Spokesman, Nottingham, England, 1980)

National Economic Conversion Commission: Responses to Subcommittee Question-naire, Report submitted by the Subcommittee on Executive Reorganization and Government Research to the Committee on Government Operations, United States Senate on S.1285, A Bill to Establish a National Economic Conversion Commission and for Other Purposes (Washington DC, 1970)

Newcastle upon Tyne Trades Council, Tyneside Anti-Nuclear Campaign and Tyneside for Nuclear Disarmament, *Jobs for a Change: Alternative Production on Tyneside* (Newcastle upon Tyne Trades Council *et al.*, undated)

Niven, Bill, *Trade-Union Strategies for Disarmament*, Paper Prepared for a Conversion Conference in Lingatan, Sweden (University of Sussex, Brighton, England, February 1983)

Niven, Bill, 'An Approach to Defence Industry Conversion', *END Papers*, Five (Spring 1983), pp. 34–45

Niven, Bill, *Defence Expenditure and Employment in Greater London* (Greater London Conversion Council, October 1983)

Norwegian Ministry of Foreign Affairs and Norwegian Committee for Arms Control and Disarmament, *The Sandefjord Report on Disarmament and Development* (Norwegian Ministry of Foreign Affairs, Norway, 1980)

Oberg, Jan, 'Disarmament, Conversion and Transformation: Some Elements of a Strategy Towards Constructive Defence and Peaceful Development', *Bulletin of Peace Proposals*, 10, no. 3 (1979), pp. 308–14

Pavitt, Keith, ed., *Technical Innovation and British Economic Performance* (Macmillan, London, 1980)

Pite, Chris, 'Employment and Defence', *Statistical News*, no. 51 (November 1980), pp. 51.15–51.19

The Potential Transfer of Industrial Skills from Defense to Nondefense Industries, A Report Prepared by the Department of Employment, State of California (ACDA, Washington DC, April 1968)

Press Release, Mikhail Gorbachev – United Nations Address – Full Text (Novosti Press Agency, London, 8 December 1988)

Prins, Gwyn, ed., *Defended to Death: A Study of the Nuclear Arms Race from the Cambridge University Disarmament Seminar* (Penguin, Harmondsworth, 1983)

'Problems of Conversion from War to Peace Production', Contributions to a Scientific Symposium held in Vienna, 30 March – 1 April 1979, Special Issue of *Peace and the Sciences*, no. 2 (1979)

Quigley, Paul, Steve Schofield and Tom Woodhouse, eds, *The Military in Manufacturing*, Studies in Defence, Disarmament and Employment no. 2 (Arms Conversion Group, University of Bradford, Bradford, November 1988)

The Relationship Between Disarmament and Development, A/36/356 (UN, New York, 1982)

Report Drawn Up on Behalf of the Political Affairs Committee on Arms Procure-ment Within a Common Industrial Policy and Arms Sales (Fergusson Report), European Parliament Working Documents 1983–1984, Doc. 1-455/83 (EC, Brussels, 27 June 1983)

Report Drawn Up on Behalf of the Political Affairs Committee on European Armaments Cooperation (Klepsch Report), European Parliament Working Documents 1978–1979, Doc. 83/78 (EC, Brussels, 8 May 1978)

Reppy, Judith, *Labour Use and Productivity in Military and Non-Military Related Industry*, Disarmament and Employment Programme, Working Paper No. 2 (ILO, Geneva, February 1986)

Rivkin, Steven R., *Technology Unbound: Transferring Scientific and Engineering Resources from Defense to Civilian Purposes* (Pergamon Press, Oxford, 1968)

Roper, John, ed., *The Future of British Defence Policy* (Gower, Aldershot, 1985)

Rose, Richard, *Public Employment in Western Nations* (Cambridge University Press, 1985)

Rosen, S., ed., *Testing the Theory of the Military–Industrial Complex* (D.C. Heath & Co., Lexington, USA, 1973)

Roswell, Judith, *Arms Control, Disarmament and Economic Planning: A List of Sources*, Political Issues Series Vol. 2, No. 3 (Center for the Study of Armament and Disarmament, Los Angeles, 1973)

Royer, Jacques, *The Long-Term Employment Impact of Disarmament Policies*, Disarmament and Employment Progamme, Working Paper No. 3 (ILO, Geneva, February 1986)

Saltman, Juliet, 'The Economic Consequences of Disarmament', *Peace Research Reviews*, 4, no. 5 (April 1972), pp. 1–84

Sampson, Anthony, *The Arms Bazaar* (Book Club Associates, London, 1977)

Schmidt, Christian, ed., *The Economics of Military Expenditures: Military Expenditures, Economic Growth and Fluctuations*, Proceedings of a Conference held by the International Economic Association in Paris, France (Macmillan, London, 1987)

Schmidt, Christian, and Frank Blackaby, eds, *Peace, Defence and Economic Analysis* (Macmillan, London, 1987)

Schofield, Steve, *Employment and Security – Alternatives to Trident: An Interim Report*, Peace Research Reports No. 10 (University of Bradford, Bradford, July 1986)

Schutt, Randy, *The Military in your Backyard: How to Determine the Impact of Military Spending in your Community* (Centre for Economic Conversion, Mountain View, USA, May 1984)

Shearer, Derek, *Swords into Ploughshares: A Program for Conversion*, Working Papers for a New Society, Reprint (Summer 1973)

Short, John, 'Defence Spending in the UK Regions', *Regional Studies*, 15, no. 2 (1981), pp. 101–10

Short, John, Timothy Stone and David Greenwood, *Military Installations and Local Economies: A Case Study – The Clyde Submarine Base*, Aberdeen Studies in Defence Economics No. 5 (University of Aberdeen, Aberdeen, Scotland, August 1974)

Skills Conversion Project, A Report Prepared by the National Society of Professional Engineers (Dept. of Labor, Washington DC, March 1972)

Smith, Dan, ed., *Alternative Work for Military Industries: Military Spending and Arms Cuts – Economic and Industrial Implication* (Richardson Institute for Conflict and Peace Research, London, 1977)

Smith, Dan, and Ron Smith, *The Economics of Militarism* (Pluto Press, London, 1983)

Smith, R. P., 'Military Expenditure and Capitalism', *Cambridge Journal of Economics*, 1 (1977), pp. 61–76

Society of Civil and Public Servants, *Defence Expenditure and Employment* (SCPS, London, 1983)

Southwood, Peter, *The UK Defence Industry: Characteristics of the Main UK Defence Equipment Manufacturers Which Are Also Relevant to a Credible Arms Conversion Strategy*, Peace Research Reports No. 8 (University of Bradford, Bradford, September 1985)

Southwood, Peter, 'Arms Conversion', in *World Encyclopedia of Peace*, edited by L. Pauling, 4 vols (Pergamon, Oxford, 1986), I, pp. 67–71

Southwood, Peter, 'Arms Conversion and the United Kingdom Defence Industry' (unpublished PhD dissertation, University of Bradford, 1987)

Southwood, Peter, and Steve Schofield, *Warship Yard Workers: A Survey of Attitudes to Defence and Civilian Work at VSEL, Barrow*, Defence, Disarmament and Employment Report No. 1 (Arms Conversion Group, University of Bradford, Bradford, March 1987)

Starr, Harvey, *et al.*, 'The Relationship Between Defence Spending and Inflation', *Journal of Conflict Resolution*, 28, no. 1 (March 1984), pp. 103–22

Statement on the Defence Estimates 1984, Cmnd 9227-I and II (HMSO, London, 1984)

Statement on the Defence Estimates 1985, Cmnd 9430-I and II (HMSO, London, 1985)

Statement on the Defence Estimates 1989, Cmnd 675-I and II (HMSO, London, 1989)

Stockholm International Peace Research Institute, *World Armaments and Disarmament: SIPRI Yearbook 1981* (Taylor & Francis, London, 1981)

Stockholm International Peace Research Institute, *World Armaments and Disarmament: SIPRI Yearbook 1982* (Taylor & Francis, London, 1982)

Stockholm International Peace Research Institute, *World Armaments and Disarmament: SIPRI Yearbook 1985* (Taylor & Francis, London, 1985)

Stockholm International Peace Research Institute, *World Armaments and Disarmament: SIPRI Yearbook 1986* (Taylor & Francis, London, 1986)

Stockholm International Peace Research Institute, *SIPRI Yearbook 1987: World Armaments and Disarmament* (Oxford University Press, Oxford, 1987)

Stockholm International Peace Research Institute, *SIPRI Yearbook 1988: World Armaments and Disarmament* (Oxford University Press, Oxford, 1988)

Stone, Timothy, *Analysing the Regional Aspect of Defence Spending: A Survey*, Aberdeen Studies in Defence Economics No. 3 (University of Aberdeen, Aberdeen, Scotland, December 1973)

Summary of Completed Military Base Economic Adjustment Projects, 1961–81: 20 Years of Civilian Reuse, Survey Compiled by President's Economic Adjustment Committee and the Office of Economic Adjustment (DoD, Washington DC, November 1981)

Taylor, Arthur, *A Better Future for Defence Jobs in the South West*, Report of a Conference held in Taunton on 23 July 1985 (Bristol, undated)

Taylor, Trevor, *European Defence Cooperation*, Chatham House Papers 24 (Routledge & Kegan Paul, London, 1984)

Taylor, Trevor, and Keith Hayward, *The UK Defence Industrial Base: Development and Future Policy Options*, A Royal United Services Institute Study (Brassey's Defence Publishers, London, 1989)

Technical and Allied Supervisory Staff Union, *Defence and Jobs* (TASS, Richmond, 1984)

Thee, Marek, *Conversion of Military-Related Industries to Socially Useful Purposes*, PRIO Report 8/83 (International Peace Research Institute, Oslo, Norway, June 1983)

Thee, Marek, 'Swords into Ploughshares: The Quest for Peace and Human Development', *International Labour Review*, 122, no. 5 (September–October 1983), pp. 535–48

Thompson, E. P., and Dan Smith, eds, *Protest and Survive* (Penguin, Harmondsworth, 1982)

Thorsson, Inga, *In Pursuit of Disarmament: Conversion from Military to Civil Production in Sweden*, 2 vols (Liber, Stockholm, 1984–85)

Topham, Tony, 'Labour Movement Strategy for Arms Conversion', *END Papers*, Five (Spring 1983), pp. 46–53

Trades Union Congress, *Discussion Paper on Defence Spending and Jobs* (TUC, London, 1984)

Trades Union Congress, *The Future Business: Britain's Research and Development Crisis* (TUC, London, May 1985)

Transport and General Workers' Union, *A Better Future for Defence Jobs* (T&GWU, London, 1983)

Trotsky, Leon, *The History of the Russian Revolution* (Pluto Press, London, 1977)

Tuomi, Helena, and Raimo Väyrynen, eds, *Militarization and Arms Production* (Croom Helm, Beckenham, England, 1983)

Tucker, A., 'Who Really Needs Eureka?', *Guardian*, 1 August 1985

Udis, Bernard, *The Economic Consequences of Reduced Military Spending* (D.C. Heath & Co., Lexington, USA, 1973)

Udis, Bernard, *From Guns to Butter: Technology Organisations and Reduced Military Spending in Western Europe* (Ballinger, Cambridge, USA, 1978)

United Nations Educational, Scientific and Cultural Organisation, *Review of Research Trends and an Annotated Bibliography: Social and Economic Consequences of the Arms Race and of Disarmament* (UNESCO, Paris, 1978)

Vickers Elswick Shop Steward Committee, *A Farewell to Arms? The Future Facing Vickers Elswick on Tyneside* (North East Trade Union Studies Information Unit, Newcastle upon Tyne, undated)

Vickers' National Combine Committee of Shop Stewards, *Building a Chieftain Tank and the Alternative* (Vickers' National Combine Committee, undated)

Vickers' North East Working Group, *Alternative Employment for Naval Shipbuilding Workers: A Case Study of the Resources Devoted to the Production of the ASW Cruiser* (Vickers North East Working Group, undated)

Von Bredow, W., ed., *Economic and Social Aspects of Disarmament: Contributions from East and West Europe* (International Institute for Peace, Vienna, 1974)

Wainwright, Hilary, and Dave Elliott, *The Lucas Plan: A New Trade Unionism in the Making?* (Allison and Busby, London, 1982)

Wallensteen, Peter, ed., *Experiences in Disarmament: On Conversion of Military Industry and Closing of Military Bases*, Report No. 19 (Uppsala University, Uppsala, Sweden, June 1978)

Wangborg, Manne, 'The Use of Resources for Military Purposes: A Bibliographical Starting Point', *Bulletin of Peace Proposals*, 10, no. 3 (1979)

Wellmann, Christian, 'Problems with the Creation of Factory Oriented Concepts of Conversion: A Selection – Using as an Example the Conflict on the Attempts to Close Down the VFW-Fokker Plant at the Town of Speyer', *Current Research on Peace and Violence*, 3, no. 2 (1980), pp. 99–117

Weston, David, and Philip Gummett, 'The Economic Impact of Military R&D: Hypotheses, Evidence and Verification', *Defense Analysis*, 3, no. 1 (1987), pp. 63–76

Wiberg, Hakan, 'JPR 1964–1980: What Have We Learnt about Peace?', *Journal of Peace Research*, 18, no. 2 (1981), pp. 111–48

Wilke, P., and H. Wulf, *Manpower Conversion in Defence-Related Industry*, Disarmament and Employment Programme, Working Paper No. 4 (ILO, Geneva, June 1986)

Wilke, Peter, and Herbert Wulf, 'Conversion of the Arms Industry', *END Papers*, Seventeen (Winter–Spring 1988), pp. 20–37

Willett, Susan, *The Future of Plessey at Ilford: A Trade Union Analysis* (Birkbeck College, London, undated)

Willett, Susan, *The Impact of Defence Procurement on the Electronics Sector: A London Case Study* (Birkbeck College, London, 1986)

Wong, C., *Economic Consequences of Armament and Disarmament* (Center for the Study of Armament and Disarmament, Los Angeles, 1981)

Woodhouse, Tom, *A Peaceful Economy? Defence Conversion and the Arms Industry in the USA: A Survey of Recent Trends*, Peace Research Reports No. 7 (University of Bradford, Bradford, March 1985)

Index

Entries are arranged in alphabetical order on a letter-by-letter basis. In almost all cases they are given in the full, not abbreviated, form.